Scottish Literature

Gerard Carruthers

Edinburgh University Press

In memory of my mother, Amalia Vincenza Tartaglia, and my father, Ernest Charles Carruthers.

Edinburgh University Press Ltd
22 George Square, Edinburgh

www.euppublishing.com

Typeset in 11.5/13 Monotype Ehrhardt
by Servis Filmsetting Ltd, Stockport, Cheshire and
printed and bound in Great Britain by
CPI Antony Rowe, Chippenham and Eastbourne

A CIP record for this book is available from the British Library

ISBN 978 0 7486 3308 1 (hardback)
ISBN 978 0 7486 3309 8 (paperback)

Contents

Series Preface

The study of English literature in the early twenty-first century is host to an exhilarating range of critical approaches, theories and historical perspectives. 'English' ranges from traditional modes of study such as Shakespeare and Romanticism to popular interest in national and area literatures such as the United States, Ireland and the Caribbean. The subject also spans a diverse array of genres from tragedy to cyberpunk, incorporates such hybrid fields of study as Asian American literature, Black British literature, creative writing and literary adaptations, and remains eclectic in its methodology.

Such diversity is cause for both celebration and consternation. English is varied enough to promise enrichment and enjoyment for all kinds of readers and to challenge preconceptions about what the study of literature might involve. But how are readers to navigate their way through such literary and cultural diversity? And how are students to make sense of the various literary categories and periodisations, such as modernism and the Renaissance, or the proliferating theories of literature, from feminism and marxism to queer theory and eco-criticism? The Edinburgh Critical Guides to Literature series reflects the challenges and pluralities of English today, but at the same time it offers readers clear and accessible routes through the texts, contexts, genres, historical periods and debates within the subject.

Martin Halliwell and Andy Mousley

Acknowledgements

I am very grateful to Sarah Dunnigan, Colin Kidd, Theo van Heijnsbergen and Matt Wickman, all of whom read and provided comment on portions of this book in draft. Conversations through the years with Carol Anderson, Carol Baraniuk, Jamie Reid Baxter, Valentina Bold, Joe Bray, Alexander Broadie, Ian Brown, Rhona Brown, John Corbett, Ted Cowan, John Coyle, Cairns Craig, Robert Crawford, the late David Daiches, Bob Davis, Frank Ferguson, Fred Freeman, Richard Finlay, Donald Fraser, Suzanne Gilbert, David Goldie, Katie Gramich, Donna Heddle, David Hewitt, Andrew Hook, Ronnie Jack, David Jago, Robert Alan Jamieson, Lynn Kelly, Innes Kennedy, Simon Kovesi, Frank Kuppner, Nigel Leask, Alison Lumsden, Kirsteen McCue, Margery Palmer McCulloch, Carl MacDougall, Alan MacGillivray, Jim McGonigall, Matt McGuire, Liam McIlvanney, Willie McIlvanney, Dorothy McMillan, James MacMillan, Alan McMunnigall, Willy Maley, Mitch Miller, Glenda Norquay, Donny O'Rourke, Murray Pittock, Chris Ravenhall, Alan Rawes, Alastair Renfrew, Julie Renfrew, Ronnie Renton, Alan Riach, David Robb, Johnny Rodger, G. Ross Roy, Patrick Scott, Ken Simpson, Jeremy Smith, Marshall Walker, Rory Watson, Christopher Whyte, Hamish Whyte, and, most of all, Douglas Gifford, have informed my ideas on Scottish Literature (even if some of the individuals here named will certainly at points disagree, probably vehemently, with aspects of these). I am hugely indebted to the numerous students and scholars of

Scottish Literature that I have encountered in my own university and in many other places; the vibrancy of the subject today and the decreasing consensus surrounding it license the more iconoclastic and revisionist parts of the following the tome. Martin Halliwell and Andy Mousley have been very wise and patient General Editors. All errors and any clumsiness are my own fault.

Chronology

The dates, people and texts listed below are, clearly, far from exhaustive and are chosen rather selectively to provide a convenient handrail through Scottish cultural history in relation to literature.

Date	Historical Events and Literary Publications and Events
84 or 85 AD	Calgacus claimed by the Roman historian Tacitus as leader of the Caledonii at the battle of Mons Graupius (84 or 85 AD).
c.500	Irish settlers, the 'Scoti', found the kingdom of Dalriada under Fergus.
c.565	St Columba comes from Ireland to found monastery on the island of Iona, a decisive moment in the establishment of Christianity in Scotland.
638	The Angles capture Din Eiden (Edinburgh), their language is the basis of what becomes Old Scots.
1066	The Norman Conquest.
1263	Battle of Largs, at which Alexander III defeats King Hakon of Norway.
1286	Alexander III falls off his horse and dies.
1296–1328	Scottish 'Wars of Independence' with England.
1305	William Wallace, leader of the resistance against the English executed in London.

1314	Battle of Bannockburn, at which King Robert the Bruce defeats the English.
1320	Declaration of Arbroath.
c.1375	Barbour writes his epic *The Brus* (or 'Bruce').
c.1420	William Dunbar born.
c.1424	*The Kingis Quair* written.
c.1450	Robert Henryson born.
1513	Battle of Flodden, where the English decisively defeat the Scots. Gavin Douglas produces his version of Virgil's *Aeneid* in Middle Scots (first printed in London in 1553).
1550s	*Ane Satyre of the Thrie Estaitis* performed.
1560	Decisive moment of Protestant Reformation in Scotland with abolition of the mass and of papal supremacy, largely under the intellectual leadership of John Knox.
1567	Publication of *The Gude and Godlie Ballads*.
1584	*The Essayes of a Prentise in the Divine Art of Poetry* written by James VI.
1603	Union of Crowns, when James VI of Scotland becomes also James I of England.
1637	*Delitiae Poetarum Scotorum* edited by Arthur Johnston published.
1638	National Covenant, drawn up and signed in Greyfriars church in Edinburgh in opposition to the attempts of Charles I to dilute the power of Presbyterian and other forms of non-Anglican worship.
1681–5	'The Killing Time' when the Covenanters are persecuted.
1684	Allan Ramsay born (d. 1758).
1688	The 'Glorious Revolution' when James II departs the British throne to be replaced by William III. The end of Stuart rule.
1706	James Watson publishes the first part of the *Choice Collection of Comic and Serious Poems* (subsequent volumes follow in 1709 and 1711).
1707	Treaty of Union, independent Scottish parliament ceases to exist and along with England is incorporated into the new United Kingdom of Great Britain, administered by the parliament at Westminster.

1710	Thomas Ruddiman publishes his edition of Gavin Douglas.
1715	First major Jacobite rising.
1745	Second major Jacobite rising; the pretender, or claimant, Charles Edward Stuart is defeated at the battle of Culloden, 1746.
1759	Birth of Robert Burns (d. 1796).
1760	James Macpherson publishes *Fragments of Ancient Poetry*.
1771	Birth of Walter Scott (d. 1832).
1768	*Encyclopaedia Britannica* first published from Edinburgh.
1786	Burns's *Poems Chiefly in the Scottish Dialect* published at Kilmarnock.
1802	Foundation of the *Edinburgh Review* (a less successful journal of the same name had previously been founded in 1755).
1804	David Irving's *The Lives of the Scotish* [*sic*] *Poets*.
1808–9	John Jamieson publishes his *Etymological Dictionary of the Scottish Language*.
1817	*Blackwood's Magazine* (the 'Maga') founded.
1814	Scott's *Waverley* published.
1824	James Hogg's *Confessions of a Justified Sinner* published (an important edition introduced by André Gide appears in 1947).
1832	*Whistle-binkie* anthology first published (ongoing until 1890).
1850	Robert Louis Stevenson born (d. 1894).
1866	Matthew Arnold lectures on 'Celtic' literature.
1882	Foundation of the Scottish Text Society.
1890–1915	Publication of Scottish anthropologist James George Frazer's *The Golden Bough*.
1892	Birth of Christopher Murray Grieve ['Hugh MacDiarmid'] (d. 1978).
1895	J. H. Millar coins 'kailyard' as a term of abuse for some recent Scottish fiction.
1913	Foundation of the Chair of Scottish History and Literature at the University of Glasgow.

1919	Signing of the Treaty of Versailles. G. Gregory Smith publishes *Scottish Literature: Character and Influence.*
1925	Foundation of the National Library of Scotland (formerly the collection of the Advocates Library, founded 1689).
1925–6	MacDiarmid publishes the collections *Sangschaw* and *Penny Wheep.*
1926	MacDiarmid's *A Drunk Man Looks at the Thistle* published.
1936	Edwin Muir publishes *Scott and Scotland.*
1947	Establishment of Edinburgh International Festival.
1958	Kurt Wittig, *The Scottish Tradition in Literature.*
1961	Muriel Spark, *The Prime of Miss Jean Brodie.*
1963	*Studies in Scottish Literature* founded in the United States.
1970	Association for Scottish Literary Studies
1971	Establishment of the Department of Scottish Literature at the University of Glasgow, the first in the world.
1981	Alasdair Gray, *Lanark.*
1993	Irvine Welsh, *Trainspotting.*
1987–8	Four-volume *History of Scottish Literature* published by Aberdeen University Press.
1995	Separate Chair of Scottish Literature established at the University of Glasgow.
1999	Election of new Scottish Parliament (established after a referendum of 1997).
2004	Edwin Morgan named by the parliament as official Scottish 'Makar' or poet.
2006	Scottish National Theatre founded (an institution aspired to since the early twentieth century).
2007	Three-volume *History of Scottish Literature* published by Edinburgh University Press.
2007	Scottish National Party forms the administration in the Scottish parliament as Holyrood.

Edinburgh Critical Guides to Literature
Series Editors: Martin Halliwell, University of Leicester and Andy Mousley, De Montfort University

Published Titles:
Gothic Literature, Andrew Smith
Canadian Literature, Faye Hammill
Women's Poetry, Jo Gill
Contemporary American Drama, Annette J. Saddik
Shakespeare, Gabriel Egan
Asian American Literature, Bella Adams
Children's Literature, M. O. Grenby
Contemporary British Fiction, Nick Bentley
Renaissance Literature, Siobhan Keenan
Scottish Literature, Gerard Carruthers

Forthcoming Titles in the Series:
Restoration and Eighteenth-Century Literature, Hamish Mathison
Contemporary American Fiction, David Brauner
Victorian Literature, David Amigoni
Crime Fiction, Stacy Gillis
Modern American Literature, Catherine Morley
Modernist Literature, Rachel Potter
Medieval Literature, Pamela King
Women's Fiction, Sarah Sceats
African American Literature, Jennifer Terry
Contemporary British Drama, David Lane
Contemporary Poetry, Nerys Williams
Postcolonial Literature, Dave Gunning

Introduction

This book deals with the contested, fabricated and vibrant subject of 'Scottish literature'. All academic disciplines in recent decades, in the sciences as well as the arts, have come under scrutiny for being not so much 'naturally occurring' as 'human constructs'. For many years, Scottish literature seen through the eyes of some was a nationalistically formulated and politically loaded project. To some extent this was true, but in the light of the new self-reflection that 'English Literature' (and all other canons of literature with a national element in their rubric) has undergone, Scottish literature in a sense suddenly finds itself on a level playing field. Even if Scottish literature is no more problematic as a concept than English literature, however, then it must also undergo the same self-reflexive scrutiny that English literature has recently been subjected to. A number of commentators have rightly diagnosed Scottish literature as a field of study which has been much slower to examine its own constructedness, and to be less immediately open to the theoretical approaches that have radicalised the foundations of literary study, generally, since the 1980s.

Chapter 1 of this book undertakes the task of uncovering and interrogating the canonical construction of Scottish literature. Paradoxically, as we shall see, many of the literary commentators who did much to establish Scottish literature as one for distinctive scholarly investigation tended to see it, at best, as representing a broken and compromised cultural tradition. This is the case in what

I will label 'generalist' Scottish literary criticism. These are treatments of Scottish literature that attempt to read historically dominant characteristics in national or even racial context. This main trunk of 'generalist' Scottish literary criticism, which sees Scottish literature as receding in authenticity, and increasingly suffering from cultural pollution and decreasingly 'national', runs from 1919 until the 1980s, and possibly beyond. As we shall see, much of this criticism is also Anglocentric in comparing Scottish literature unfavourably to an 'English literary tradition' that is over-idealised as a more complete cultural entity. As we shall see, modern Scottish literary criticism in its original quest for a culturally *distinctive* tradition stemmed from Matthew Arnold's late nineteenth-century postulation of 'Celticism' as a distinctive component in British culture. As I discuss in the following chapters, the idea of a Celtic-informed Scottish literature has often been conceived as different from, but eventually decidedly inferior to, English and other national literary traditions which are supposedly more organically full or completely developed. The discussion starting in Chapter 1 raises such questions as: What is authenticity in literature, Scottish or any other? Is a national context important? Or, alternatively, might it be often irrelevant to literary writers?

This book takes the view that although national context is not all-defining, and indeed has been often over-read by Scottish critics, it is still an important one. The notion of nation may be to some extent mythic, but 'myths' often occupy a position somewhere between truth and falsity, in that the successful ones become, in a sense, reality. People believe such defining stories, act on them in the world and promulgate them in their expression. We find such active myths as the 'fighting Scot', the 'freedom-loving Scot', the 'primitive Scot', the 'puritanical Scot' and the 'civilised Scot', all of which will appear prominently as we chart the literary history of Scotland.

Chapter 2 takes a seemingly rather obvious plank of national identity – the Scots language – and looks at its interrelations with the rise of a literary identity from the fourteenth century which is closely groomed by national interest. Literature in Scots from the medieval period to the present is often associated with a sense of core identity, and yet this literature has historically been as manufactured or, we might say with some dramatic emphasis, 'imposed' upon the Scottish people as English literature has supposed to have been. Is there much point in arguing, as many have done, that the English language (and literature) has been part of a colonising effect in supplanting the Scots language, when that Scots language previously, in large measure, supplanted Gaelic? Might we not merely adopt the multicultural argument to suggest that Scotland has all of these languages (as well as others now in their infancy, such as Punjabi and Lithuanian) in which people in Scotland are writing? Also, as Chapter 3 shows, Scottish literature in English is often as concerned with, or is as sensitive to, a 'Scottish' agenda, as literature in Scots. Scotland as elsewhere is a melting pot for languages and literatures. However, surely questions about power and domination remain? It would be naïve not to acknowledge an Anglocentricity (exercised as much by Scottish as English people) that sees Scots as lacking in the full expressive possibilities of English. Any language, however, does not have greater or lesser expressive possibilities than any other, so much as having greater or lesser cultural power. Political pull from London (or sometimes even from Edinburgh) has meant that naturally, in a manner of speaking, the Scots language was historically forsaken (especially as a language of non-fiction prose). Literature in Scots has come and gone in cycles, however, which might be seen to disprove the notion that it is inherently more limited as a medium than English.

If we are to be less concerned than we once were with 'tradition' and 'continuity' and fixed national cultural characteristics or modes of expression, we might also more easily begin to subject Scottish literature to new approaches. We might deconstruct its texts; we might apply feminist and other modern critical approaches to these (as Chapter 4 begins to exemplify). We might also bring Scottish literature more into the realm of 'Comparative Literature' (as Chapter 5 explores). New theoretical and comparative approaches can move the discussion of Scottish literature forward and away from simply the concerns of 'nationality' or 'Anglo-Scottish relations'. Both historically and theoretically, however, the belief acted upon in this book is that all of these areas – national, Anglo-Scottish, literary theory and comparative literary studies – are important to the ongoing development and value of the subject of Scottish literature.

CHAPTER I

The Rise of Scottish Literature

In the last two decades of the twentieth century self-reflexive scrutiny of the discipline of 'English Literature' and 'English Studies' became a strongly marked feature in academic study. Within the framework of literary theory, this practice has sought to identify the ideological intent lying behind the rise of English as a subject in the nineteenth century, and its eventual supplanting of the classical humanities as the central arena in which literary criticism was conducted.[1] It is fairly obvious that canons, or selections of writers and texts for study on courses and in critical writing, are both inclusive and exclusive, and seek to narrate a cultural 'story'. A narrative foregrounded in the 'English' label is that of one particular nation among others in the British Isles, and yet English courses have long continued to include such 'non-English' writers as James Joyce, Dylan Thomas and Muriel Spark.

Might it be, then, that 'English' refers primarily to a *lingua franca*? And if this is the case, what is to be done, for example, with writing in Scots? Is this a different language from English or merely a 'dialect' of it? If it is the former, then presumably the need exists for a subject of 'Scots Literature'? If it is the latter, then why have this dialect and its rich creative literature, along with many other dialects of English, been largely excluded from the study of English literature? In other words, in recent years scholars have worried over the dominant canonical logic lying behind English Literature and its comfortable narrowness, and one of the results has been the rise of courses in historically marginal areas of English, whether American, Australian, Canadian, Caribbean, Commonwealth, Irish, New Zealand or Scottish literature (and language). These national or (in the case of Commonwealth literature, most obviously) post-imperial labels represent the decentralisation of metropolitan or 'high' English literary culture in which, previously, emphasis had been placed upon the cultural production and standards of London and the Home Counties' English departments in schools and universities throughout the world.[2]

CELTICISM

The construction of Scottish literature, of its own dominant canon, also raises questions about inclusiveness or homogeneity, and of bias in geography, language, ethnicity, gender, sexuality and religion. This chapter critically examines the different perceptions of Scottishness and Scottish literature that have informed nineteenth- and twentieth-century literary criticism. The principal aim of this investigation will be to locate the political and ideological assumptions on which these perceptions rest.

It is crucially to the second half of the nineteenth century that we must look for the modern rise of the subject, which is attendant also on the rise of English literature. One of the prime architects of English literature as an academic discipline was Matthew Arnold (1822–88). Poet, critic, schools inspector and cultural activist, Arnold worried over a number of tendencies in the mid-Victorian period, which might be summed up in the title of one of his own books as a looming crisis between *Culture and Anarchy* (1869). New and various waves of nationalist and proto-socialist political unrest had been unsettling Europe for two decades (one notorious outcome just around the corner was to be the establishment of the ideology of Communism in the early 1870s). Revolutions in scientific ideas, such as discoveries in geology which proved the world was much older than claimed by traditional Christian theology, and the theory of evolution (Charles Darwin's *The Origin of Species* had been published in 1859) were also conspiring to unsettle the old believing order of things. Faced with disruptive new political movements and increasing doubt about the existence of a Supreme Creator, Arnold looked for some kind of new cultural, or even spiritual, centre around which the labouring class of Victorian Britain (to say nothing of its expanding empire) might be made culturally cohesive. If Christian scripture was increasingly unsafe ground in this respect, then 'English Literature' might fill the void.

For Arnold, English poetry, especially, was full of cultural wisdom and good taste. Also, it could be cheaply and widely administered, presenting fewer of the exclusive problems raised by Classical studies (Greek and Latin) through which appreciation of the literary aesthetic was more usually accomplished at university, public, grammar and even parish school level. With much less of a barrier in respect of language, the increasingly fractious masses filled with the doubts of the age might be taught vernacular English literature as a civilising subject. Arnold's broad thinking made him perhaps the first fully-fledged theoriser of appreciation of English literature as a matter of 'social rather than purely individual' cultivating education.[3] His writings and efforts as a man of educational policy galvanised the rise of English Literature in the latter part of the nineteenth century in the universities, in schools, even in the Mechanics' Institutes (training colleges for an increasingly diverse class of artisans), and also as part of that important British imperial mechanism, the Indian Civil Service examinations.[4]

To a great extent, unsurprisingly, the fault-lines in Victorian and European culture and society (and Arnold's writings in response) registered in Scotland. For a start, the Scots were frequently enthusiastic in their support of the British state and empire. Scotland joined in the new enthusiasm for the teaching and promotion of English literature, to the extent that Robert Crawford has declared the 'Scottish invention of English literature' (a project he sees as extending from the eighteenth-century Enlightenment through the nineteenth century).[5] Leaving aside this notion of a Scoto-centric invention of English literature as a subject, this chapter is more interested in the Anglocentric invention of Scottish literature. We can begin charting this Anglocentric influence by observing that there arose in Scotland a new literary nativism which took its cue from Arnold's thinking generally, but with reference to one of his works in particular, his lectures *On the Study of Celtic Literature*, first delivered at Oxford in 1866. Arnold's lectures stand as testimony to the rise of scientific racism and the particular influence of the French Orientalist Ernest Joseph Renan, who was determined, amidst the renewed nationalist enthusiasm of the mid-nineteenth century (following on especially from the nationalist rebellions across Europe in 1848), to argue for distinctive characters and traditions within particular cultures and individual nations. Renan's emphatic distinctions with regard to Aryan and Semitic cultures inspired Arnold to venture into similar sweeping statements in cultural genetics. Establishing the long-rooted tradition of English culture or 'genius' that had produced its great literature, Arnold identified as keynotes 'Saxon' 'honesty' and 'energy' derived from 'Celtic' and 'Roman' sources.[6] Arnold's basic motivations here are obvious enough. He acknowledged the heterogeneous cultural history of Britain, though at the same time he homogenised, as 'English' culture was comprised for him of previously competing historic cultural elements; the Celtic gene was strongly associated with the other nations of the British Isles which England over time had incorporated or subjugated. The Roman component is at first glance, perhaps, perplexing until we realise that this adds, in a way particularly useful in combating or appeasing the Classicists, a dash of ancient venerability, which enhances the pedigree of English culture and literature.

Arnold sparked a late nineteenth-century enthusiasm for 'Celticism', which contributed strongly to effects that he did not particularly intend, including the revival of Celtic cultural nationalism in Ireland, Scotland and elsewhere. A plethora of studies in Scottish literature over the next half-century adopted Arnold's language as these attempted to stamp a Celtic identity upon Scotland. A few examples are quickly revealing. John Ross's *Scottish History and Literature* (1884) posited the 'Celtic fervour and enthusiasm' lying behind the course of Scottish national character and creative utterance.[7] Telling also is the overall theme of *The Feeling for Nature in Scottish Poetry* (1887) by John Veitch. Arnold had suggested that a Celtic influence informed English poetry's 'turn for natural magic, for catching and rendering the charm of nature in a wonderfully near and vivid way'.[8] George Douglas's *Scottish Poetry* (1911) finds in Scottish writers sometimes too much of an 'academic' direction associated with ('Saxon') England in contrast to 'a native energy, simplicity and spontaneity' (a Celtic sign, obviously) found most triumphantly in the Scots language poets of the eighteenth century.[9] One of the most flamboyant of the Arnoldian-influenced Scottish Celticists was Patrick Geddes (1854–1932), whose four-part periodical, the *Evergreen* (1895–6), was themed upon the seasons and inhabited the idea of Celtic closeness to nature. The magazine's title also recalled a two-volume anthology of poetry, *The Ever Green* (1724), edited by one of Geddes's heroes, Allan Ramsay. Geddes's invocation of a 'Scottish' tradition through echoing Ramsay's publication is a nice example of a widespread historical phenomenon with its roots in the eighteenth century which has carried on until the present day, the facile and convenient elision of Celtic (Highland or Gaelic) and Lowland Scottish identity (the latter being that, essentially, to which Ramsay's anthology spoke). In his keynote essay to the first issue of the *Evergreen*, Geddes saw his own activities in the context of a British Isles-wide awakening in Celticism:

> Our new 'Evergreen' may here and there stimulate some newer and younger writer, and hence beside the general interests common to all men of culture; it would fain now and then add a fresh page to that widely reviving Literature of Locality to which the kindly firesides of Thrums and Zummerzet, the wilder dreamlands of Galway and Cadder-Idris, of Man and Arran are ever adding their individual tinge and glow.[10]

In hailing a new 'Literature of Locality' Geddes can be marked out as something of a *fin-de-siècle* pre-modernist. One influential aspect of modernism, as it was to emerge fully in the early twentieth century, was its challenge to ideas of 'progress' and 'civilisation'. Such ideas were largely the product of eighteenth-century Enlightenment thinking which sought to formulate human thought and philosophy along the lines of reason, and against older (sometimes religious or supernatural) forms of belief, which it saw as often superstitious and non-progressive. From the late eighteenth century the Romantic movement, with its greater emphasis upon subjective states of mind, or feelings, had begun a reaction against this sometimes arid

Enlightenment emphasis upon reason. The late nineteenth century saw an intensification of this reaction, which looks towards the eventual emergence of modernism. The proto-modernist critique of civilisation from this time derived much energy from the work of the Scottish anthropologist of 'primitive' cultures James George Frazer in his pioneering work *The Golden Bough* (1890–1915), and new psychological work beginning to focus upon 'the unconscious', most obviously in the work of Sigmund Freud (also publishing in the 1890s). Emerging at this time, then, was a powerfully posited identification of a post-Enlightenment rationality that had caused the Western mindset to lose touch with more primeval and regionalised (that is, non-metropolitan) culture. Broadly, in a cultural coinage still current today, it was in this new cultural terrain that Geddes and others attempted to situate the Celtic apprehension as something close to the natural margins, the 'wilder dreamlands' that speak poetically, or with an irrational wisdom.

Some contemporary critics, noticeably Andrew Lang (1844–1912) one of Scotland's foremost men of letters and himself deeply interested in mythology (particularly fairy stories), expressed strong reservations about the new racial turn being taken in the description of (Celtic) Scottish identity by Geddes and others. Writing of the 'Celtic Renascence' in *Blackwood's Magazine* in 1897, Lang warned: 'Races have been too long mixed, and the history of race is too profoundly obscure. When we bring race into literary criticism, we dally with that unlovely fluent enchantress, Popular Science.'[11] Nothing daunted, late Victorian Scotland swathed itself comfortably in its newfound Celtic blanket of racial identity. The seamlessness of this garb might best be seen in the nation's cemeteries. In Glasgow's great 'Necropolis', for instance, can be found a sudden rash of Celtic crosses dating from the 1880s and 1890s and under these previously thought-to-be rather 'popish' icons are buried some of the most respectable citizens of douce, Presbyterian Glasgow. This aesthetic trend of Celticism, aided and abetted by the emergent sensibilities of *art nouveau*, represented a renewed 'indigenous' cultural confidence in Scotland. It made also, however, for a rather undiscriminating homogenisation of Scotland's self-image as it adopted the symbols (or pseudo-symbols) of an originally Gaelic-speaking culture, which the course of Scoto-British history since at least the defeat of the last Jacobite rebellion of 1745–6 had done much to subjugate. Indeed, it might be argued that Scotland's late nineteenth-century adoption of Celticism marks the completion of the 'safe' or neutering appropriation of that culture.

We shall return to the discourse of 'Celticism', or 'Highlandism', and another relation, the 'Kailyard' strain of literature, all of which have been seen by commentators as marking a strongly pronounced culture of denial and escapism in eighteenth-, nineteenth- and twentieth-century Scotland.

GENERALIST SCOTTISH LITERARY CRITICISM

In the early twentieth century the criticism of Scottish literature continued, crucially, in Arnold-inspired racial vein. There is an important but little noticed pamphlet, published for the Scottish Branch of the English Association: an indication that the promulgation of 'Scottish Literature' was also very much part of the promotion, after Arnold, of vernacular literary studies in Britain. J. C. Smith's *Some Characteristics of Scots Literature* (1912) pronounced:

> If humour implies, as it seems to do, some perceived incongruity between points of view, then Scottish humour lies above all in the perception of incongruity between the romantic and the vulgar, the general and the personal, the sacred and the profane. Some of these differences, it is not to be denied, correspond to differences between the Celtic and Saxon temperaments, and in the clash of these temperaments Scottish humour finds one of its choicest fields.[12]

We have here an acknowledgement of the plural history of Scottish culture (Celtic *and* Saxon). This is reasonable enough, but, at the same time, Smith's confidence that racial characteristics can be identified with such separate certainty is less credible to modern eyes. Smith's essay, in fact, is the missing link between Arnoldian Celticism and the dominant trajectory of what we shall call 'generalist' Scottish literary criticism for much of the rest of the twentieth century. Generalist Scottish criticism attempts to describe the continuity, or lack of this, in a way that is concerned with an over-determined or over-anxious sense of tradition.

THE CALEDONIAN ANTISYZYGY OF G. GREGORY SMITH

Not usually noticed is the foundational influence of the passage quoted above upon the most famous work of criticism in Scottish literature, *Scottish Literature: Character and Influence* (1919) by G. Gregory Smith (1865–1932), Professor of English at Queen's College, Belfast. Part of the late nineteenth-century wave of renewed scholarly attention to Scottish history and literature, Smith was general editor of the Scottish Text Society from 1899 to 1906, experience that he put to use in the width of reading in his book, which is the first extended generalist treatment of Scottish literature. It might be inferred that Smith's attempts to bring an overarching theoretical synthesis to his topic stemmed from dissatisfaction with a book which he had read in proof by a law lecturer at Edinburgh University, J. Hepburn Millar's *Literary History of Scotland* (1903); this book with its compendious, non-emphatic approach, largely unconcerned with the idea of any continuous tradition, actually looks much more modern today than Smith's. As Robert Crawford has discerned, Smith's approach to literary studies differed in some significant aspects from that of Arnold and his followers, but the fact remains that, in the 'Character' of the book's subtitle and in the central 'characteristics' that he discerned in the main trunk of Scottish literature, an Arnoldian racial lineage remains central.[13] Smith's book was written during 1918–19 and was consonant with the new *zeitgeist* in which the Treaty of Versailles and its encouragement of the national and cultural independence of smaller nations was soon to be signed. In line with this mood, Smith sought to emphasise the historic distinctiveness of Scottish creative utterance. Often with great humour, Smith coined the idea of the 'Caledonian Antisyzygy'. He used this label to gather together the two moods, the 'polar twins' of Scottish literature, realism and fantasy.[14] In an oxymoronic configuration where these two propensities coexist, often with a 'sudden jostling of contraries', the hallmark of great Scottish literature is identified from the time of the medieval 'makars' down to the late nineteenth century.[15] Smith infers that this configuration of realism and fantasy is testimony to a continuing 'medieval' outlook, where 'the Scot, in that medieval fashion which takes all things as granted, is at his ease in both "rooms of life"'.[16] The crucial coexistence between the rational and the irrational suggests a kind of continuity not usually so strongly argued either before or after Smith, given the large-scale historical disruptions such as the Wars of Independence with England, Reformation, Unions of Crown and Parliament which many commentators have seen as undermining Scottish cultural stability.

Smith's formulation, though, might be seen as a sleight of hand as it posits stability of constant instability. Standing behind Smith's account is anxiety about turbulent cultural interruption as he writes of

> the contrasts which the Scots shows at every turn, in his political and ecclesiastical history, in his polemical restlessness, in his adaptability, which is another way of saying that he has made allowance for new conditions, in his practical judgement, which is the admission that two sides of the matter have been considered.[17]

Smith's book is full of this kind of overarching generalisation, where it is far from clear whether the Scot is constitutionally unstable or merely open-minded to the point of incoherence. Smith is determined, however, to cast a largely positive spin on the Scottish cultural 'character', posing a kind of creative dialectic:

> The Scot is not a quarrelsome man, but he has a fine sense of the value of provocation, and in the clash of things and words has often found a spiritual tonic. Does any other man combine so strangely the severe and tender in his character, or forgo the victory of the most relentless logic at the sudden bidding of superstition? Does literature anywhere, of this small compass, show such a mixture of contraries as his in outlook, subject and method; real life and romance, everyday fact and the supernatural, things holy and things profane, gentle and simple, convention and 'cantrip', thistles and thistledown?[18]

To which questions an entirely reasonable answer might be: 'Who knows?' What is clear is that via J. C. Smith, G. Gregory Smith contorted new and extended usage from Arnold's original dichotomy of Saxon and Celtic characteristics.

Gregory Smith's account does one thing particularly that deeply roots subsequent generalist Scottish literary criticism. His quasi-racial musings set Scottish criticism off on the path of mass psychology, which led later Scottish critics into absolute pessimism about the viability of Scottish culture and literature. Smith also presents us with one of the basic problems of attempting to argue too strongly for the cultural distinctiveness of any nation or of enduring native tradition: that this runs the risk of separating it from Western or world cultural history, by painting limited locality instead of an arguably more vibrant cosmopolitanism.

Smith's account provoked the scepticism of T. S. Eliot, who, reviewing Smith's book from the point of view of a stable literary tradition, realised that Smith, in projecting continuity out of discontinuity (or instability), was building a house on sand.[19] A question which will surface again in this book is the extent to which healthy culture or literature requires a well-functioning nation or society, but this intuitive and common-sense assumption is one that underpinned Anglo-American literary criticism (largely resting upon the Arnoldian foundation) for much of the twentieth century. The poet Hugh MacDiarmid, however, revelled in the 'Caledonian Antisyzygy'. It seemed to MacDiarmid to provide the disruptive creative licence and Scottish national difference that his brand of modernism and nationalism required. In 1926, in his long poem *A Drunk Man Looks at the Thistle*, MacDiarmid declared himself 'aye [always] to be whaur extremes meet'.[20] It is no surprise, then, that he broke off all relations with his one-time collaborator in the 'Scottish Literary Renaissance' (the revival of Scottish literature in the 1920s and 1930s), Edwin Muir (1887–1959), when Muir declared that, because of the historical instability besetting Scottish culture, Scottish literature no longer truly existed. Muir, a close follower of T. S. Eliot, set out his influential ideas which, along with those of G. Gregory Smith, were to be the most seminal in twentieth-century Scottish generalist criticism, in his *Scott and Scotland: The Predicament of the Scottish Writer* (1936).

THE COMPLETE DESPAIR OF EDWIN MUIR

True disciple of Eliot in his desire for a stable and settled national culture, Muir borrowed from his master the phrase 'dissociation of sensibility' to describe Scotland's cultural catastrophe, which stemmed from the fatally altered national character brought about by the Protestant Reformation of the sixteenth century.[21] For Muir, then, in contrast to Gregory Smith, what had been precisely interfered with or destroyed was Scotland's medieval mindset. Muir saw the puritanical Calvinist form that the Reformation predominantly took in Scotland disrupting an organic socio-cultural harmony in which literature previously had sat quite naturally:

> For some time more or less corresponding to the reign of James IV, Scotland had a major poetry, written in a homogenous language in which the poet both felt and thought naturally . . . Once the language was broken up, the old fusion between thought and feeling was lost and a far reaching dissociation set in . . . [22]

For Muir, Calvinist hostility to creative utterance *per se*, and the introduction of the English vernacular Bible, meant that the golden age of literature in Scots under James IV was irremediably the end of a rooted native literary tradition in Scotland. More sober reflection on the facts, however, might have us pause with regard to Muir's diagnosis. He lambasted the introduction of the English Bible as undermining the authority of the Scots language; however, we might counter this idea with the fact that a rich Scots was still to be heard in Scottish pulpits well into the nineteenth century, at least. More widely, his notion of a homogeneous national language at the time of James IV ignores the complex linguistic situation where Latin is the language of law and church, and where French in Scotland, as elsewhere at this time, is in many ways seen as the language of high culture. And this is to say nothing of the troublesome existence of Gaelic, still spoken in the 1560s across more than half of the Scottish land mass.

Muir peddled bad sociolinguistics and bad literary linguistics, as history shows us that many writers are able to write in more than one language. His idea of 'homogeneous language' was also, in its insistence upon 'fusion between thought and feeling', disrupted after the Reformation (a new spin on G. Gregory Smith's dangerous mass-psychological approach). Muir was explicit about the disaster to the Scottish psyche and his own critical schooling; he wrote in his conclusion that 'feeling' and 'intellect' were placed in 'disastrous confrontation' by the Reformation, a collision 'for which Gregory Smith found the name of the "Caledonian Antisyzygy"'.[23] This is a licentious usage of Smith's term, just as Smith was licentious with his Arnold-derived vocabulary of cultural bifurcation, or split. Muir was a much more thorough prosecutor of organicist logic than Smith. He realised that the vicissitudes of Scottish history amount to a great deal of linguistic, literary, political and cultural turbulence out of which it is difficult to argue for any consistently enduring central Scottish cultural and literary traditions. In the background of Muir's account is Scottish history seemingly disabling Scottish literature with alarming regularity, particularly the Reformation (when it would be difficult to disagree that Calvinist hostility to drama stunted opportunity for Scottish theatre down to the twentieth century), the Union of Crowns of 1603 (when James VI, committed royal literary patron, is lost to Scotland as he goes south to England and sponsors a rich Jacobean literature) and the Union of Parliaments of 1707 (which becomes increasingly significant for critics who follow Muir, as it is seen to allow the Scottish Enlightenment with its supposed hostility to vernacular Scottish culture and literature). All of these are moments in cultural history which I discuss in this book, but for the moment we might simply bear them in mind as the bases for Muir's insistent narrative of Scottish cultural recession or of national circumstances becoming ever more diluted.

We might begin to counter Muir's pessimism by observing the Anglocentrism embedded in his reading of Scottish literary history. Muir's Anglocentricity becomes particularly apparent in his idealisation of two broad periods: the Renaissance and the Romantic in English literary history. Muir finds an index of England's important cultural progress in the case of the former in Elizabethan drama, which he claims spawns a vitally intimate expressive continuity through seventeenth-century metaphysical verse and into the lyricism of Romantic poetry. Finding a developmental or organic relationship here, Muir identified the hub of an English literary imagination that speaks of a tolerant 'humanist' creative intelligence, which helped to situate England at the centre of healthy Western civilisation.[24] In Scotland, on the other hand, the 'Scottish dramatic urge', according to Muir, went underground during the seventeenth century and fed into the rich folk tradition of the ballads. Muir believes in natural cultural development – for instance, the fact that a nation collectively will (and ought to) have a 'dramatic urge' – and that the progress of English literary history, essentially, represents the natural course of things. However, why should Scottish literary history necessarily be analogous to that of England? We can also pose the question: might it be that the literary history of any nation for better or worse is actually rather accidental? Literature, perhaps, is not naturally in operation according to any kind of absolutely given trajectory. More particularly, we might notice that Muir overemphasises *system* (or a rather monolithic idea of tradition) with his idea of a deformed Scottish dramatic sensibility re-routed into the ballads. In fact, Muir did not compare like with like. The ballads are not 'literature' in the print sense, and Muir, for all his often expressed admiration of the ballads, is actually guilty in his systematic approach of disrespecting these as an entity which is *lesser than*.

With regard to the Romantic period, in *Scott and Scotland* Muir regards two of Scotland's most internationally successful writers, Robert Burns and Walter Scott, as inauthentic because they lack a healthy national background. At a stroke, Muir suggested that Romanticism in Scotland (the claims for which would largely centre on Burns and Scott) does not exist. This is typical of Muir's far-fetched logic and implies a deep negation of Scottish literature in his writing.

CONTINUING THE LAMENT: JOHN SPEIRS, KURT WITTIG, DAVID CRAIG AND DAVID DAICHES

Muir's is the central work in twentieth-century Scottish criticism proposing the impossibility of Scottish literature. Hugely influential, his ideas were adopted and adapted by numerous critics. John Speirs's *The Scots Literary Tradition* (1940) sides with Edwin Muir in seeing the Scots language as, historically and ideally, the most important medium for Scotland's literature. By the twentieth century, he sees this as not viable. Speirs said of Muir's arch-opponent MacDiarmid (Christopher Murray Grieve): 'the weakness of such of Grieve's work as is in his "Synthetic Scots" can at once be traced back to the fact that he himself does not speak "Synthetic Scots", nor does anyone else.'[25] It is telling that Speirs lists prominently in the acknowledgements to his book the 'editors of *Scrutiny* . . . and especially Mr. and Mrs. F. R. Leavis'. The Leavises had founded their journal, for which Speirs was a reviewer, in Cambridge in 1932. F. R. Leavis was one of the most influential English critics until the 1970s and promulgated a view of the 'great tradition' in the English novel which has been seen subsequently as singularly elitist. On the other hand, he believed that literature should be more widely appreciated by members of modern mass society, for whom cheap cultural substitutes had taken its place. For Leavis this was a tragedy; he believed that literature spoke as deeply of the human condition as any of the widely approved utilitarian disciplines of the sciences or social sciences. In his anxiety that literature should be more integral to mass society and his discernment of a proper line of historical literary tradition, Leavis's influence was not only upon Speirs but also the *Scrutiny*-reading Edwin Muir. What we should keenly notice is Leavis's diagnosis that England had lost much of its connection with its great literary past. He demonstrates, then, that the lamenting of lost literary sensibility is far from an exclusively Caledonian phenomenon in the early twentieth century. In fact, from Arnold's to Leavis's time uncertainty as to the integrity of the cultural health of the nation in wider British terms is mirrored by similar anxiety in Scotland.

Kurt Wittig's *The Scottish Tradition in Literature* (1958) is another much read, long account of Scottish literary history.[26] Wittig's work is divided into three parts according to the metaphor of seasonal change: 'Spring Tide', 'Autumn Tide' and 'Another Spring?', and so carries on something of the Arnoldian idea of Celtic or Scottish closeness to nature. Wittig's project is essentially to define further the modalities of Scottish literature as first described by Gregory Smith. For Gregory Smith's 'fantasy' Wittig prefers the 'grotesque' (or 'exaggeration'); for Gregory Smith's busy realism he prefers 'formal intricacy'.[27] Complicating Wittig's portrait of Scottish expressive predilection, though, is what he finds to be the pervasive quality of 'direct statement' (which shades into the grotesque, often in the mode of 'flyting', the exchange of poetic insults). Wittig also promulgates the myth of Scotland as essentially a proto-Protestant nation for this quality of 'direct statement'. For Wittig, the medieval poet Robert Henryson is 'perhaps the greatest of all Scottish poets',[28] and he shows his deeply Scottish nature in 'using a tone of intimacy that clearly foreshadows the Presbyterians and their daily reckoning with God'.[29] Henryson also 'shares the old wisdom of the folk, their poetry, proverbs, and lore'.[30] Wittig conceded that Henryson 'writes art poetry' but has also a 'closeness [to] folk poetry . . . most evident in his many points of contact with the ballads'.[31] Often a shrewd critic, nonetheless Wittig provides an overarching characterisation of the Scottish literary tradition. The antisyzygical modality of the 'grotesque' and 'intricate ornamentation' set in a context of Protestant primitiveness is yet another general and historically desensitised account of Scottish literature. We should note in Wittig the emergence, much more explicitly than in any critic before, of the idea of Scottish culture as a small 'no-nonsense' culture (at its best close to 'the folk'), somewhat resistant to the metropolitan guile of the outside world, whether Rome or England.

Wittig did, however, see moments of overwhelming cultural pollution in Scottish literature. Most especially, he made some landmark judgements with regard to cultural splitting in the eighteenth century:

> whereas poetry is part of a living tradition, made up of symbols, allusions, values felt and recognised by the community out of which it grows, the Anglo-Scottish neo-classicism of the North Britons was primarily a deliberate intellectual attitude; and it is small wonder that Ramsay, Fergusson and Burns wrote good poems in Scots, but invariably bad ones in English . . . Much of the eighteenth century Scots poetry embodies the tunes, verse forms, and rhythms of popular song

> and dance – a consequence of the fact that it was not so much literary as communal poetry: it grew out of the interactions between the individual and the community in the village pub or in the club at Edinburgh.[32]

Later chapters will consider the claims that eighteenth-century Scots poets cannot write in English, that theirs was an expression 'not so much literary' and that neoclassicism was baneful in Scotland. For now we simply need to notice the ideas, reiterative in twentieth-century Scottish criticism, of compromised authenticity and cultural split, and the especial emergence in Wittig's commentary of Scottish literature being different (more folk-based), even implicitly less crafted, than was the case in England.

David Craig (b. 1932), in *Scottish Literature and the Scottish People* 1680–1830 (1961), is hugely influenced by Muir and Wittig, even though he explicitly criticises the latter for 'forced Scotticising'.[33] Like these predecessors Craig diagnosed a deeply fractured Scotland. Craig idealised what he calls the 'old communal culture' which he found in the eighteenth century where, in contrast to England, the poets Allan Ramsay, Robert Fergusson and Robert Burn 'inhabit the ordinary pubs and market places, centres of gaming, drinking, eating, small business deals, the coming and going of farmers, chapmen (pedlars), and lawyers looking for work'.[34] Craig's emphasis on the strength of documentary realism in Scottish literature at its best reveals his Marxist outlook, where literature ought primarily to be concerned with the realities of class and economics. England, on the other hand, he suggests, has a much more rarefied literary culture, in the eighteenth century, especially where country house patronage was widespread. Craig also seems to find a positive spin for Scottish culture and literature with regard to Protestantism. Whereas for Muir the great villain of Scottish culture is the Reformation, for Craig, Calvinism is to be rehabilitated to some extent as an outlook of protest and dissent in the face of urbanisation and the embourgeoisement of Scotland during the eighteenth century. Time and again, Scots poetry inhabits what he calls the 'reductive idiom', or a mode of satirical levelling which draws upon both folk wit and the iconoclasm towards hierarchy found in Calvinism. He sums up:

> The style used . . . plainly draws directly on spoken, unliterary Scots. That kind of sceptical downrightness is in fact what became the standard idiom of Scottish poetry. . . . It is always present, suggesting a kind of norm of common-sense (what Burns called 'countra wit'), even in the most abandoned comic flights. My point here is that it is through such processes in the sensibility, rather than outward censorship, that 'Calvinism' mainly affected the deeper life of the country.[35]

Calvinism, then, might be puritanical towards artistic expression, taking the view that such utterance is vane and profane in the face of the earth being a fallen place where humans do not exist to enjoy themselves. Unintentionally, however, it provides a predominantly sardonic mode to Scottish literature which is commendable and enjoyable.

However, Craig could not sustain his positive interpretation for long, as he vaunted his Marxist idea of a positive literature of protest. He is also, true to his mentors (as with Speirs and the Leavises with whom he worked closely at Cambridge), a believer in the ideal of a healthily socialised 'great tradition'.[36] Clearly, for Craig dissent cannot be wholesomely sustained forever, as he concludes that eighteenth-century poetry in Scots is ultimately compromised:

> The *form* of 18th century Scottish poetry tends to be incommensurate with wholeness of experience . . . The range of the forms used is rather restricting . . . A result of the taste for forms based on social festivities is to limit the kind of life, and the attitude to it, that can be expressed. Conviviality, the drink, music, and good fellowship of the pub, the fun and knockabout of the public holiday – such things form the situation and state of mind from which most of the vernacular poetry at least starts. One cannot but feel that it is at the expense of the more inward and settled and abiding concerns of the people.[37]

What Craig means by his last statement is that the reaction of poetic conviviality does not provide an adequate platform for reflecting the serious and sometimes tragic plight of 'the people' in Scotland. For instance, starvation was a potential fact of life for a substantial part of the population well into the nineteenth century. Craig reiterated belief in an organic culture and even, somewhat bizarrely, contrasted the inadequate context of eighteenth-century Scottish poetry with that of the more wholesome context of Alexander Pope and Jonathan Swift. Pope and Swift were as scurrilous and as streetwise in their utterances and themes as Robert Burns, for instance, 'but it is perhaps better for such wholeness of culture that such low life should intermingle openly with the polite. The result of the Scottish language split was that the upper classes in effect disowned a great deal of what went on in their own country'.[38] In other words, it is a pity that eighteenth-century Scotland did not have the country house patronage that English literature enjoyed in the same period. This is perhaps a not altogether cogent position for a Marxist such as Craig to maintain.

For Craig, not only is there an 'alienation from things native' in the upper classes but also, and perhaps more crucially, in the Enlightenment middle classes: the philosophers, historians, scientists and improvers who resided in an Edinburgh that was in its time celebrated as a great centre of culture and knowledge.[39] On this view, these *literati* – men such as David Hume and Adam Smith – are ultimately *Scottish* failures, whatever successes they might score in the cosmopolitan world of learning:

> several generations of the 'great Edinburg' made up a body of remarkably talented men, working and living together as a conscious intelligentsia who led their country in many fields of thought and professional work. Moreover they had a character and ethos of their own, distinctive in idiom and social attitude. The manners and idiom of their milieux did not feed a polite literature of any quality, and this correlates with their anxious awareness of a powerful culture near by, very different from their own yet appealing to them as a model civilisation – a culture less tied than their own to a backward country and one, too, which had a more articulate character and powers of expression . . .[40]

Here is maintained the long-standing vocabulary in twentieth-century generalist criticism of what is 'natural' and 'unnatural' in

Scottish culture and literature. Leaving aside the literature (most often in English) associated with the Enlightenment and to which we shall return, we simply record here that a second major unnatural mentality emerged in Scottish life: Craig's Enlightenment, a polluted outlook rivalling that of Muir's Calvinist Reformation. Peculiarly, then, by the 1960s, Scottish literary commentators were lamenting periods in Scottish cultural history that had previously been seen as formative components in modern Scottish identity. There is a level of specific literary detail here which we shall need to consider later, but it is worth noting that yet again a Scottish critic outlined a recessionist narrative, as Craig saw Scotland's history as largely a story of cultural pollution and decline.

David Daiches (1912–2005) can be said, in Andrew Hook's estimation, to be 'the finest and most creative scholar and critic of Scottish literature in the twentieth century'.[41] However, Daiches overarching view of Scottish culture and literature is ultimately a story of severely limited imaginative output. No one did more to confirm the longstanding critical idea of bifurcated or split Scottish culture, most especially with regard to the eighteenth century, and Daiches's *The Paradox of Scottish Culture* (1964) introduced a new piece of negative vocabulary to be applied to Scottish literature to sit alongside the rubric of 'antisyzygy', 'dissociation' and 'reductive idiom'. This new idiom was 'paradox': the idea that following the Union of 1707 and down to the twentieth century, much of the most notable literary creativity emerged in reaction or, paradoxically, to less than propitious national circumstances. Ultimately, Daiches saw this factor as unhealthy. His paradox-in-chief is that the eighteenth century (as with David Craig) revealed Scottish literature, in both its Enlightenment English sides and in its Scots poetry revival, to be a time of false achievement. Time and again, according to Daiches, separated or isolated strands of Scottish culture assumed a kind of unnatural prominence. So it is, he claimed, that the Scottish legal profession which did so much in the eighteenth century to assume civic and cultural leadership and an institutional centre of pride in the absence of the old parliament was, nonetheless, unable to provide 'a basis for a national culture or for any culture that took into account all the relevant and available traditions of thought and culture'.[42] Leaving aside the particulars attached to this judgement, what is apparent in yet another Scottish critic is the idealisation of a complete or organic cultural holism. It is easy with modern multicultural eyes to respond to this by asking: is any group or centre in any nation or society ever capable of delivering the kind of complete culture that Daiches like so many Scottish critics before him demands? Paradoxical (or hollow) creativity is diagnosed by Daiches in eighteenth-century Scottish culture in many passages that clearly reveal his own critical lineage, for instance:

> If you talk and, as it were, feel in Scots and think and write in standard English, then your Scots is likely to be sentimental and self-indulgent and your English is likely to be highly formal and in some degree de-natured. The expository, historical, and philosophical prose of eighteenth century Scotsmen is often very fine, because these are area of communication in which the formal discipline of a method of expression acquired at school was helpful. Scottish poetry, when written in English, was often (but not invariably) derivative and stilted, and when written in Scots was always in danger of being self-consciously humorous or low or 'quaint'. Eighteenth century Scottish literary criticism, which is almost entirely concerned with rhetoric, with the study of formal devices for stirring the emotions, is generally quite incapable of dealing with the more subtle and impressive devices of combining rational and emotional appeal to achieve richness of expression and tends to mistake floridity for eloquence, pathos for tragedy, and sentimental declamation for poetry. The reception of Macpherson's *Ossian* is evidence of this or, to take a more particular case, Henry Mackenzie's review of Burns's Kilmarnock volume in *The Lounger*, which praised some of the weakest and most sentimental of Burns's stanzas as being 'solemn and sublime, with . . . rapt and inspired melancholy'.[43]

Scottish inability to manage language, then, because of the respective status of Scots and English, leads to a kind of mass psychological confusion and an inability in aesthetic judgement. Another critic, Kenneth Simpson, in 1988 takes the Daiches thesis even further, arguing that eighteenth-century Scottish literature is largely the manifestation of a 'crisis of identity'.[44] Simpson, like Daiches, a fine critic of particular Scottish writers, perhaps delivers the final insult to Scottish literature in his anxiety to make an all-encompassing statement. In the fields of culture and literature, the Scots (in the eighteenth century and down to the present) are out of control, wrongly programmed automata, knowing little of the value of what they are expressing, aping the English or inhabiting their own denuded and psychologically incomplete Scottish utterance.

A number of critics and commentators in the last twenty years, whose work will be discussed subsequently, have begun to provide alternatives to the pessimism of the generalist Scottish literary and cultural critical tradition of the twentieth century, and to these different perspectives we shall return. A true paradox resides in the fact that (largely well-meaning) critics seeking to explore Scottish literature further have, due to their idea of a tightly-bound literature and nation, found Scottish literature ultimately to be unsustainable. Strangely, any academic seeking to espouse the view that 'there is no such subject as Scottish Literature' might well have enlisted Muir's or even Daiches's work to help prove their point.

The formal (especially university-level) discipline of Scottish Literature should very briefly be put into historical perspective. A landmark event in the modern establishment of Scottish Studies was the founding at the University of Glasgow in 1913 of the Chair of Scottish History and Literature, in keeping with the renewed nativist confidence in the late nineteenth and early twentieth centuries described at the beginning of this chapter. Indeed, its origins can be specifically traced to William Freeland, founder of the Glasgow Ballad Club in 1908, a society that sought to throw renewed light on, among other things, traditional folk culture and literature.[45] This professorship had an historical emphasis, though, and it was not until 1995 that the university established a separate chair of Scottish Literature. We should notice, then, something of a time-lag, which is borne out by other telling details. The Scottish Text Society (STS) came into being in 1882 (as an element in the founding of modern post-Arnoldian Scottish Studies) and until the present day has produced around 150 volumes. Scottish literature, then, might seem to be well served during the past century or so. However, again, the STS has been resolutely a project of historical retrieval, reaching only very slowly in focus from the medieval period into the eighteenth century.

Scottish Literature as an academic discipline and as opposed to being principally an adjunct of historical enquiry has only really come into being since the 1960s. G. Ross Roy in the United States founded its first journal, *Studies in Scottish Literature*, in 1963; the Association for Scottish Literary Studies (ASLS) was formed in Scotland in 1970; and the autonomous Department of Scottish Literature at the University of Glasgow came into being in 1971. This remains the only separate department in the world, though its existence, as with the ASLS, can be said to owe much to the burgeoning of courses in Scottish Literature at the universities of Aberdeen, Dundee, Edinburgh, St Andrews, Stirling and Strathclyde from the late 1960s, as well as a new mood of nationalist politics in this period.[46]

More recently, courses in Scottish Literature are to be found in universities in Italy, New Zealand and the United States. Provision at the beginning of the twenty-first century remains fairly strong in Scotland, but is patchy outside the country, though there are signs of new recognition with growing attention being paid to Scottish literature at the large American annual Modern Language Association conference.

The rise of the critical study of Scottish literature has been (and remains) something of an uncertain story and is one that we shall trace in the chapters that follow, as we now turn our attention to the primary matter of Scottish literature.

SUMMARY OF KEY POINTS

- The contemporary discipline and study of 'Scottish Literature' sits in tension with 'English Literature', but the historical rise of these two traditions is deeply entangled.
- The idea of the 'Caledonian Antisyzygy', the yoking of opposites as a predominant feature in Scottish literature, has its ancestry in Matthew Arnold's nineteenth-century identification of 'Saxon' and 'Celtic' characteristics in 'English' culture.
- Turbulence in national cultural history (particularly the Reformation, the Union of Crowns and the Union of Parliaments)

is seen by a succession of twentieth-century critics to be disabling in the literary sphere.

- Strengths in an otherwise compromised Scottish literary tradition are often rooted in folk culture and a closeness to 'the people'. Conversely, the synthetic aping of 'English' expression is often seen to represent an inauthentic form of Scottish literature.
- The generalist twentieth-century tradition of Scottish criticism provides an overarching sense of Scottish literature in relation to the nation that is too systematic and allows little space for the creativity of the literary artist.

NOTES

1. A classic account is Chris Baldick, *The Social Mission of English Criticism* 1848–1932 (Oxford: Clarendon Press, 1983). See also Baldick's *Criticism and Literary Theory,* 1890 *to the Present* (Harlow: Longman, 1996).
2. For an astute and wide-ranging engagement with these issues, see Robert Crawford, *Devolving English Literature* (Oxford: Clarendon Press, 1992).
3. Baldick, *The Social Mission*, p. 54.
4. For a much fuller description of Arnold's English project and its background, see ibid., pp. 18–58.
5. Crawford, *Devolving English Literature,* pp. 16–44.
6. Matthew Arnold, *Lectures and Essays in Criticism*, ed. R. H. Super (Ann Arbor, MI: University of Michigan Press, 1962), p. 341.
7. John Ross, *Scottish History and Literature to the Period of the Reformation* (Glasgow: J. Maclehose and Sons, 1884), p. 2.
8. John Veitch, *The Feeling for Nature in Scottish Poetry* (Edinburgh: Blackwood, 1887); Arnold, *Lectures and Essays in Criticism*, p. 361.
9. George Douglas, *Scottish Poetry: Drummond of Hawthornden to Fergusson* (Glasgow: J. Maclehose, 1911), pp. 66, 155.
10. Patrick Geddes, 'The Scots Renascence', *Evergreen: A Northern Seasonal* 1, Spring 1895, p. 131.
11. Andrew Lang, 'The Celtic Renascence', *Blackwood's Magazine* 926, February 1897, p. 191.

12. J. C. Smith, 'Some Characteristics of Scots Literature' (London: the English Association, 1912), p. 7.
13. Robert Crawford, 'Scottish Literature and English Studies', pp. 225–46 in *The Scottish Invention of English Literature*, ed. Robert Crawford (Cambridge: Cambridge University Press, 1998).
14. G. Gregory Smith, *Scottish Literature: Character and Influence* (London: Macmillan, 1919). See pp. 4–27 for the diffusive description of the Caledonian Antisyzygy.
15. Smith, *Scottish Literature: Character and Influence*, p. 20.
16. Ibid., p. 35.
17. Ibid., p. 4.
18. Ibid., pp. 19–20.
19. T. S. Eliot, 'Was there a Scottish literature?' *The Athenæum*, 1 August 1919.
20. Hugh MacDiarmid, *A Drunk Man Looks at the Thistle*, ed. Kenneth Buthlay (Edinburgh: Scottish Academic Press, 1987), ll. 141–2.
21. Eliot actually coined this phrase in 'The Metaphysical Poets' (1921) to refer to a process in English poetry during the seventeenth century where 'the language became more refined [and] the feeling more crude': Eliot, *Selected Prose*, ed. John Hayward (Harmondsworth: Penguin, 1953), p. 288.
22. Edwin Muir, *Scott and Scotland: The Predicament of the Scottish Writer* (Edinburgh: Polygon, [1936] 1982), p. 72.
23. Ibid., p. 36.
24. Ibid., pp. 47–51.
25. John Speirs *The Scots Literary Tradition*, 2nd edn (London: Faber and Faber, [1940] 1961), p. 155.
26. Kurt Wittig, *The Scottish Tradition in Literature* (Edinburgh: Oliver & Boyd, 1958); reprinted in identical pagination in 1978 by James Thin.
27. Wittig's identification of the grotesque is diffuse in his book; his most concentrated view of it from the medieval poem 'Christ's Kirk on the Green' down to the twentieth-century novelist Eric Linklater is to be found in ibid., pp. 329–30.
28. Ibid., p. 52.
29. Ibid., p. 50.

30. Ibid., p. 52.
31. Ibid., p. 52.
32. Ibid., pp. 160–2.
33. David Craig, *Scottish Literature and the Scottish People* 1680–1830 (London: Chatto & Windus, 1961), p. 310.
34. Ibid., p. 19.
35. Ibid., p. 76.
36. See the foreword to *Scottish Literature and the Scottish People 1680–1830*, p. 9.
37. Ibid., p. 95.
38. Ibid., p. 63.
39. Ibid., p. 63.
40. Ibid., p. 52.
41. Andrew Hook, 'David Daiches on Scottish Literature', in *David Daiches, A Celebration of His Life and Work*, ed. William Baker and Michael Lister (Eastbourne: Sussex Academic Press, 2007), p. 71.
42. David Daiches, *The Paradox of Scottish Culture: The Eighteenth Century Experience* (London: Oxford University Press, 1964), p. 66. See also Daiches's *Literature and Gentility in Scotland* (Edinburgh: Edinburgh University Press, 1982), which is essentially an expansion of his views in his earlier book, taking into similar negative account the effects of the Union of Crowns of 1603.
43. Daiches, *The Paradox of Scottish Culture*, pp. 21–2.
44. Kenneth Simpson, *The Protean Scot: the Crisis of Identity in Eighteenth Century Scottish Literature* (Aberdeen: Aberdeen University Press, 1988).
45. For a very illuminating account of the foundation of this Chair and many of the early twentieth-century energies consonant with those described at the beginning of the present chapter, see Edward J. Cowan, 'Scottish History and Scottish Folk', Inaugural Lecture, 15 March 1995.
46. A fascinating account of the genesis of the Department of Scottish Literature at Glasgow and the provision of Scottish Literature courses elsewhere is to be found in David Robb, *Auld Campaigner: A Life of Alexander Scott* (Edinburgh: Dunedin Academic Press, 2007), especially pp. 67–96.

CHAPTER 2

Scottish Literature in Scots

MEDIEVAL, REFORMATION AND RENAISSANCE PERIODS

One expression of Scottish literature is writing in Scots, which has a number of periods of particular fruition. The medieval period is the earliest of these, where literature in Scots can be seen to accompany a prominent national or dynastic agenda, 'nation-building' as I will call it. What is usually taken to be the earliest extant fragment of poetry in Scots (though from a fifteenth-century printed source) concerns the death of King Alexander III in 1286, when the Scottish monarch had fallen from a horse. Alexander had definitively ended Norse claims on Scotland by defeating King Hakon of Norway at the Battle of Largs in 1263. A shrewd politician, he had in turn married an English princess and a French noblewoman as he played a balancing game between much larger kingdoms and, for a time, deflected imperial English eyes from Scotland. The narrator of the poetic fragment bewails catastrophe:

> Qwhen Alexander our kynge was dede
> That Scotland lede in lauche and le, [law protection]
> Away was sons of alle and brede. [plenty]
> Off wynne and wax, of gamyn and gle. [play joy]
> Our golde was changit in to lede. [lead]
> Crist, borne in virgynyte,

Succour Scotland, and ramede, [cure]
That stade is in perplexite. [stood][1]

We might notice here the organic outlook of the medieval world, which we have seen Edwin Muir idealise. The king is dead and so all fails: the good times and even nature. Scotland has been a kind of paradise, but there has been a fall from grace and a new hellish reality is abroad as even gold is changed into lead. Scotland has been cast out of its Edenic state and all the poet can do is appeal to Christ to redeem the situation. The writer may well be personally devout, but we should notice a larger agenda. He (presumably) wishes, as with all self-respecting national or even regional commentators across much of Europe in this period, to couch his nation as an exemplary Christian kingdom even in its suffering.

The ensuing Wars of Independence from 1296 to 1328, when Scotland struggled to resist English incursion, cast up two national icons, William Wallace (c.1272–1305) and Robert the Bruce (1274–1329), who long feature in Scottish Literature with their saviour-like propensities. Bruce, by now King Robert I of Scotland, famously defeated the English army of Edward III at Bannockburn in 1314, and this paved the way for the Declaration of Arbroath in 1320, an address in Latin from the Scottish nobles to the Pope asserting Scotland's right to rule itself. The document is in itself, as a missive to the centre of Christendom, an assertion of Scotland as a civilised, cultured, Christian place (when imperial English propaganda had often previously suggested it to be a barbaric area ripe for subjugation). A number of interesting tropes or myths present themselves in the Declaration of Arbroath, which long endure in Scottish culture and literature. To take only two of these, the document claims that Edward has been treacherous and that at Bannockburn God has made his displeasure known on this front.[2] The idea of the betrayal of Scotland (as the only means of defeating it, implicitly) is joined by the martial myth: despite the Scots winning precious few battles after Bannockburn, the idea of the Scots as ferociously successful fighters, in time the myth of the 'fighting Jock', is an important one. This is due not so much to historical reality but as a convenient cultural and literary (or expressive) site of resistance. One of the boasts of the Declaration is that the Scots have arrived after journeying, first of all, from overseas in the northern parts of Britain, somewhat after the fashion of a wandering tribe, the lost tribe of Israel perhaps, a part of the Chosen People. They defeat the indigenous Picts and then hold the land against many other potential invaders, thus demonstrating their ordained lot in the world. We have, then, in another part of the Caledonian martial myth the idea of Scottish invincibility, which had been given convenient warrant by the Roman historian Tacitus writing around 80 AD of the small tribe of Caledonii led by Calgacus, who resisted Roman domination even though hopelessly outnumbered. The Declaration, in a rousing statement that is famously picked up in the Hollywood film *Braveheart* (1995), says: 'For so long as there shall but one hundred of us remain alive we will never consent to subject ourselves to the dominion of the English', and so harks back to the Tacitus-originated myth of the indomitable, freedom-loving Scot.

Unsurprisingly, there is an alternative reality underlying the ideas set out as fact in Tacitus and at Arbroath. Calgacus may not have existed, instead being a convenient mythical, muscular, heroic figure for the historian to set against a first-century Roman Empire which he believed was becoming bloated and unhealthily luxurious. The medieval Scots, though, seized upon the character, and vigorously promoted the notion of the unyielding Scot. Many ethnic and demographic complexities might be considered in a critique of the Declaration, which claims that 'This kingdom hath been governed by an interrupted succession of 113 kings, all our own native and royal stock, without the intervening of any stranger'. For a start, the term 'Scots' refers originally to the Irish immigrants who settled first in the ancient kingdom of Dalriada (Argyll) under Fergus, the first 'Scottish king', in 500 AD and the Scots more likely intermarried with the Picts rather than extirpating them. Also, 800 years until the Declaration leaves hardly enough time for '113 kings'. Perhaps more pertinently, however, both Wallace and Bruce, whose martial exploits allowed the letter to the Pope to come about, are *nouveau* Scots of Norman or French ancestry. Their families, like so many members of the thirteenth-century Scottish nobility, had arrived north in the wake of the Norman Conquest of the British Isles in 1066. Most pertinently, Wallace was probably as fluent in French, not only his ancestral language, but also the chief language of culture alongside Latin in medieval Europe, as in 'English' or 'Scots', a language that had also arrived in the north of Britain after 1066 as a variation of Anglo-Saxon brought by the native retainers and servants of the Norman nobility (though we should be aware that 'Older Scots', as an offshoot of the language spoken by the Angles who had invaded East Lothian, had been around since the seventh century). It is the language of 'Middle Scots', dating from the eleventh century on, however, more so than the ecclesiastical and aristocratic medium of Latin or French, which is used in medieval Scottish Literature in a project that we might, in retrospect, call nation-building.

During the 1370s John Barbour (c.1320–95) produced his epic poem *The Bruce* celebrating the exploits of Robert I and his grandfather against the English. Clearly, this text delighted Robert II, grandson of the Bruce, who awarded Barbour £10 in recognition. The poem's extensive use of the Scots language in the mode of *chansons de geste* (song of heroic deeds) made it both distinctively national and fashionably French: the *chansons de geste* genre associated strongly, for instance, with the deeds of the chivalrous knight Roland, was popular throughout Europe from the eleventh to the fourteenth centuries. The literary celebration of Roland's deeds often involved conflict between Christians and Moors, whereas, of course, Barbour's poem is about Anglo-Scottish tension, but this analogue, clearly, was in no way thought to be reductive of the Bruce's exploits (at least in Scotland), but rather to confer upon them the same sense of spiritual struggle as was to be found in the battle with the 'heathen' in the Holy Land. A consistently enjoyable tale of derring-do told with considerable narrative panache, Barbour's text is also carefully propagandistic, incorporating, for instance, the line 'Quhen Alexander the king wes deid'. This intertextuality, then, recalls the royal disaster that Bruce's messianic coming had now put to rights.[3] Striking also is the use of a certain trope:

> A! Fredome is a noble thing
> Fredome mays man to haiff liking [permits happiness]
> (I, ll.225–6)

Scotland we might say needed an Epic, one that used the most up-to-date European literary modes (*chansons de geste*, chivalry, Romance) to celebrate a very Scottish hero, but also incorporated a language (Middle Scots) intelligible to a growing burgess class as well as nobles, which was necessary at this time to the formation of Scottish civic and national pride. This text reminded the Scottish 'race' of their most celebrated characteristic, as lovers of freedom, albeit that this word, in its medieval usage, did not mean quite the same thing as the modern term, but rather the ability to dispose of one's own possessions according to one's own wishes. Robert II's gift to Barbour clearly demonstrates his awareness of the poem's nationally propagandistic accomplishment. Apparently, Barbour wrote a further two epic pieces, now lost, one of which is *The Stewartis Original*, claiming that the lineage of the Stewart dynasty, which arises through Bruce's line, can be traced back to Banquo, the character murdered in Shakespeare's early eleventh-century-set *Macbeth*, when the Stewart dynasty only really had a claim to regal prominence from the fourteenth century. The other text is *The Brut*, telling of Brutus, descendant of Aeneas, arriving from Troy in the British Isles. The large implication here is that the Britons (a term sometimes supposedly derived from 'Brutus'), a people increasingly concentrated in Gaelic-speaking areas such as Scotland, are true racial ancients, both in British Isles terms and in terms of their classical world origins. These in time set their faces in resistance against the Anglo-Saxon invasions that eventually swept through England. Again, then, we notice the emphatic concern with venerable, ancient pedigree.

Other major writing in Scots during this period also exhibits a clear patriotic purpose. *The Kingis Quair* (c.1424) ('the King's Book') may well have been written by, as it is attributed to, King James I (1394–1437), grandson of Robert II. The poem is the first of several high-profile, sovereign-authored texts in Scottish literary history that imply national pride in the idea of the monarch as literary figure. *The Kingis Quair* opens with the narrator reading *The Consolation of Philosophy* by Boethius, the Roman philosopher who was put to death in 524 AD and who wrote his text cheerfully from his prison cell. Boethius for the best part of the next millennium was read as a classic of Christian resignation to the will of God, and many historians have suggested that in the Middle Ages his book was second only in popularity to the Bible. Not only through this detail do we have a generally cultured, Christian narrator (James I), however, we also have a more specific claim to Scottish culture and spirituality vying with the case of England. This is because Boethius's work had been translated, or at least overseen, into Anglo-Saxon from Latin by King Alfred, a monarch who, with much justification, was long held by the English to be the epitome of educated, enlightened and religious monarchy. Alfred certainly believed in such a cultural formation, albeit that his own levels of actual literacy stand in some historical doubt. A further translation of Boethius was completed by Geoffrey Chaucer, whose standing with Scottish as well as English poets in the medieval period was hugely influential. We see Chaucer's example in *The Kingis Quair* in its use of rhyme royal, the seven-line stanza in iambic pentameter rhymed ababbcc, a form that is very well suited to an elegant turn of expression, and which Chaucer had used to great effect in his *Troilus and Criseyde*. However, the stanza is reputedly named after the usage of King James, the epithet thereafter taking on some coinage in England as well as Scotland. Generations of critics down to the present day have learned to call James I and a number of Scottish poets following him the 'Scottish Chaucerians', and the influence of Chaucer is undeniable. However, the implication that these Scottish poets are (perhaps rather slavishly) imitating a master craftsman who is essentially English is arguably not only an imperious insult, but a misplaced one. Chaucer, like James I, as with all English and Scottish poets at this time, is part of a wider cosmopolitan poetic culture, where, if anything, the French influence is *the* crucial impetus. We might turn to 'The Goldyn Targe' ('shield') by William Dunbar (c.1420–c.1513), where the narrator, concluding a long moral allegory concerning reason and sensuality, says:

> O reverend Chaucere, rose of rethoris all [rhetoricians]
> (As in oure tong ane flour imperiall) [vernacular; Superlative]
> That raise in Britane evir, quho redis rycht, [(for) anyone who interprets well]

Thou beris of makaris the triumph riall; [bear the victor's crown among poets]
Thy fresche anamalit termes celicall [polished figures divine]
This mater coud illumynit have full brycht. [topic; have shed light upon]
Was thou noucht of oure Inglisch all the lycht,
Surmounting every tong terrestriall,
Alls fer as Mayis morrow dois mydnycht?

O moral Gower and Ludgate laureate, [crowned with laurels]
Your sugurit lippis and tongis aureate
Bene to oure eris cause of grete delyte.
Your angel mouthis most mellifluate
Oure rude langage had clere illumynit [crude; enlightened]
And fair ourgilt oure speech, that imperfyte [beautifully gilded over; imperfect]
Stude, or your goldyn pennis schupe to write; [before; prepared]
This ile before was bare and desolate
Or rethorike or lusty fresch endyte [writing][4]

Here we see that the term 'makar' (adopted more and more aggressively by certain cultural activists during the twentieth century), as a distinctive Scottish term for 'poet', was a label extended by Dunbar to that great English writer Chaucer. Dunbar also has an awareness of the poetic canon in which he belongs in the context of 'Britane'; and, generally, in his mind the language of 'Inglisch' accommodates writing on both sides of the River Tweed. We should not, however, therefore simply read Dunbar, a man of proud patriotic presence at the Scottish Stuart court, as 'politically' British; for him it is quite clear that poetry and indeed language can have a trans-border commonality. We might notice also that Chaucer, who fought in the English campaigns in France in the 1350s, was similarly porous-bordered in cultural mentality as he derived much influence from French literature, even translating, for instance, *Roman de la Rose*. Chaucer's friend John Gower wrote more fluently in French and perhaps even in Latin than in English, and John Lydgate, English court poet, mentioned above by Dunbar, derived his major influences equally from Chaucer, from French literature and the history of the Trojan Wars. Dunbar, like these poets, was a man of international culture with a strong Scottish accent. It is perhaps fair to say that cultural (as opposed to racial) roots and origins mattered little to many medieval poets, cradled as they were in a common Greco-Roman Christian Europe in which for most of the period the pre-eminent modern literary 'nation' was France. It is interesting that a long distinguished line of Dunbar criticism often deals with the vibrant influence that the poet exerts in Scotland (and elsewhere) and his embroilment in Scottish court politics without worrying over any distinctive Scottish national agenda in his work.[5] Perhaps in a different way from that which Edwin Muir described, the Scottish medieval period really was, in a sense, a helpfully 'unselfconscious' literary time.

The mid-fifteenth to the early sixteenth centuries were an astonishingly productive creative time, perhaps never surpassed by any other such Scottish time-span in poetic output. Shared practice with much of the rest of western Europe gives rise to 'The Buke of the Howlat' (owl), written between 1445 and 1452 by Richard Holland (fl. 1482), a landmark, accomplished text of thirteen-line alliterative verse which was popular also at this time in early fifteenth-century England, though arriving a little later in Scotland and a form still in use later than in the southern kingdom as in Alexander Montgomerie's 'The Flyting of Montgomerie and Polwart' (c.1580). The form was influential within a relatively limited, importantly court-centred, national literary scene. 'The Buke of the Howlat' is a very specific piece of arch, local, political crowing, chillingly relishing the violent end of the dynastic rival to the poet's patron family, even as it is in the ubiquitous mode of 'bird assembly' poems, and is part of the most shocking piece of Scottish literature ever produced. In the same verse form, the anonymous 'The Taill of Rauf Coilyear' (late fifteenth century) tells the tale of the great Holy Roman Emperor of the late eighth and early ninth centuries, Charlemagne, being separated in a storm from his retinue at Christmastime, made vulnerable and encountering Rauf the coalman. Unaware of whom he harbours, Rauf takes the emperor home, but delivers blows to him when Charlemagne offers precedence to Rauf after the coalman has made it clear that the stranger is an honoured guest. A topsy-turvy tale appropriate to Yuletide (a poem perhaps even recited or performed at the Scottish court), the comedy of a beaten Charlemagne, last word in chivalry and Christian witness in the Middle Ages, represents, clearly, a very broad farce. Not only this, however, there is a deeper Christmas message, which Charlemagne is wise enough to imbibe; the emperor does not even reveal himself when the collier serves up to the king his own deer, poached earlier, but ultimately knights Rauf for his rescue services. Even amidst the satire of romance and chivalry there is a Nativity message about the king humbled (Christ the King is born in a stable) and the fragility of the human world. These effects of mode and theme written in Middle Scots demonstrate the confident vibrancy of literature in the vernacular language of Scotland at this time.[6]

We might also note here a 'tradition' of poetry with its roots in mid-fifteenth- century Scotland, the perception of which is one of the cues to those generalist critics noted in the previous chapter who seek to emphasise a demotic and particularly nativist propensity in Scottish literature. In the late twentieth century Allan H. MacLaine edited *The Christis Kirk Tradition: Scots Poems of Folk Festivity*.[7] MacLaine's anthology marks a recurrent issue in the definition of Scottish literary tradition in that it identifies a certain phenomenon but overdrives its significance. From the fifteenth to the eighteenth centuries, it is true that Scots poets often used the Christ's Kirk mode. MacLaine, however, reads this as a form of protest literature, especially in the face of puritanical but 'triumphant Calvinism'.[8] He reads the Christ's Kirk mode as a reactive, over-exuberant comedy pitched against po-faced Protestantism, and so yet again we find a version of 'dissociation' being diagnosed in Scottish culture. However, MacLaine's own anthology features, for instance, Alexander Scott's rollicking 'The Justing and Debait up at the Drum Betwix William Adamsone and Johine Sym' (c.1560) from a poet who was also a sincere Scottish reformer, William Drummond's 'Polemo-Middinia inter Vitarvam et Nebernam' (c.1645), a macaronic poem (and so an interesting deviation from the usual Scots language of Christ's Kirk productions) which, albeit in comic voice, celebrates the pleasantness of Scotland; and Robert Fergusson's 'Hallow-Fair', a work that, up to a point, depicts the healthy, non-luxurious living of the Scottish peasantry. Fergusson's poem, like Drummond's, is far from a poem of reactive holiday excess, which a number of the Christ's Kirk productions admittedly feature, and the trait upon which MacLaine places undue critical prominence in spite of the evidence of his own anthology. The idea of the often satirical (or 'reductive' to use David Craig's favourite term) Christ's Kirk genre in Scotland is mapped onto that familiar idea of the reactive, cornered but defiant Scottish people snarling in beleaguered or less than whole cultural – or national – circumstances. Continuity in these essentially negative terms is actually bought at the price of surrendering the diversity in detail and the variety that in many ways represents a more interesting facet of the Christ's Kirk 'tradition'.

The 'Christ's Kirk' genre has also been an important location in recent attempts to apply the critical perspective of carnival, as initiated by the Russian critic Mikhail Bakhtin. Christopher Whyte has offered extended carnivalesque readings of 'Peblis to the Play' (a 'Christis Kirk' poem written before 'Christis Kirk on the Grene', the former dating from c.1430–50, the latter most likely between 1490 and 1510), and also writings by the eighteenth-century poets John Skinner, Robert Fergusson and Robert Burns.[9] For Whyte, the carnival space at its most radical is a fairly comprehensive one where 'the relations between different social and commercial groups and castes, normally mediated conceptually, through ideology and language, [are] replaced by a free bodily contact'.[10] In other words, hierarchy and other divisions such as gender, or borderlines between high and low languages, are disrespected as everyone takes a holiday from the normal, respectable and social rigidities of life.

Where Whyte is most convincing is in his observation of the incursions of folk (especially rural) culture (with its pagan associations) into the urban space (his two chosen medieval poems are set in towns). However, there are details that do not seem to fit the carnival reading. For instance, Whyte claims that 'the women in "Christis Kirk" do not behave in a characteristically feminine way'.[11] The women in the poem, though, are seen at the beginning of the text 'weschin clene [washed clean] / In thair new kirtillis [gowns] of gray, / Full gay' (ll.7–9), which is as stereotypically female virginal and preening as one could wish. True, later on they fight and act in vulgar fashion, but are such transgressions so uncommon? Might we not simply be talking of social satire, to some extent anti-feminist satire, which is therefore not as radically transgressive as Whyte wishes us to believe? He also claims of 'Peblis to the Play' that the deep and comprehensive sense of carnivalesque inclusivity wholeheartedly involves the author also and is seen in an aspect of 'direct speech . . . as if the poet had simply allowed the language of the festivities to spill over into his poem'.[12] The text ends with the narrator saying he would tell more about the debauchery of the day, but the sun has gone down and the people have dispersed. One would assume that some of the characters, at least, have left to continue their fun, so why is the narrator coyly left behind if he is so implicated in the carnivalesque situation? What is at stake here is a reading of literature where Whyte (a critic especially interested in queer readings of texts) sees huge majority dissent from social (including sexual) 'normality' supplanted by much more 'anarchistic' bodily inclinations. He reads the laughter of inclusive hedonism rather than the ridiculing of human folly. This is an interesting alternative to consider; we shall return to discuss in depth a medieval text of deviant sexuality and bodily interest in Chapter 4.

Three major poets represent the power of the medieval makars at their height. The first of these is William Dunbar whose stylistic range is wide and who is sometimes seen, as a result, as 'showy' or, in better light, as a 'poet's poet'. Probably part of the Scottish delegation to London in 1501 negotiating the betrothal of the English princess Margaret Tudor to King James IV, Dunbar commemorated the marriage in a poem that has become known as 'The Thrissill and the Rois' (1503). If Richard Holland's 'The Buke of the Howlat' is literature as intimidation, Dunbar's text, somewhat in the same mode of Dame Nature overseeing the proper, ordered articulation of fauna and flora, is poetry as a lush diplomatic device insinuating the advantage of dynastic alliance (although there may also be a modicum of sly one-upmanship in the celebration of a happy union of Scottish male monarch and English royal spouse). Much more enigmatic, and indeed ambiguous about femininity, is Dunbar's 'The Goldyn Targe' (early 1500s), an elaborate aureate dream allegory where the male narrator has his reason assaulted and overcome by female beauty. It is a text that shows the natural landscape, as well as femininity, as sensual and sinister in equal measure. With its magnificent ambidextrousness, including also a brilliantly managed procession of Greek and Roman deities so that the reader (similarly to the narrator) is assaulted with allegorical, or sensory, overload, the text represents one of the high points of Middle Scots literary expression.

Exuberant and philosophical also, though in rather different mode, is Dunbar's longest work, 'The Tretis of the Twa Mariit Wemen and the Wedo' (early 1500s), to which we shall return in the context of the portrayal of women. Through the first decade or so of the sixteenth century Dunbar could be scurrilously humorous, as in the text just mentioned, socially observant, deeply contemplative or religiously devout. In this last context we might notice especially his joyous Christianity in works such as 'Done is a Battell on the Dragon Blak' or 'Ane Ballat of Our Lady'. The ornate, alliterative, tightly rhyming, mantra-like Latinate Scots of the latter attests to the Scottish medieval Catholic mindset which was soon to be swept away in the Reformation:

> Hale, sterne superne, hale in eterne [celestial star]
> In Godis sicht to schyne;
> Lucerene in derne for to discerne [lamp; darkness; by which to see]
> Be glory and grace devyne
> Hodiern, modern, sempitern, [for this day this age and evermore]
> Angelicall regyne [queen]
> Our tern inferne for to dispern [gloom infernal; disperse]
> Helpe, rialest rosyne.
> *Ave Maria, gracia plena.*
> Haile, fresche floure femynyne; [womanly]
> Yerne us guberene, virgin matern [govern us diligently; maternal]
> Of reuth baith rute and ryne. [pity; root and bark][13]

Robert Henryson (c.1450–c.1505) is often paired with Dunbar as equals in the extensive possibilities of poetry in Middle Scots.

In a title accorded posthumously, his *The Morall Fabillis of Esope the Phrygian* (1480s) shows the easy, cosmopolitan confidence of the Scottish writer of this time. With the coming of printing, the first large-scale collection of Aesop, a bilingual version in Latin and German, appeared in 1476–7, followed by a French translation in 1480, translated into English by William Caxton in 1483–4. Henryson's Scots version, then, complements this pattern of vernacular translation. No mere translations of a single author, however, as the title of the collection might lead us to believe, Henryson's thirteen fables (plus a prologue) are diffuse in source. They owe as much to the cycle of beast fables, *Le Roman de Renart*, as to Aesop and are often highly individual in their development of animal 'character' as well as in their (often deliberately) difficult moral interpretation. In one of the most celebrated texts of Henryson's sequence, 'The Cock and the Jasp', a fowl discards a jasp (or jewel) as he scratches around a midden heap for his dinner, since, logically enough, it is no good to eat. The reader is likely to commend the bird's lack of interest in worldly wealth, but it is not until the 'moralitas' at the end that we are given the proper interpretative key. The jasp, allegorically, has been 'wisdom' to which the dumb animal has paid no heed. For humans, however, the message is that we do not live on bread alone, but by the spirit and the mind as well. The reader may well feel somewhat cheated by this turn of events, but Henryson's overarching point is that humans, if they are wise, ought not to feel that they have wisdom always or very easily within their grasp. With such serious playfulness, reflection on the appetites, reason and the nature of the universe, Henryson's fables proceed with a delightful facility in both narrative and characterisation that allows a full gamut of moods from farce to tragedy.

Among the rest of Henryson's output, his 616-line narrative poem 'The Testament of Cresseid' (late fifteenth century) stands out. Extending the story of Chaucer's great 'Troilus and Criseyde', Henryson's text deals with the fate of Cresseid after she betrays her faithful lover Troilus amidst the epic Trojan wars. Cresseid, complaining to the gods after Diomeid, for whom she has left Troilus, discards her, is afflicted with leprosy. She eventually dies of this, but not before having charity bestowed upon her by Troilus who, encountering her, fails to recognise her other than as someone deserving pity. Much divided critical interpretation has been expended on Henryson's text, not least on its attitude to women. The most orthodox reading, taking into account Henryson's medieval Christian faith, is that the lives of both the central protagonists end in bitter disappointment in worldly terms, but that a moment of grace, indicating that Troilus and Cresseid are truly and eternally spouse to one another, completes the action of the poem, bringing if not happy then at least appropriate moral closure.

The classicism of medieval Scottish literature is arguably seen at its zenith in the writing of Gavin Douglas (1476–1522), scion of the aristocratic Douglas family and from 1515 Bishop of Dunkeld. As great a writer as Dunbar and Henryson, his work has perhaps not endured as accessibly as theirs, maybe because what has survived of his poetry is relatively narrow in scope. His 'The Palice of Honour' (1501) involves an elaborate quest for the abstract quality of the text's title with many abstruse difficulties on the way. The end of the poem features an invocation of three Scottish and three English poets alongside Latin masters, and yet again demonstrates the naturally elastic, catholic canonical mindset of the medieval Scottish writer. Douglas's *Eneados*, his rendition of Virgil's epic *Aeneid*, was completed by 1513, the same year as the Battle of Flodden when English incursions into Scotland led to the catastrophic defeat and death of James IV. Douglas's Middle Scots translation is often rather 'free', including the interpolation of prologues before each of its thirteen books. In its creativity, continuous narrative and alliterative energy it shows medieval Scottish literature reaching a highpoint in confidence at a moment that otherwise spells disaster for Douglas's native country.

A remarkable phenomenon can be observed with regard to the 'early period' of Scottish literature. In 1988 R. D. S. Jack edited a volume of critical essays of enduring fineness, *The History of Scottish Literature. Volume 1: Origins to 1660* (first of a comprehensive four-volume project under the general editorship of Cairns Craig).[14] Part of a much needed revisionist agenda which saw some more continuity between the medieval, Reformation and Renaissance periods than had been often the case, the 'origins' part of the rubric, which meant in Jack's anthology the fourteenth century, came to be precisely challenged a decade later. This happened in an anthology of primary texts translated into English, edited by Thomas Owen Clancy, *The Triumph Tree: Scotland's Earliest Poetry AD* 550–1350.[15] Pointedly, the one piece in Scots included is that often described as the earliest fragment in the language on the death of King Alexander, to which we have already alluded. This is situated nearly 300 pages into the anthology and so, accurately, it is quite clearly signalled that the Scots language is a 'Johnny-come-lately'. As *The Triumph Tree* demonstrates, the land that we know today as 'Scotland' is something of a palimpsest, Pictish, Latin, Welsh, Gaelic, and even Norse all being for a time settled and, in time, unsettled literary languages within its borders. A truly canon-bending anthology, one of its most provocative gestures is the inclusion of the sixth-century Welsh classic 'The Gododdin' since 'the kingdom at the heart of this literary work . . . is that of the Gododdin who occupied the territory of the Lothians, and had as their main fortress Din Eidyn (Edinburgh)'.[16]

Even more challenging, perhaps, is the inclusion (also in English translation) of that famous piece of literature in Old English, 'The Dream of the Rood', 'first represented carved in runes on a splendidly sculpted free-standing cross at Ruthwell in Dumfriesshire' (*The Triumph Tree*, p. 121). A phrase from the poem gives the anthology its name and this is to be made sense of in two ways. First of all, metaphorically the triumph of the tree is that it has many different branches of language and literature, a most acceptable message in terms of contemporary multiculturalism. Secondly, however, the title, in alluding to the cross upon which Christ was crucified, reminds Scotland of its cultural origins as a Christian country, most especially with regards to the coming of St Columba from Ireland to Scotland and so the bringing of Gaelic and gospel, literature and liturgy (Columba features prominently in the anthology as subject-matter). In 1998, the year after Scotland had voted for a devolved parliament and the year before it was established at Holyrood in Edinburgh, this was a gesture whose significance warrants some reflection. For a start, Clancy and his other collaborators in the anthology are scholars of the earliest 'Celtic' periods and are perhaps justifiably annoyed at the successfully enduring medieval attempt to draw to itself the idea that it represented a long-standing, settled Scottish culture.[17] Just how successful Clancy et al. have been in shifting the boundaries is shown in a more recent three-volume literary history of Scotland whose first volume period boundaries are 'from Columba to the Union (until 1707)'.[18]

If there has been something of a movement to work back before the medieval period, conventionally demarcated in terms of Scotland's literary history, there has also been, since the late twentieth century, a strong tendency to re-examine what comes after. The Reformation, Renaissance and the seventeenth century are seen to have more of literary substance going on than the main-stream Scottish literary critical tradition with its narratives of fatal disruption and discontinuity has sometimes allowed. This is true even of John Knox (?1512–72), the leader of the Scottish Calvinist Reformation and so often associated with hostility to literature. Knox had been accused in his day by the Catholic apologist Ninian Winzet (c.1518–92) of being hostile to the Scots language itself as his writing is a Scots-inflected English reflecting the fact that his style developed while he was living in exile as a Protestant preacher in the England of Edward VI. The polemics of Knox have returned to the fore in recent years, which is not to say that these have been retrieved necessarily as things of unalloyed goodness, but that these prose writings in their imaginativeness represent strong rhetorical and literary expressions which might, for instance, be critiqued in their gender suppositions.[19] The 'Gude and Godlie Ballads' (published in 1567), compiled by the three Wedderburn brothers, represent another notorious expression of the Scottish Reformation. These included adaptations of folk songs for sacred purposes and although seen by Edwin Muir and others as representing the puritanical policing of profane expression, these hymns are a sincere expression of Protestant belief in the God-centred world. They provide, in fact, a strong depository of Scots vernacular religious texts resorted to for over one hundred years, something that gives the lie to the claim that the Scottish Reformation absolutely crushed the Scots language. Worthy of mention in this context are the fine Scots love lyrics of Alexander Scott (c.1515–83), work of a reform-minded individual, which fly in the face also of the supposed Puritanism of the Protestant sensibility.

The most famous literary text associated with the Reformation in Scotland is the drama *Ane Satyre of the Thrie Estaitis* (1552) by

David Lindsay (c.1486–1555). Although he perhaps remained theologically more Catholic than otherwise, Lindsay, in his play, ridiculed the venal corruption of the medieval church. As Sarah Carpenter points out, he featured amidst a very obviously allegorical cast in an earlier performed version, a Poor Man appealing for justice against the avaricious church directly to the King.[20] In the final rendition of the play, John the Commonweil emerges as the greatest plaintive against the church urging action from King Humanitie, the earthly (Scottish) monarch who has to navigate a court scene beset with vices before deciding that reformation is required in morality and statehood. Often performed in the twentieth century, frequently taken to embody quintessentially Protestant and demotic sympathies, it is seen as another text in the canon, as Wittig would see it, of no-nonsense, earthily realistic Scottish expression. Drawing on traditions of English morality play and French *moralité-sottie*, as well as utilising a widely expressive Middle Scots language, Lindsay's play is a complex, cosmopolitan Scottish literary work with genuine anger in its belly.[21]

If the Reformation milieu has been only very slowly critically revisited in recent decades, quicker-paced activity has surrounded appreciation of the Renaissance in Scotland. It might be argued that the roots of this period are to be found in the humanist bias (where classical models are utilised) in poets such as Dunbar, Henryson and Douglas of the period of James IV. Certainly by the time of King James VI (1566–1625) we have very visibly in place a culture of learned, exuberant, even mannered, literary expression associated with the European Renaissance. James was himself a talented poet who wrote his *The Essayes of a Prentise in the Divine Art of Poetry* (1584) containing *Reulis and Cautelis* [Rules and Directions] *in Scottis Poesie*, a treatise in Scots patriotically promoting a national culture of poetry that was also in accord with the most modern literary innovation of Europe. Showcased here and among the numerous poets James encouraged at his court, or through its general influence upon even some poets who never met him, was the fine jewel of Renaissance writing, the sonnet. James's favourite (though eventually in disfavour for his militant Catholicism), Alexander Montgomerie (?1555–1597), was particularly experimental with his sonnet rhyme schemes, contemplative and rhetorically showy in equal measure, writing with great thematic width about love, nature, theology, human moods and even complaining that the king has not been paying him his promised pension. John Stewart of Baldynneis (1550–1605) is also a subtle and subject-wise supple sonneteer, along with William Fowler (1560–1612) and Montgomerie penning the cream of many hundreds of sonnets written in Scots during the late sixteenth and early seventeenth centuries. Fowler chose to imitate Italian (especially Petrarchan) models, while the other two, more typical of the writers around James VI, followed the French lead (especially the example of the more classically inclined Pierre de Ronsard). This French fashion follows the initiative of James, as result of the enduring 'Auld Alliance', Scotland's traditional friendship with France. Another striking 'national' predilection was the use, including by James VI, of the sonnet rhyming scheme of ababbcbccdcddee, often said to originate with the Anglo-Irish Edmund Spenser, but used by the Scots before the latter's supposed pioneering usage.

Other literary modes also abounded around the Scottish Jacobean court, for instance, Montgomerie's long religious/love allegory (best read as expressing the author's Catholic sympathies amidst the turmoil of post-Reformation Scotland), *The Cherrie and the Slae* (late sixteenth century), the stanza of which was to become seen later as one of the cultural signatures of Scottish writing. We might also mention Stewart of Baldynneis's *Roland Furious* (late sixteenth century), a long narrative poem based on Ariosto's *Orlando Furioso*. One other writer might be briefly mentioned, Alexander Hume (c.1556–1609), whose finely wrought poem 'Of the Day Estivall' (1599) projects both a beauty and latent sinister sensuality as it surveys the landscape on a summer day. Hume's gradual retreat from both the fringes of James's court and from poetry itself, it has been suggested, signals something of the increasingly Calvinist mistrust of the world that was abroad in the Scottish mentality from this period. James's accession to the throne of England in 1603 affords the convenient narrative of a recession point, when literature, supposedly sometime protected in the oasis of the Scottish Jacobean court, is thereafter afforded too little protection and rapidly declines. We shall return to this idea, but for now we might simply ask whether there are other concerns that might as justifiably concern the critic as much as 'national narrative' or modal criticism, in medieval, Reformation or Renaissance Scotland, such as, for example, gender and sexuality.[22]

THE EIGHTEENTH CENTURY

The eighteenth century sees a vigorous return to literature in Scots, often described as the 'vernacular revival'. In traditional criticism, this is seen as Scotland returning to a kind of cultural and literary authenticity, though, as we have seen, existing within a rather limited and ghettoised space. The term 'vernacular', actually, is rather unhelpful in its primary socio-linguistic definition of 'the native language of a people'. For one thing it is doubtful if literature, in its creative licence and special genres, is ever really written in such a language. If we examine what is undoubtedly a renewed emphasis upon the Scots language in literature in the early eighteenth century, we ought to be aware too of an agenda surrounding it that is arguably subscribed to by only a minority of the Scottish 'people'. In 1706, James Watson (d.1722), an Edinburgh printer, produced the first of three volumes of the *Choice Collection of Comic and Serious Scots Poems* (the other volumes following in 1709 and 1711). Watson's *Choice Collection* was hugely popular in its day and became a foundational text in eighteenth-century Scots poetry. It published 'Christ's Kirk on the Green', which it explicitly attributed to King James V, and 'The Life and Death of the Piper of Kilbarchan, or the epitaph of Habbie Simson', attributed to Robert Sempill of Beltrees (c.1595–c.1665) and which features the Habbie Simson or, as Allan Ramsay renames it, the 'standard Habbie' stanza. These two stanzas, with, to a lesser extent, the 'Cherrie and Slae' stanza (Watson also published Alexander Montgomerie's poem), became the cultural signatures of eighteenth-century poets writing in Scots. We should note, however, that Watson published more material in English than in Scots, including translations from Scottish Latin works, and was particularly heavy in his selection of poems by Robert Aytoun (1570–1638), who followed James VI to England, and is buried in Westminster Abbey. Aytoun represents part of a strong Scoto-Latinist tradition and is anthologised in *Delitiae Poetarum Scotorum* (1637) edited by Arthur Johnston (1587–1641) and John Scot of Scotstarvit (1585–1670). To Aytoun is also attributed 'Old-Long-syne', which going through a series of transformations became by the end of the eighteenth century in the hands of Robert Burns 'Auld Lang Syne', the most famous of all Scottish songs.

Watson's *Choice Collection* demonstrates two very interesting things Scottish criticism has been largely slow to notice. It is a volume that sees little possibility of a Scots language-led national literature and, indeed, is not much concerned with the idea of a national language, or 'vernacular'. If anything, following on from the work of Johnston and Scot of Scotstarvit, it venerates Latinity, as well as writers such as George Mackenzie (1636–91), who is until well into the nineteenth century a figure of hate among Scottish Presbyterians, being nicknamed 'Bluidy Mackenzie'. Mackenzie, like a number of others in Watson's anthology, is a Stuart loyalist (and as well as James V's, the poetry of James VI is published in the *Choice Collection*). The second thing we should be aware of, then, are the ideological credentials being laid down by Watson. He is a Catholic and a Jacobite, loyal to the deposed Stuart line of James II or VII, deposed from the British throne in the Glorious Revolution of 1689. Stuart loyalty is found throughout Watson's three volumes as the Tory, aristocratic ideals of the good life, which includes both 'high' (including Latin) literature and drinking songs and comical, even bawdy, verse. This is a sensibility largely forged amidst the tension of the English Civil War (1642–6) where the Royalist or 'Cavalier' side often saw itself representing both a more civilised and sensuous culture in opposition to the supposedly more puritanical, dissenting Protestant forces of the Parliament. In the Scottish context, by the time Watson was editing the *Choice Collection*, Stuart loyalty was seen to be all the more urgent in the face of a particularly puritanical Calvinist Scottish church. This had largely welcomed the Glorious Revolution and the ascent to the British throne of William, Prince of Orange, as William III, seen by most Protestants in Scotland as a guarantor against the supposed absolutism and Catholicism of the last Stuart king. Exiled in Europe, the Stuarts also opposed the Union of Parliaments between England and Scotland in 1707, so that a conjunction of Jacobitism and anti-Unionism came to exist in the early years of the eighteenth century and became a motor force in the revival of eighteenth-century poetry in Scots.[23]

Producing the first volume of the *Choice Collection* a year before the Union of 1707, Watson's anthology was in the vanguard of cultural resistance to that coming event. His likeminded circle in Edinburgh included Archibald Pitcairne (1652–1713), atheist, physician (an expert especially on the circulation of blood) and Latinist, profiling the rationalist, Tory Jacobite mentality which despised uncultured superstition and fanaticism. This it routinely equated with the Presbyterian church in Scotland. Pitcairne had attacked the Scottish church in his play *The Assembly* (1692), satirising the General Assembly of the Church of Scotland in a way that consciously echoed David Lindsay's attack on the medieval church in *Ane Satyre of the Thrie Estaitis*. Pitcairne's play owes much to the Jacobean dramatist Ben Jonson lampooning the Puritans of London, and so we should be aware of a cross-border cultural mentality that owes more to confessional or religious allegiance (and indeed repugnance) than to national identity. In characters such as Timothy Turbulent, Pitcairne caricatures the factionalism and even the sexual hypocrisy of Scottish Presbyterianism in a way that reverberates through the eighteenth century and into the next, as we shall see. Similar in outlook, though a believing Episcopalian (adherent of a Protestant church with bishops, very similar in theology to the established Church of England), was Thomas Ruddiman (1674–1757). Through Pitcairne's influence, Ruddiman became a copyist in the library of the Faculty of Advocates (the Scottish legal profession) in Edinburgh in 1700. This library, which in 1925 became the National Library of Scotland, had largely been the brainchild of George Mackenzie, and so we should be aware of the important institutional cultural continuity in this period among a circle loyal to the House of Stuart.

Ruddiman became an important editor and printer in the Scottish capital, in 1710 seeing through the press a gorgeous edition of Gavin Douglas's *Eneados*, which included a glossary of the Scots language which played an important part in reigniting Scots poetry. We should notice with this publication the conjoining of pride in both the Scots language and the heritage of Scottish classicism, and in this Scoto-Latinity or Scottish Humanism we see the cradle of the eighteenth-century Scots poetry revival.[24] For Ruddiman, like his contemporary and ally James Watson, though, there was not as yet any pronounced notion that Scots had necessarily been in the past, or might be in the future, *the* national literary language. Ruddiman displayed his ideological colours yet again in producing in 1711 an edition of the works of the seventeenth-century Scottish poet William Drummond of Hawthornden, Stuart loyalist but a writer who wrote largely in English. Another production was his edition in 1715 of the *Opera Omnia* of George Buchanan (1506–82), who had been a royal tutor, including under his charge Mary, Queen of Scots. Ruddiman, in this publication of the man who was often regarded as the greatest European dramatist in Latin of the sixteenth century, permits national pride to overrule the suspicion of Buchanan's proto-Presbyterianism. That showcase of Scottish Latinist pride, the aforementioned *Delitiae Poetarum Scotorum*, for instance, had ignored Buchanan altogether.

Out of the circle of Watson, Pitcairne and Ruddiman, however, emerged the first great poet in Scots of the eighteenth century, Allan Ramsay (1684–1758). Lost from sight for over 200 years, Ramsay's first-known published work, 'A Poem to the Memory of Archibald Pitcairn, M.D.' (1713), shows fairly precisely the Jacobite, anti-Unionist context from which Ramsay emerged. This is a profile sitting somewhat at odds with the traditionally emphasised, rather nebulously framed idea of Ramsay as a poet of the dissenting, proto-demotic energy of Old Town Edinburgh. Ramsay, indeed, was a cultural dissenter, but from the perspective of the Tory, Stuart-loyal sensibility.[25] Ramsay's poem to Pitcairn is prefixed by a quotation from Douglas's *Eneados* and laments that certain individuals have sold their nation's independence in 1707 for English gold. These men are very unlike Pitcairne, whom Ramsay places in the pantheon of Scottish heroes alongside Bruce, Wallace and John Graham of Claverhouse (c.1649–89) ('Bluidy Clavers'), along with George Mackenzie, deplored in the Scottish Presbyterian cultural narrative as a brutal suppressor of religious freedom. Written in elegant English couplets, it seems that, as yet, Ramsay, often regarded as the 'father' of the Scots poetry revival of the eighteenth century, had not grasped the possibility of Scots as a particularly viable literary medium. Much criticism of the 'crisis of identity' kind sees Ramsay as rather conflicted in his identity, as throughout his entire poetic career he writes variously in Scots, English and perhaps even a kind of Scots-English. An often cited piece of evidence with regard to Ramsay's mentality is his adoption of the club name 'Isaac Bickerstaff' (the pseudonymous editor of Richard Steele's London periodical, *The Tatler*), and his later change in *nom de guerre* to 'Gawain (or Gavin) Douglass'. These monikers were adopted in the context of the Easy Club, which paid for the publication of Ramsay's poem on Pitcairne. This anti-Unionist, Jacobite drinking and literary club based in Edinburgh took the view that eighteenth-century Scotland was being laid waste culturally as well as politically by the puritanical Whigs or Presbyterians, and the club's veneration of the periodical culture of early eighteenth-century England associated with Richard Steele and Joseph Addison (the Easy Club took great delight in Addison's journal, the *Spectator*) was part of this asserted outlook. Literary culture, whether English or Scottish, and perhaps especially Latinate, they believed needed to be reborn in their nation. It is not the case that Ramsay's shift in club pseudonyms, then, shows any conflicted cultural identity, but rather a continuous one, albeit one of heightened Scottish patriotism by the time Ramsay decides to adopt the name of Douglas.

Ramsay's Scots language poetry takes off in publishing terms in 1718 when he produced an edition of 'Christ's Kirk on the Green', adding a canto, or section, of his own to an original two cantos. He had immersed himself for some time in the antiquarian endeavours of Watson and Ruddiman, being particularly fascinated by Ruddiman's glossary to *Eneados*. His expansion of 'Christ's Kirk' marks the dovetailing of his own historic studies with a contemporary creativity, which he took further in the same year with the publication of a series of comic elegies in Scots. His 'Elegy on John Cowper' was in the mode of Ben Jonson's and Pitcairne's mockery of puritanical hypocrisy, as it depicted a kirk treasurer's man, collector of fines for immorality on behalf of the Presbyterian church, whose 'whore-hunting' (l.13) is a *double entendre* slyly signalling Cowper's alleged abuse of his office.[26] 'Elegy on Maggy Johnston' laments the death of a tavern-keeper and brewster who had previously kept the narrator and his cronies in happy insobriety; one of those poems that has often seen Ramsay portrayed as a straightforward celebrator of mindless drunkenness, it is actually more a protest poem than a hymn to hedonism, cocking a snook, yet again, at the po-faced mentality of Calvinist Edinburgh. Of this sequence of poems, all employing the 'Habbie Simson' stanza, Ramsay's finest production is 'Lucky Spence's Last Advice'. A catalogue of complaint against the non-Stuart, 'Whiggish', Presbyterian cultural powers of the day, this poem portrays the dying words of a madam of a brothel as, in the diction of a real mother, she urges her 'loving lasses' (Vol. I, l.7) to heed her good advice. This includes threatening clients who refuse to pay with reporting them to the colleagues of John Cowper (so the church has its 'uses'), as well as saving money for a rainy day. In the mindset of a Jacobite Tory like Ramsay, early eighteenth-century Britain is ruled by Whigs who care only about commerce and money, so that, ironically, in the poem Spence is couched to some extent as an important and successful 'Whiggish' business-woman. Capping this list of rotten authority, the madam urges her girls to avoid soldiers since, she says, they are more or less lawless. Scatological and farcical in its humour, the poem nonetheless diagnoses misrule, and Ramsay was perhaps not without some justification in his identification of contemporary cultural narrowness. His own attempts as Scots poet, bookseller, encourager of theatre and of painting were ferociously attacked in pamphlets and from pulpits by the more conservative factions of the Church of Scotland.

Ramsay's most famous work is his pastoral drama *The Gentle Shepherd* (1725), which celebrates the Restoration of the Stuarts in 1660 and features a series of folk songs; it remained hugely popular well into the nineteenth century. It is curious that over time Ramsay's ideological impetus, an aristocratic-leaning one, was largely erased in popular consciousness. By the twentieth century he is seen much more prominently, and in keeping with the nationalist and left-leaning predilections of Scottish criticism, as more prominently a pioneer of 'folk' culture. If he is, indeed, an important editor of everyday song, he is also important in the eighteenth-century rediscovery of medieval and Renaissance Scottish verse, in his anthology *The Ever Green* (1724). This makes extensive use of the hugely important Bannatyne manuscript (works gathered together by George Bannatyne in 1568) so that Henryson and Dunbar are prominently featured, having been previously largely ignored in Watson's *Choice Collection*.

Ramsay is the most prominent of a number of important Scots language poets in the first seven decades of the eighteenth century. One living contributor to Watson's anthology was William Hamilton of Gilbertfield (1665–1751). His exchange of verse epistles with Ramsay marks a moment of high literary confidence in Scots, though his translation in 1722 of the medieval epic *Wallace* by Blind Harry (c.1440–92) from Middle Scots into English shows an artist less sanguine than Ramsay about Scots as a literary medium. In 1768 Alexander Ross (1699–1784) produced the longest poem in Scots of the century, *Helenore, or the Fortunate Shepherdess*, which is largely realistic to the customs of country life in the north-east of Scotland and, at the same time, a work deeply indebted to traditions of classical pastoral, and so exemplifies yet again the tradition of Scots Humanism. John Skinner (1721–1807), an Episcopalian clergyman and so, in Scottish terms, a cultural and religious dissenter, who suffered much official harassment throughout his life, wrote with equal facility in Scots, English and Latin. His 'The Christmass Bawing of Monimusk' (1739) is the most accomplished poem of the first half of the eighteenth century in the Christ's Kirk stanza.

The greatest Scots language poet of the eighteenth century before Burns is Robert Fergusson (1750–74), ambidextrous in writing fine work in English as well, although this has been largely ignored by Scottish critics. A legal clerk in Edinburgh who died in squalid circumstances in Edinburgh's Bedlam, mystery surrounds his death, perhaps from injuries sustained from a fall or a beating some weeks earlier; perhaps, it has been argued, out of Calvinist guilt that he had been so iconoclastic towards the Presbyterian faith in which he had been brought up. There is little evidence for the latter view, and it is interesting that Fergusson's ideological allegiances are almost identical to those of his predecessor, Ramsay. Indeed, the nephew of Ramsay's cultural kindred spirit, Thomas Ruddiman, Walter Ruddiman (1719–81) was the first to publish Fergusson in his *Weekly Magazine*. As with Ramsay, Fergusson is often taken to be a celebrator of Edinburgh conviviality and even excess, but there is both a strong recommendation to the moral, cultural and political good life in, and a darker edge to, his poetry. His 'Habbie Simson' performance, 'The King's Birth-Day in Edinburgh' (1772), exemplifies both features. A poem prefaced with a quotation from Drummond of Hawthornden's 'Polemo-Middinia' (a signal of Stuart loyalty) and going on to essay a scandalously riotous 'celebration' of the reigning monarch in the Scottish capital, it depicts a rotten cultural reality. The city magistrates, still in the 1770s of strong Calvinist tincture, are abused by the citizenry, veteran soldiers are ragged beggars and the city police force (or guard) is comprised of unruly Highlanders, both inept and violently oppressive, who have served Britain in recent wars. What we have, then, is a portrait of Hanoverian misrule and disorder. One comical moment has also a sinister undertone in the metaphor of rape, as the City Guard, whose Highland pronunciation of English is mocked, overload the gun being symbolically fired in royal salute:

> Oh willawins! Mons Meg, for you,
> 'Twas firing crack'd thy muckle mou; [large mouth]
> What black mishanter gart ye spew [misfortune; made]
> Baith gut and ga'? [gall]
> I fear they bang'd thy belly fu' [full]
> Against the law.[27]

Fergusson's poem ends with the idea that the muse does not belong in the malfunctioning Scottish capital, but needs to retreat to the country to seek refuge from urban conditions that are not amenable. In spite of using Edinburgh as a site of cultural dissent and distaste, Fergusson also, clearly, loves the city. His 'Auld Reikie' ['Old Smokie'] (1773) is a long *tour de force* Scots poem in couplets peddling both documentary realism of the sights and sounds of the capital and philosophical insight. With this poem and with Fergusson's work, generally, eighteenth-century poetry in Scots reaches a previously unparalleled point of achievement.

Along with Ramsay, Ross, Fergusson and Burns, one other Scots language poet and activist deserves particular note: Alexander Geddes (1737–1802). It is telling that these five poets all feature prominently in David Irving's *The Lives of the Scotish* [*sic*] *Poets*

(1804). After the first edition of a book that became hugely influential on the nineteenth-century perception of Scottish literary history, however, Ross and Geddes have the space allotted to them edited severely in the second edition.[28] The Tory, anti-Presbyterian, Jacobite sensibilities of Ramsay and Fergusson were increasingly 'written out' by the nineteenth-century Scottish mentality that begins to see the apotheosis of the eighteenth-century Scots revival as the Presbyterian, peasant poet, Robert Burns. There is, then, alongside this conception, no place for Alexander Geddes, Catholic priest from the north-east and one of the heirs of the tradition of Scots Humanism. Geddes's greatest poetic achievement in Scots is his 'Epistle to the President, Vice-Presidents and Members of the Scottish Society of Antiquaries' (1792), a sweeping survey of Scottish cultural history. Also notable is his *Three Scottish Poems with a Previous Dissertation on the Scoto-Saxon Dialect* (1792), where Geddes makes the claim that Scots is less bland than contemporary English and has more extensive expressive possibilities. This makes for a highly interesting moment in the history of eighteenth-century Scots, as it flies in the face of the idea that he and his contemporaries were, or felt, linguistically ghettoised.

The great fruition and also the complicating of the legacy of eighteenth-century Scots poetry are found in Robert Burns (1759–96). Inspired by Ramsay, Fergusson, Ross and others, Burns transplants to Presbyterian Ayrshire what was essentially in the eighteenth century alien poetic technology. On the one hand, Burns was at odds with the communion in which he had been brought up as he wrote 'Holy Willie's Prayer' (written in 1785) mocking Calvinist hypocrisy in a manner that can be traced back at least as far as Pitcairne in the Scottish tradition. This poem, seen as supremely scurrilous so as never to be officially published in the poet's lifetime, depicts a man ostensibly praying but actually, in the belief that he is one of the Calvinist Elect (vouchsafed salvation at the beginning of time by God), boasting of his status. He even rationalises the visitation of the sins to which he is 'confessing' as God's way of preventing him from being too perfect. Incorporating his insight that Burns imbibed from the interest in psychology of the Scottish Enlightenment, Willie vaunts his membership of the church in seemingly orthodox language. The reader should be aware that, ironically, Willie is crowing of his male sexual prowess:

> Yet I am here, a chosen sample,
> To shew thy grace is great and ample:
> I'm here, a pillar o' thy temple,
> Strong as a rock,
> A guide, a ruler, and example
> To a' thy flock.[29]

Based on real-life events in Burns's locale and passed around in manuscript form among farm workers and townspeople in a way that irritated the local church, the poem's popularity proved that the Presbyterian heartlands were not now, if ever they had been, entirely puritanical. Over time, Burns's usage of the 'Habbie' stanza, in this and many other poems, becomes so accepted as to be known as the 'Burns stanza'.

The success of Burns's *Poems, Chiefly in the Scottish Dialect*, published in Kilmarnock in 1786, shows the poet, supported in the subscription list for his volume by local lawyers, teachers and shopkeepers, to be part of the Ayrshire Enlightenment. Burns's volume projected humanity as closer to nature than it was sometimes thought to be. For instance, in 'To a Louse' the narrator mock-berates an insect for its cheek in crawling upon a finely dressed beauty in church, when the point of the text, of course, is that it is humanity in all its finery and pretension that is presumptuous rather than the dumb beast. As well as satire, Burns peddles 'sympathy', the doctrine of which he had been schooled in by reading the philosopher Adam Smith. Thus it is that he is also able in 'The Cotter's Saturday Night' to defend the unpretentious, sincere, Bible-centred worship of the Presbyterianism in which he had been cradled. This was largely a manoeuvre that no major Scots poet before Burns would have contemplated, and he is expansively even-handed in his human sympathy elsewhere in his poetic career. Fergusson may have mocked the Gael in his portraits of Edinburgh's Highland police force, but Burns protests against the despised status of the Highlander in several poems and is also one of the key revivers of Jacobite song for a Scottish market wider than the traditional Highland, Episcopalian and Catholic audience for such material. Despite his notorious reputation with the opposite sex, Burns included several (upper-class) women among his most trusted correspondents as he debated ideas with, and tried out his poetry on, them.

If Burns's widely even, deeply sympathetic sensibility can be argued, it is in the area of his reputation as a 'peasant poet', naturally inspired ('this Heaven-taught ploughman' as Henry Mackenzie labelled him in a celebrated review) that Burns is seen to be the epitome of literary democracy and novelty. The downside here is that, as we see in the labelling of the 'Burns stanza', the traces of the poet's literary antecedents are kicked over. Burns is, indeed, a great tradition-bearer of folk culture, but this is largely through his role (equally important to that of poet) as a song collector and songwriter. In his poetry dealing with the country customs of the people we find a poet very much 'schooled' in the modes of the eighteenth-century poetry revival (to say nothing of his very wide and catholic reading of all the mainstream poets of eighteenth-century Britain) and wielding a mentality that very much pertains to the contemporary Scottish Enlightenment. In 'The Holy Fair' (1786), a poem that depicts a Presbyterian field-gathering (where the pious would come to listen to numerous long sermons), Burns utilises the carnivalesque 'Christ's Kirk' stanza and an undercut religious language to pinpoint the real reason for such human congregations:

> O happy is that man, an' blest!
> Nae wonder that it pride him!
> Whase ain dear lass, that he likes best,
> Comes clinkan down beside him! [jingling]
> Wi' arm repos'd on the *chair* back,
> He sweetly does compose him;
> Which, by degrees, slips round her *neck*,
> An's loof upon her *bosom*, [hand]
> Unkend that day. [unnoticed][30]

By the end of the eighteenth century Burns had successfully widened the appeal of poetry in Scots from its previously narrower ideological identity. A telling marker here is 'Auld Lang Syne', which passed through various older versions by Robert Aytoun and Allan Ramsay, and which was essentially a Cavalier drinking song. In Burns's hands, this pro-Stuart context is largely erased as it becomes a generalised hymn to the parting of friends, very appropriate for an age of increasing, worldwide mobility for the Scots as well as others.

After Burns, the story of poetry in Scots is often couched as one of long decline. Certainly, the most overwhelmingly popular Scottish poet in the generation immediately after Burns is Walter Scott with his gothic, medieval romance-reviving productions, such as 'The Lay of the Last Minstrel' (1805) in English. In Scots, Burns helped inspire poetry that took up the causes of radical politics following the French Revolution in 1789. One such was Alexander Wilson (1766–1813), driven into exile in America for his outspoken views against the British political system. More typical, perhaps, however, was a conservative continuation of the Burnsian legacy where Burns Clubs of conservative, anti-radical, British patriotic energy sprang up from the early 1800s, and numerous poets besotted with the 'Burns stanza' and steeped in the phraseology of the works of 'the Bard' advocated piety, sobriety and political caution (three counts upon which Burns himself was of shaky reputation). There is also the work of William Tenant (1784–1848), whose 'Anster Fair' (1812) attempts to make more respectable the eighteenth-century Scots tradition of works on the festive theme, written as it is in English and sanitises as it does the hedonistic intensity of folk celebration. James Hogg, perhaps the best poet in Scots immediately after Burns, writes antiquarian tales of witchcraft and ancient romance, a kind of Scots-language counterpart to the work of Walter Scott. As the major Stirling-South Carolina edition of Hogg's work has begun to show in recent years, in Hogg's Scots poetry, as elsewhere, he is an even more important Scottish and Romantic artist than has commonly been realised.

Standard critical narratives see the systemic, infantilised descent of Scots poetry in the nineteenth century exemplified by the hugely popular *Whistle Binkie* anthologies (1832–90), in which Scots is seen as the preserved area for sentimental, mawkish and comic observation (most notoriously, 'Wee Willie Winkie' by William Miller (1810–72) features in one *Whistle Binkie* volume). More recently, though, critics have detected to some extent a more socially engaged, mature poetry in Scots in the nineteenth century, albeit by poets who often have to be somewhat disinterred from the periodical press and forgotten pamphlets.[31] It is also true that the most vibrant, enduringly read literary Scots usage is to be found as dialogue and sometimes as interpolated narrative within the English prose fiction of Walter Scott, James Hogg, John Galt and Robert Louis Stevenson during the nineteenth century.

THE TWENTIETH CENTURY

The twentieth century saw another significant revival of the Scots language in literature. Activists of the movement that came to be known as the 'Scottish Literary Renaissance', so labelled by the French critic Denis Saurat, most especially Hugh MacDiarmid (the pseudonym adopted by Christopher Murray Grieve (1892–1978)), felt themselves encumbered linguistically by an unusable past. For MacDiarmid, Scots had been compromised by Anglicisation and by its conservative literary usages since at least and including the time of Burns. Believing that there had once been a somewhat abler intellectual and cultural age for Scots, MacDiarmid issued the rallying cry 'Back to Dunbar!' In 1922–3, he published a periodical, *Scottish Chapbook* ('chapbooks' being cheaply produced pamphlets of tales, poems and songs sold door to door by chapmen, or peddlers, which were especially part of the Scottish cultural scene during the nineteenth century). In choosing *Chapbook* for his title, MacDiarmid was gesturing towards a culture that was, while popular, more underground, demotic and less official than the rather bourgeois, or mainstream, culture as expressed by the *Whistle Binkie* phenomenon. In his periodical MacDiarmid published poetry by a range of hands and his own agenda-setting essays which he called 'Causeries'. In one remarkable essay he attempts to position the Scots language *à propos* literature:

> The Scots Vernacular is a vast storehouse of just the very peculiar and subtle effects which modern European literature in general is assiduously seeking . . . The Vernacular is a vast

> unutilised mass of lapsed observation made by minds whose attitudes to experience and whose speculative and imaginative tendencies were quite different from any possible to Englishmen and Anglicised Scots to-day. It is an inchoate Marcel Proust – a Dostoevskian debris of ideas – an inexhaustible quarry of subtle and significant sound.[32]

Here we see MacDiarmid attempting to position literature in Scots within the modernist movement. The idea of the alternative psychological or the subjective, peripheral, fragmented, irrational state famously comes to occupy the world of artistic expression during the modernist early decades of the twentieth century. Another exemplar of this kind of thinking on MacDiarmid's part was his repeated adoption across his poetry of Gregory Smith's idea of the Caledonian Antisyzygy. This as a badge of honour, the poet's positive spin upon it suggesting that it was advantageous that Scotland and its literature had been somewhat out of step with more normative, centred, metropolitan English cultural development. With considerable early panache, MacDiarmid set about demonstrating that the Scots language was a powerful site of modernist lyricism. His first collections, *Sangschaw* ['Songshow'] (1923) and *Penny Wheep* ['Penny Whistle'] (1926), exemplify MacDiarmid's Scots-language primitivist sophistication, where he sought to discuss universal or philosophical matters through the perspective of a medium that had supposedly been superseded. It is worth quoting one of the early poems, 'The Bonnie Broukit Bairn', in full:

> Mars is braw in crammasy, [beautiful; crimson]
> Venus in a green silk goun, [gown]
> The auld mune shak's her gowden feathers, [old; moon; shakes; golden]
> Their starry talk's a wheen o' blethers [pack of (spoken) nonsense]
> Nane for thee a thochtie sparin' [none; thought]
> Earth, thou bonnie broukit bairn [pretty; neglected; child]
> — *But greet, an' in your tears ye'll droun* [cry; drown]
> *The haill clanjamfrie!*[33] [whole; collection]

The expressive compression here, indeed the reductive 'conceit' of the planets as a group of frivolous idlers at a social gathering, perhaps a grand ball, owes much to the contemporary rediscovery of the English metaphysical poets of the seventeenth century such as John Donne by T. S. Eliot. A large part of Eliot's reinstatement of the metaphysical poets had to do with his apprehension of a later seventeenth-century 'dissociation of sensibility', where the English literary tradition had become aridly rational in expression, and so again we should be aware of the influential relationship between the 'English' critical and literary mentality and the taste and thinking of Scottish literary 'renaissance' activists like MacDiarmid. In his poem, MacDiarmid utilises a simple, insistent four-stress rhythm familiar from the ballads, another referencing of the 'primitive' context for his revival of Scots, and inhabits also, seemingly, the homely, 'nursery rhyme' idiom that he and others were critiquing as the cul de sac into which the vernacular had steered itself in the preceding century.

Cleverly, however, MacDiarmid is both registering this familiar, debased coinage and elevating its usage (here quite literally) to reach the cosmos. This boldly huge trajectory shows MacDiarmid as *par excellence* the transformer and reinscriber of poetry in Scots. The other planets are devoid of life, whirling silently in space, while Earth, the blue planet of water and of tears of suffering, is a place of renewal and rebirth (indicated in its status as a 'bairn'). The message of the poem is both straightforward and profound: humanity for all its travails, for all its emotional strife and, implicitly, its tragic history, is something positive. 'The Bonnie Broukit Bairn' is typical of MacDiarmid's early lyrics in evincing a large philosophical proposition in few, albeit nicely arch, movements. And this in a way that recalls elements of past Scots literary history while forging a new abstract lyricism that electrified the contemporary literary scene.

MacDiarmid's gentler sensibility as seen in the poem just discussed is evident in many of the early, short lyrics, though a more abrasive tenor is apparent also from the start of his career. He vented much splenetic prose throughout his life not only against those he regarded as among the numerous historical cultural traitors to Scotland, but including too such contemporaries as Neil Munro, James Bridie and Edwin Muir. Late in life, in 1962, he famously attacked the young existentialist writer Alexander Trocchi as 'cosmopolitan scum', utilising a fashionable Soviet insult of the day, which carried with it also anti-Semitic overtones. If MacDiarmid's terminology was extreme he was not without provocation, Trocchi having just announced from a shared public platform with the older poet that he himself had produced the only worthwhile 'Scottish literature'.[34] There was some irony in Trocchi's declamation as it was very similar to the kind of messianic literary presence that MacDiarmid had often previously utilised for himself. Politically volatile, MacDiarmid had been a founder member of the National Party of Scotland in 1928, had eventually joined the Communists, was in turn expelled from both parties, and rejoined the Communist Party in 1956 after the repressive Russian invasion of Hungary. If this latter fact has quite rightly tarnished his reputation, as might some of his utterances about the English that today strike us as racist, MacDiarmid has a largely positive status at the dawn of the twenty-first century. In 2000, when newspaper polls sought the 'Scot of the millennium', he garnered much support and, as a thriving critical industry attests, there are those who would argue he is the greatest Scots, and indeed Scottish, poet of all time. Most neutrally, one might offer that MacDiarmid was the most influential and indefatigable cultural activist in twentieth-century Scottish literature.

One facet of this, however, has been his major contribution alongside the Scottish critical tradition we have already examined in Chapter 1 to the over-discriminating attempts to identify writers who are truly, seriously Scottish. For instance, his early dismissal of Neil Munro as a mere purveyor of Celtic romance, when the work of this fine writer is much more than anything so simplistic did much lasting damage to Munro's acceptance within a serious Scottish literary canon. Again, there is some irony here, as MacDiarmid himself, though repudiating the late nineteenth-century revival of Celticism in Scotland as something *ersatz*, espoused a form of the same not least in his choice of pseudonym which he took as a moniker in keeping with Scotland's supposedly more essential Gaelic identity. Likewise, as Douglas Gifford has argued, MacDiarmid was rather grudging in his acceptance of fellow writers of the literary renaissance, including especially such pioneers of Scottish Modernism as Catherine Carswell and the likes of Violet Jacob (1863–1946),

Marion Angus (1866–1946) and William Soutar (1898–1943), all of whom are careful craft-workers in Scots poetry.[35]

As Gifford and others have recently suggested, these and other Scots language poets, including the earlier work of Robert Louis Stevenson, ought to be seen as part of a wider, deeper and more continuous Scottish literary context than MacDiarmid was wont to allow. MacDiarmid perhaps ought to take some blame for painting too bleakly the Scottish literary wasteland preceding him and too narrow a corridor of Scottish creativity in his own time. MacDiarmid's terminal spat with Edwin Muir is interesting, as it represents surely a conscious attack upon the former by the latter. After publication of Muir's *Scott and Scotland* in 1936, which claimed that serious literature was now impossible in the Scots language, the two poets, former friends and allies, fell out forever. If Muir's pessimism was too absolute and seen understandably by MacDiarmid as an insult to his own contemporary work, MacDiarmid, perhaps tellingly, turned to writing in English with increasing frequency the longer his career went on. Generally, we might even conclude that both Muir and MacDiarmid represent in their key pronouncements a similarly over-prescriptive approach to Scottish literature which has not always been helpful.

If MacDiarmid might be charged, at times, with unreasonable egotism, he is also undoubtedly a courageous poet and great galvaniser of literary endeavour. His *A Drunk Man Looks at the Thistle* (1926), a poem of 2,685 lines, replays to some extent the drunken excursus of Burns's 'Tam o' Shanter' though in much more inebriated as well as in more explicitly philosophical voice. MacDiarmid's narrator sees Scotland all the more clearly for his irrational state, since the nation's culture too is deeply murky and compromised, especially by 200 years of Scotland having thrown in its lot with the British imperial and industrial complexes. The most ambitious poem of the Scottish modernist period, on a scale that no other contemporary had the gumption to attempt, it is a text of perhaps mixed intellectual and prosodic effects, but at its best it is a funny and serious critique of the state of Scotland, the vigour of its Scots language unfailing. One might also highlight at the apex of MacDiarmid's irrepressible ambition, 'On a Raised Beach' (1934), a virtuoso usage of geological terminology amidst a meditation on life and death, though tellingly in an English-language context principally. One might suggest that this poem is a marker of the point at which MacDiarmid dispenses with Scots for any extensive poetic purpose.

MacDiarmid's closest literary collaborator for a time was Lewis Grassic Gibbon (pseudonym of James Leslie Mitchell (1901–35)). Together, the pair produced *Scottish Scene* (1934), a collection of essays and short stories that summed up much of the left-leaning cultural dissent offered by the Scottish literary renaissance. Particularly notable among the contents is Gibbon's Scots prose fiction, which, together with his trilogy of novels, *Sunset Song* (1932), *Cloud Howe* (1933) and *Grey Granite* (1934) (collectively entitled *A Scots Quair*), makes the most distinguished corpus of literature in the vernacular of the twentieth century, alongside, and perhaps even surpassing, the efforts of MacDiarmid. The story 'Smeddum' ('spunk') is typical of Gibbon's 'Diffusionist' outlook. Generally, the Marxist-flavoured anthropological theory of Diffusionism held that 'civilisation' was a compromised entity, arising with the ancient irrigation of the River Nile leading to the establishment of a settled farming culture and with it a hired labour system which signalled the beginnings of capitalism. For Diffusionists, the coincident superseding of the independent 'hunter-gatherer' represented a fatal loss for the human spirit and its freer way of life. 'Smeddum' features Meg Menzies, a force of nature, giving birth to nine offspring, but standing ambiguously within the Mearns community of the north-east, where all of Gibbon's Scots-language fiction is set. We are invited both to marvel and laugh at Meg as she does much of the work around the farming homestead which her work-shy, alcoholic husband refuses to undertake:

> However, he drank himself to his grave at last, less smell on the earth if maybe more in it. But she broke down and wept, it was awful to see, Meg Menzies weeping like a stricken horse, her eyes on the dead, quite face of her man. And she ran from the house, she was gone all that night, though the bairns cried and cried her name up and down the parks in the sound of the sea. But next morning they found her back in their midst, brisk as ever, like a great-boned mare, ordering here and directing there, and a fine feed set the next day for the folk that came to the funeral of her orra man.[36]

Typical of Gibbon's modernist period writing where humanity is emphatically yoked with nature rather than a separated sphere of human situation, Meg is equine, as well as a mother-earth figure, both tender and resilient. Her dysfunctional husband is only one of a number of male authority figures in the story, the others a veritably full cast of bourgeois patriarchy: teacher, doctor and minister, all of whom she bests in one fashion or another. Her feminine strength is a kind of residue of pre-civilised, humanity and her 'orra' ('spare') man confirms this independence not only in Meg's love for the disreputable creature, but also in the fact that his status, we learn at the end of the story, is 'orra' too in the sense that Meg has never actually married him. Revealing this eventually to her assembled children, most of whom are attempting to make 'respectable' lives for themselves, she enjoys their horror and prepares for the arrival of her 'black sheep' daughter Kath, who is coming to borrow money and say farewell prior to emigrating with her lover and live with him, marrying him only 'if I feel in the mood'.[37] Kath clearly is, like her mother, nonconformist, liberated femininity enjoying superior freedom in mind and in body.

Gibbon's *Scots Quair* is a more extensive exploration of off-centre perspective, as it features peasant female central protagonist, Chris Guthrie, intelligent and instinctual, challenging patriarchal, metropolitan views in her off-beat perception of the senselessness of the First World War. Related is her explicit enjoyment of her sexuality and in her lyrical awareness of the timelessness of the land, even as she registers the changing human use of it, in contrast to the restlessly fluid movement of civilisation, to say nothing of her unsentimental love and sometimes contempt for the humans she encounters. One of the most shocking things about *Sunset Song* when it appeared (and Gibbon genuinely scandalised the Scottish nation, most especially the folk of his native Mearns, many of whom regarded him as mud-raking *à propos* his native culture) was his portrayal of Chris's first husband, Ewan. Ewan goes from tender lover who had helped Chris escape from a brutal, incest-attempting father to a man brutalised by his experience in the army returning on leave and becoming a wife-beater. His eventual desertion from the front, intending apparently simply to walk back to Chris, for which he is shot as a coward, is seen alternatively by Chris as an act of redemption. This stunned the 1930s Scottish public, for whom the carnage of the Great War was very fresh, with a portrait that very precisely undercut that enduring symbol of national pride, the Scottish soldier. Narrated, as all Gibbon's Scots fiction is, in a voice he labelled 'the Speak', this gossipy, brutally clear-sighted, often nasty, inaccurate narrator was conceived as emanating from within the community whose events it narrates with all the simultaneous intimate insight and partiality that this implies. Unreliable, subjective and lyrical, Gibbon's narrative voice represents both a usage of literary Scots as mature as any in history, while being also one of the triumphs of British modernism.[38]

In one of many 'third-person' narrated (though character-focalised) passages, which accommodates epiphany, even something approaching stream of consciousness, Chris reflects upon the fragmented experience to which she is subject:

> that was Chris and her reading and schooling, two Chrisses there were that fought for her heart and tormented her. You hated the land and the coarse speak of the folk and learning was brave and fine one day; and the next you'd waken with the peewits crying across the hills, deep and deep, crying in the heart of you and the smell of the earth in your face, almost you'd cry for that, the beauty of it and the sweetness of the Scottish land and skies. You saw their faces in firelight, father's and mother's and the neighbours' before the lamps lit up, tired and kind, faces dear and close to you, you wanted the words they'd known and used, forgotten in the far-off youngness of their lives, Scots words to tell to your heart how they wrung it and held it, the toil of their days and unendingly their fight. And the next minute that passed from you, you were English, back to the English words so sharp and clean and true – for a while, for a while, till they slid so smooth from your throat you knew they could never say anything that was saying at all.[39]

For Chris, the Scots language situation is merely one factor among others, including class and gender, that speak collectively not so much of simple 'national' disgruntlement but a marginalisation of identity born of the 'progress of civilisation' and the centralising, colonising, metropolitan tendencies of modern culture.

After the striking modernist innovation of MacDiarmid and Gibbon, use of the Scots language in any central sense, or for 'high' purpose, is most fully seen in the accomplished poetry of Robert Garioch (1909–81) and Sydney Goodsir Smith (1915–75). They represent a post-MacDiarmid generation of writers where Scots is emphatically acceptable for the most cerebral thought. Following their heyday in the 1940s and 1950s, however, the legacy of later twentieth-century literature in Scots is patchy, at least in terms of the agenda of cultural nationalism engendered by MacDiarmid and of which these writers are apostles, where what was being espoused was Scots as *the* national language. In the second part of the twentieth century the most critically acclaimed 'Scots' literature is, in one sense, a regional affair. From the 1960s, the poetry of Tom Leonard (b.1944) foregrounded Glasgow patois, for some of the purists who had followed MacDiarmid a kind of debased, urban, sometimes even Irish-English inflected, non-'classical' form of Scots. Indeed, Leonard explicitly mocks the insularity of such people in a 'poster-poem':

> Makars' Society
> GRAN' MEETIN'
> THE NICHT
> TAE DECIDE THE SPELLIN'
> O' THIS POSTER[40]

Leonard's Glaswegian-voiced poetry proceeds from two major premises. The first, seen for instance in several poems where football fans unselfconsciously wax lyrical over a goal scored by their team, is that working-class patois is as expressive as any other argot. The second, where Leonard operates on this assumption often by means of a stereotypically aggressive narrator, angrily reacts against cultural snobbery. We see this in the third of his series in a sequence, 'Unrelated Incidents', which operates as critique of colonial power relations within the British Isles:

> this is thi
> six a clock
> news thi

man said n
thi reason
a talk wia
BBC accent
iz coz yi
widny wahnt
mi ti talk
aboot thi
trooth wia
voice lik
wanna yoo
scruff.[41]

Not prolific in poetic output, and perhaps his finest piece, 'A Priest came on at Merkland Street', is in English, Leonard has been an inspirational revisionist critic, most especially with regard to nineteenth-century Scottish literature, and has paved the way for numerous 'working-class' poets in a plethora of late twentieth-century magazines to express themselves in 'dialect'. As much because he is a student of mid-twentieth-century American experimental poetry, especially Carlos Williams Carlos, Leonard has been a Scottish trailblazer *à propos* formal freedom, including the foregrounding of naturalistic conversation and sound in his poetry.

Leonard's close friend and ally James Kelman (b.1946) has been both the most celebrated and derided of Scots language writers in the second half of the twentieth century. Kelman regards as telling of the unhealthy cultural hegemony that there is so much comment on his language choice, where critics marvel that Glasgow patois should be writ large in novels that feature a kind of late Modernist commitment to intense, subjective realism. Kelman is a 'Kafka of the Clyde' in one repeated epithet. Alternatively, commentators have loudly deplored the replete 'obscenities' in Kelman's fiction, as shown in the furore surrounding his Booker Prize-winning novel of 1994, *How Late It Was, How Late*, where, unusually, the judges had a very public disagreement over the book's merits. Some newspapers joined the bandwagon that saw Kelman's work as angrily rebarbative for no good reason. It is not without some irony that

Rabbi Julia Neuberger slammed the pointlessness of the novel, as it follows a blinded unemployed man as he attempts to negotiate his way around Glasgow in a way that replays the Old Testament scenario of Samson, interrogating similarly the idea of vulnerability to the power ambition of others.[42] Kelman's political and artistic commitment in his fiction and elsewhere are almost puritanically clear-sighted. His best novels, *The Busconductor Hines* (1984) and *A Disaffection* (1989), provide fascinatingly intense interior monologues by individuals beleaguered by uncaring, post-industrial capitalism, their situations unpleasantly aided and abetted by the aspirational bourgeois mores also of many of the people who are being oppressed under this system. Crushingly, sensitivity and intellect are little allowed by society in Kelman's fiction to his male working-class central protagonists who possess these characteristics. Like Leonard, Kelman is one of the most adept essayists in modern literature of the male psyche, vulnerable even as it might often appear assertive.

Of a number of Scottish novelists following the influence of Kelman, Irvine Welsh (b.1958) has been the most notably successful, speaking as he does to a youth market all the more open to him after the huge film success of his first novel, *Trainspotting* (1993).[43] Renton, played by Ewan McGregor in the film, however, is much less densely accented as the same character of unremitting Edinburgh–Leith patois in the novel. For all the ironies of this novel, with which we shall deal in a later chapter, Welsh's work, alongside that of Leonard and Kelman, not through any fault of these writers, confirms for many the status of Scots as the language of the urban gutter. All of these writers, however, like Ramsay, Fergusson or Burns before them, are very *literary* writers, a fact perhaps sometimes forgotten in equal measure by champions and detractors alike. Less controversial has been the unbroken usage of Scots in the context of drama over most of the twentieth century. Plays of historical and social realism such as *The Anatomist* (1930) by James Bridie (1888–1951), the work of the Fife miner Joe Corrie (1894–1968), *Jamie the Saxt* (1937) by Robert McLellan (1907–85), *Men Should Weep* (1947) by Ena Stewart Lamont (1912–2006), *The Jesuit* (1976) by Donald Campbell (b.1940), the trilogy *The Slab Boys* (1978–82) by John Byrne (b.1940) and *Mary Queen of*

Scots Got Her Head Chopped Off (1987) by Liz Lochhead (b.1947) represent a rich theatrical tradition where language politics are to the fore, certainly, but where Scots usage has shown itself to be continuously as dynamic as ever, to say nothing of its ability to attract a large audience.[44]

SUMMARY OF KEY POINTS

- The Scots language, which results primarily from the incursion of Anglo-Saxon after 1066, is used from the fourteenth century in a project of literary nation-building.
- Patriotism and the drawing upon European literary values coexist in literature in Scots from the medieval period to the end of the sixteenth century.
- The eighteenth-century Scots poetry revival is powered to begin with by a particular Jacobite ideological agenda, rather than being a more generally 'nationalist' reaction against the Union of Parliaments of 1707. It develops into a very full literary usage during the eighteenth century, most especially in the work of Robert Burns.
- From the starting point of literary Scots used to express cultural nationalism in the first part of the twentieth century, its usage has continued to the present with no less fervent, though different ideological aims. It has featured as part of the modernist aesthetic, and to convey regional and urban realism and the politics of cultural and linguistic power.
- Scots remains a potent literary language.

NOTES

1. Thomas Owen Clancy (ed.), *The Triumph Tree: Scotland's Earliest Poetry* AD 550–1350 (Edinburgh: Canongate, 1998), p. 297.
2. See the English translation of the Declaration in Gordon Donaldson (ed.), *Scottish Historical Documents* (Glasgow: Neil Wilson Publishing, 1974), pp. 55–8.

3. John Barbour, *The Bruce*, ed. A. A. M. Duncan (Edinburgh: Canongate, 1999), Book I, l.37.
4. See the text in R. D. S. Jack and P. A. T. Rozendaal (eds), *The Mercat Anthology of Early Scottish Literature* 1375–1707 (Edinburgh: Mercat Press, 1997), pp. 134–5, a superb surveying anthology with an excellent introduction to texts and critical issues.
5. A recent collection, which in its series of essays on the full range of Dunbar's writing, is instructive here, Sally Mapstone (ed.), *William Dunbar, 'The Nobill Poet'* (East Linton: Tuckwell Press, 2001).
6. For a survey of Scottish alliterative verse in its full panoply of operation, see Felicity Riddy, 'The Alliterative Revival', in *The History of Scottish Literature*. Volume 1: *Origins to* 1660, ed. R. D. S. Jack (Aberdeen: Aberdeen University Press, 1988), pp. 39–54.
7. Allan H. MacLaine, *The Christis Kirk Tradition: Scots Poems of Folk Festivity* (Glasgow: Association for Scottish Literary Studies, 1996). It is revealing that in the preface MacLaine acknowledges the originator of the idea for his volume to be that arch-theoriser of ghettoised and compromised space in Scottish literary history, David Daiches (see p. iii).
8. *The Christis Kirk Tradition*, p. ix.
9. Christopher Whyte, 'Bakhtin at Christ's Kirk: Carnival and the Scottish Renaissance', *Studies in Scottish Literature* XXVIII (1993), pp. 178–203; and 'Bakhtin at Christ's Kirk (Part II) Carnival and the Vernacular Revival', *Studies in Scottish Literature* XXIX (1996), pp. 133–57.
10. Whyte, 'Bakhtin at Christ's Kirk', p. 179.
11. Ibid., p. 190.
12. Ibid., p. 191.
13. *The Mercat Anthology of Early Scottish Literature* 1375–1707, p. 172.
14. Jack (ed.), *The History of Scottish Literature. Volume* 1.
15. Jack's volume appeared around the same time as Priscilla Bawcutt and Felicity Riddy (eds), *Longer Scottish Poems. Volume One:* 1375–1650 (Edinburgh: Scottish Academic Press, 1987), these two volumes together performing cognate functions in

countering the old Scottish critical canard that the Reformation had spelled the end, for the time being at least, of meaningful Scottish literature.

16. *The Triumph Tree*, p. 46.
17. Clancy and one of his translators in *The Triumph Tree* had earlier produced: Thomas Owen Clancy and Gilbert Márkus (eds), *Iona: The Earliest Poetry of a Celtic Monastery* (Edinburgh: Edinburgh University Press, 1995).
18. Thomas Owen Clancy and Murray Pittock (eds), *The Edinburgh History of Scottish Literature. Volume 1: From Columba to the Union (until 1707)* (Edinburgh: Edinburgh University Press, 2007).
19. See, for instance, C. Marie Harker, 'John Knox, *The First Blast*, and the Monstrous Regiment of Gender', in Theo van Hiejnsbergen and Nicola Royan (eds), *Literature, Letters and the Canonical in Early Modern Scotland* (East Linton: Tuckwell Press, 2002), pp. 35–51. The prose riches from this period to the end of the seventeenth century are highlighted, typically, by the brilliantly helpful R. D. S. Jack in his anthology, *Scottish Prose 1550–1700* (London: Calder & Boyers, 1971).
20. Sarah Carpenter, 'Early Scottish Drama', in *The History of Scottish Literature*, Vol. 1, pp. 199–211.
21. See the excellent introduction in David Lindsay, *Ane Satyre of the Thrie Estaitis*, ed. R. J. Lyall (Edinburgh: Canongate, 1989).
22. See two recent books, particularly, Sarah M. Dunnigan, C. Marie Harker and Evelyn S. Newlyn (eds), *Woman and the Feminine in Medieval and Early Modern Scottish Writing* (Basingstoke: Palgrave Macmillan, 2004); and Sarah Dunnigan, *Eros and Poetry at the Courts of Mary Queen of Scots and James VI* (Basingstoke: Palgrave Macmillan, 2002).
23. The work of Murray Pittock has been especially cogent in teasing out the Stuart/Jacobite background in Scottish literature. See his *Poetry and Jacobite Politics in Eighteenth Century Britain and Ireland* (Cambridge: Cambridge University Press, 1994), especially pp. 133–86; and *The Invention of Scotland: The Stuart Myth and Scottish Identity, 1638 to the Present* (London: Routledge, 1991), especially pp. 30–61.

24. For an excellent essaying of this background, see F. W. Freeman, *Robert Fergusson and the Scots Humanist Compromise* (Edinburgh: Edinburgh University Press, 1984), Chapter 1.
25. F. W. Freeman and Alexander Law, 'Allan Ramsay's First Published Poem: The Poem to the Memory of Dr Archibald Pitcairne', *The Bibliotheck*, 9, No. 7 (1979), pp. 153–60.
26. *The Works of Allan Ramsay* 6 volumes, ed. Burns Martin, John W. Oliver, Alexander M. Kinghorn and Alexander Law (Edinburgh and London: Blackwoods for the Scottish Text Society, 1951–74), Vol. I, p. 15.
27. *The Poems of Robert Fergusson*, ed. M. P. McDiarmid, 2 volumes (Edinburgh: Blackwoods for the Scottish text Society, 1955–56), Vol. II, p. 53.
28. David Irving, *The Lives of the Scotish* [*sic*] *Poets* (Edinburgh: Alexander Lawrie, 1804).
29. *Burns: Poems & Songs*, ed. James Kinsley (Oxford: Oxford University Press, 1969), p. 57.
30. Ibid., p. 105.
31. See, for instance, the poets dealt with by Tom Leonard in his anthology *Radical Renfrew: Poetry from the French Revolution to the First World War* (Edinburgh: Polygon, 1990). See also essays by William Donaldson, William Findlay and Edwin Morgan, in Douglas Gifford (ed.), *The History of Scottish Literature*: Volume 3, *Nineteenth Century* (Aberdeen: Aberdeen University Press, 1988); and material in Douglas Gifford, Sarah Dunnigan and Alan McGillivray, *Scottish Literature in English and Scots* (Edinburgh: Edinburgh University Press, 2002), for the reappraisal in recent years of nineteenth-century poetry.
32. Hugh MacDiarmid, *Scottish Chapbook* 1.8 (March 1923), reprinted in *Hugh MacDiarmid: Selected Prose*, ed. Alan Riach (Manchester: Carcanet, 1992), pp. 22–3.
33. Hugh MacDiarmid, *Selected Poetry*, ed. Alan Riach and Michael Grieve (Manchester: Carcanet, 1992), p. 9.
34. For a fascinating account of this exchange, see Andrew Murray Scott, *Alexander Trocchi: The Making of the Monster* (Edinburgh: Polygon, 1991), p. 108.
35. See Douglas Gifford, 'Remapping Renaissance in Modern Scottish Literature', in Gerard Carruthers, David Goldie and

Alastair Renfrew (eds), *Beyond Scotland: New Contexts for Twentieth Century Scottish Literature* (Amsterdam and New York: Rodopi, 2004), pp. 17–38.

36. Lewis Grassic Gibbon, *Smeddum: A Lewis Grassic Gibbon Anthology*, ed. *Valentina Bold* (Edinburgh: Canongate, 2001), p. 37.
37. Ibid., p. 44.
38. If Gibbon has been under-appreciated beyond Scotland, Raymond Williams has been one critic who has seen that his artistry is 'especially important' (p. 271) in his discussion of *A Scots Quair* in *The Country and the City* (London: Hogarth Press, 1985), pp. 268–71.
39. Lewis Grassic Gibbon, *Sunset Song*, introduced by Tom Crawford (Edinburgh: Canongate, 1988), p. 32.
40. Tom Leonard, *Intimate Voices* 1965–1983 (Newcastle upon Tyne: Galloping Dog Press, 1984), p. 53.
41. Ibid., p. 88.
42. For an excellent account of the awkward politics of reading Kelman and of the Booker Prize controversy, see Simon Kovesi, *James Kelman* (Manchester and New York: Manchester University Press, 2007), especially pp. 155–62.
43. Other especially powerful users of Scots in their fiction are Iain Banks (b.1954) and Thomas Healy (b.1944).
44. For some of these plays, see the very convenient anthology, *Twentieth Century Scottish Drama*, ed. Cairns Craig and Randall Stevenson (Edinburgh: Canongate, 2001). See also John Corbett and Bill Findlay (eds), *Serving Twa Maisters: Five Classics Plays in Scots Translation* (Glasgow: Association for Scottish Literary Studies, 2005) for the continued vibrancy of literary translation into Scots.

CHAPTER 3

Scottish Writing in English

With Scottish literature in Scots we have a fairly obvious marker of a cultural, at least geographic, distinction. However, from the seventeenth century at least there is the complicating phenomenon of the Ulster-Scots language out of which has developed a very worthwhile literature on the island of Ireland. We might also consider the fact that William Wordsworth, when first encountering the poetry of Robert Burns, claimed that this was a language very familiar to him because of the kinship of his native Cumbrian 'English'. The fact remains, however, that since the eighteenth century to the present a far greater quantity of creative literature published by Scottish people either in or furth (outside) of Scotland has been written in English. Very often this literature has been as interested in Scottish subject-matter as any other writing in Scots or Gaelic, and has been frequently accepted into the Scottish literary canon. As we have seen, however, some writing in English by Scottish people has seemed to some critics either indifferent to, or even worse to be a perversion of, the national interest in some sense. This brings us to pose some large questions: must Scottish literature always speak to Scotland specifically, as opposed to 'merely' the world at large, and must it do so in some properly pro-Scottish fashion?

THE SEVENTEENTH CENTURY

The first phase of extensive Scottish writing in English coincides with the reign of James VI and his court culture. From the 1580s James encouraged poets who developed the Petrarchan sonnet in Scotland and who seem to have decided that the English language was the appropriate medium to utilise. If we look to the sonnet writing of Sir William Alexander of Stirling (1567–1640), Sir David Murray of Gorthy (1567–1629) or Alexander Craig of Rosecraig (c.1568–1627), all writing in the early 1600s, we can see a fairly stark language contrast with the Scots of Alexander Montgomerie fewer than twenty years earlier.

It does seem that the new language choice was associated with the cultural pull of England, where the Scottish king was crowned James I of Great Britain and Ireland in 1603, but this did not mean that the writers just mentioned were not patriotic. It is interesting that Craig defined himself as 'Scoto-Britane' on the frontispiece of his *Poeticall Essayes* (1604), perhaps the first instance of hyphenated Scottish literary identity. Postcolonial theory has noted such hybridity and wondered whether the combination of unequal cultural parts constitutes surrender or opportunity, often concluding that opportunity really means opportunism on the part of the colonised embracer of hybrid identity. With Craig, however, we might note his thoughtful address to both nations – hence the use of English. Craig, a sincere Protestant, inhabited the loss felt by England with the death of Queen Elizabeth, champion of anti-Catholicism, but pointed out that, with the succession of James, Scotland has lost its distinctive monarch for ever and so is wounded even more:

> Now rivall *England* brag, for now, and not till now
> Thous has compeld unconquered harts & sturdy necks to bow.
> What neither wits, nor wars, nor force alone could frame,
> Is now accomplisht by the death of thy Imperiall Dame.
> Eliza faire is gone, into the land of rest,
> To that *Elisium* predecried and promis'd to the blest;
> And *England* for her sake now weares the sabill weede,

But *Scotland* if thou rightly looke thou has more cause
indeed.[1]

Another poet who, like Craig and others, followed King James to London was Sir Robert Aytoun, who is associated with the English metaphysical poets and whose work shows similarly skilful compression in meaning. As previously mentioned, Aytoun is one of the sources for Burns's 'Auld Lang Syne' and a contributor to the tradition of Scoto-Latinity. In one sonnet he depicts the sovereign power of James flowing across the River Tweed as essentially a natural phenomenon, but these waters continue to flow around Melrose Abbey also, which houses the heart of Robert the Bruce:

Till his high tydes these flowing tydeings tell;
And soon will send them with his murmering sounds
To that religious place, whose stately walls
Does keepe the heart which all our hearts inthralls.[2]

It is interesting that James's court-poets such as Aytoun were among the first to suggest and write towards countering cultural misshaping following 1603 in a corpus of work that remains critically under-explored. A Stuart loyalist, a lover of the history of Scottish independence, a classicist and an enjoyer of the English wits of the Inns of Court, Aytoun was culturally ambidextrous but realised that the Union of Crowns would complicate the position of the Scottish nation.[3]

William Drummond of Hawthornden (1585–1649) is Scotland's greatest poet of the seventeenth century. He was someone whom we have already seen as important to eighteenth-century revivers of poetry in a supposedly deracinated Scotland (see Chapter 2) and whose influence lies behind even the eventual reflourishing of poetry in Scots. Little noticed is the fact that at one point Allan Ramsay's bookshop featured outside it a sign with two heads, Drummond's and Ben Jonson's, testifying to a famous literary friendship exemplifying cross-border sensibilities that matched in their royalism and dislike of Puritanism. We have already mentioned Drummond's 'Polemo-Middinia' with its celebration of Scotland's marine resource wealth. This line of thinking is yet another way in which Drummond fed into later Scottish poetry as Allan Ramsay in 'The Prospect of Plenty' (1719) and Robert Fergusson in 'The Rivers of Scotland' (1773), both critically little noticed productions because they are written in Scots-English and English, respectively, also peddled a kind of water patriotism. England may have its 'green and pleasant land' and Scotland may be a place of scanter agricultural resources, but it had good things in its seas and rivers.

As R. D. S. Jack has noted, Drummond features in some versions of Scottish literary history as a 'canonical villain'.[4] This has to do not only with some Scottish critics betraying an inadequate grasp of the ideology of eighteenth-century poets in Scots and the way in which they derive sustenance from the seventeenth century, but also with the fact that Drummond is too 'mannered', European or even classical. It is probably fair to say that the 'dissociation of sensibility' identified by T. S. Eliot as emanating from fractures in seventeenth-century British culture, where religious accord is shattered into many pieces during that fevered, sectarian period, has had a longstanding effect of marginalising the literature of this period. Scottish commentators (Edwin Muir and many others) have been especially suspicious of the seventeenth century in Scotland. This not only means the long-enduring critical attacks on the nation's Calvinism, seen as so baneful to literary production, but also, in a strange paradox, with a kind of puritanical distaste for the supposedly florid *de haute en bas* productions of Drummond. What we might identify here again is the quasi-Presbyterian, populist mistrust of anything too self-consciously 'literary', such as we have seen in some Scottish critics in Chapter 1.

Drummond's major poetic work includes the collection *Poems, Amorous, Funereall, Divine, Pastorall in Sonnets, Songs, Sextains, Madrigals* (1614), as its title suggests a self-conscious, eye-catching showcase of formal and thematic suppleness; *Poems* (1616), where many of the texts deal with the narrator's lover and the landscape in sensuous, perfervid and melancholic combination; and *Flowres of Sion* (1623), deeply meditative and comprising some of the best religious poetry ever written in Scotland. A poet who felt that after 1603, Scotland, and to some extent increasingly Britain too, was something of a cultural wasteland (he also wrote political squibs against those he took to be enemies of the Stuart monarchy),

Drummond is somewhat the poet in retreat. He was a gentleman virtuoso building a fine library in his home in which he wrote, largely removed from the world. Like many figures of his age, Drummond was a man of sometime fluctuating political sympathy. Having been a signatory to the National Covenant of 1638, which opposed the innovation of Charles I as he attempted to make the church in Scotland as well as England conform to models that paved the way to High Anglicanism, he was later staunchly on the Cavalier side in the Civil War. Drummond's aloof, aristocratic persona led to him being seen as someone essentially apart from the story of Scottish literature which, as we have observed, sets so much store by communitarian principles. Scottish literary criticism has not really known what to do with his exquisitely crafted poetry in English as it speaks of a largely solitary sensibility.

If Scottish criticism has often failed to recognise, arguably, its most accomplished writer of the post-1603 century, English criticism has dealt with Drummond mainly as a footnote, especially in Ben Jonson studies. Drummond is one of those writers who is awkward for Scottish and English critics alike in his 'problematic' Scottish culture, and so fails to feature as largely as he ought in accounts of seventeenth-century literature. With Drummond we see exposed not only the fault-lines in his own cultural profile but within those of both English and Scottish criticism, equally suspicious of one another and neither in any real sense, arguably, willing to mount a more neutral cross-border account of British Isles literature and culture.

THE EIGHTEENTH CENTURY

As with the seventeenth century, eighteenth-century Scottish literature in English is read by some critics as alien. This designation goes as far as to see the English, or sometimes merely the Scots-English, productions of Ramsay, Fergusson and Burns dismissed as automatically inferior to the Scots-language texts of these poets. As suggested, this leads even to the excision of Scottish patriotic discourse, such as is found in Ramsay's 'The Prospect of Plenty'.[5] We might also suggest more generally, and as we have seen in the Scottish literary critical tradition, that there is often dismissal or neglect of anything that seems 'Augustan'. This, one might counter, is to concede an important literary sensibility to be the preserve of English or of French literature when 'Augustanism', in fact, was far from absent in Scotland.

The Augustan age in England and France was neoclassical in impetus in a variety of ways. The pastoralism which was a strong feature of the milieu had much to do with the idealisation of a simple, healthy, bucolic lifestyle that reacted, generally, against the previous catastrophic European religious strife of the seventeenth century. It can be argued that this predilection provided the wide context into which fitted the valorisation of country living, seen in the Scots language literature of all of Ramsay, Fergusson and Burns. Another aspect of the Augustan project was the verse-epistle in which Burns excelled (to say nothing of his prose letters, written for the overwhelming part in polished, witty, 'standard' English). So too we might note the strong strain of eighteenth-century Augustan didacticism, often satirical, to which these poets are heirs rather than to David Craig's supposedly native Scottish 'reductive' idiom. What is long overdue is some appreciation of the way the Augustan mentality is at large in eighteenth-century Scotland, in both Scots and English. This has for long been resisted, though, due to a critical attitude that reads Augustan neoclassicism as too consciously literary, sitting at odds with the couther, more homespun untutored creature that literature in Scots is read to be during the eighteenth century. One of Allan Ramsay's finest productions, never anthologised, is his 'Wealth, or the Woody' (1720) ('woody' means 'the gallows'), a Scots-English Augustan poem that satirises, in keeping with Ramsay's anti-Whiggish sensibility, the way in which Britain had gone money-mad. From the opening invocation of the appropriate classical muse 'Thalia' (associated with cheerfulness) through the poem's blend of Scots and English, to say nothing of its absence of specific Scottish location, it is easy to see why the poem is not treated seriously or extensively by traditionally Scottish critics of Ramsay:

> Thalia, ever welcome to this Isle,
> Descend, and glad the Nation with a Smile;
> See frae yon Bank where South-Sea ebbs and flows,
> How Sand-blind Chance Woodies and Wealth bestows;

Aided by thee, I'll sail the wondrous Deep,
And throw the crowded Alleys cautious creep.
Not easy task to Plough the swelling Wave,
Or in Stock-jobbing Press my Guts to save:
But naething can our wilder Passions tame,
Wha rax for Riches or immortal Fame.[6]

Here we have the Scottish poet speaking as a worldly-wise Briton practising a compact wit, typical of the Augustan period, where the 'swelling' of the sea and of supposed 'riches' are yoked together. Ramsay also here, and throughout the rest of his poem, ironically couches his poetic mission as a 'no[t] easy task' to essay deep-running passions (a standard idea of what the insightful poet must attempt). In fact, though, as is playfully signalled to the reader, the wild passion of greed is not all that mysterious. In a poem replete with the imagery of nature, Ramsay castigates the unnatural passions of the 'South Sea Bubble' in which members of the government, out of vested interest and personal greed, had urged British citizens to invest over-confidently in an overseas stock company. The resultant stock crash confirmed Ramsay in his diagnosis of the hollow rottenness of post-1707 Britain and allowed him the opportunity to exercise his wit in a poem that was enjoyed by English writers such as Alexander Pope and John Gay. Scottish criticism, though, has largely failed to accommodate this poem, where an eighteenth-century Scottish writer seizes successfully upon the opportunity to broadcast views about and to Britain at large.

James Thomson (1700–48) is remarkable in being, arguably, the most internationally influential Scottish poet of all time, while being little accepted as a Scot. His *The Seasons* (1726–30), a long poem charting the annually changing landscape and human world, is important in establishing a theme taken up subsequently in art, music and other expressive genres (a theme that becomes so ubiquitous it is difficult for the modern mindset to grasp that this is an innovation, essentially, of the eighteenth century). Not the first writer to depict flora and fauna in poetry, of course, but the first to do so as extensively and also to couch his whole treatment in didactic terms, Thomson has a reach through the Western imagination that is certainly unsurpassed by any fellow Scot, with the possible exception of Walter Scott. Thomson, though, is never forgiven by some Scottish critics for writing in English, indeed operating out of London, and writing in a moral or didactic mode, which again (contrary to the full evidence of how Ramsay or Burns actually write) is assumed to be the antithesis of the more anarchic predilections of eighteenth-century poetry in Scots.[7] Thomson is also one of those poets whose circumlocutory over-description is deemed after the Romantic period to be all too euphemistic (though all the major Romantic poets, especially Wordsworth, read Thomson).

Let us observe Thomson in his 'Autumn' sequence depicting his native land:

See Caledonia in romantic view –
Her airy mountains from the waving main
Invested with a keen diffusive sky,
Breathing the soul acute; her forests huge,
Incult, robust, and tall by Nature's hand
Planted of old; her azure lakes between,
Poured out extensive, and of watery wealth
Full; winding deep and green, her fertile vales,
With many a cool translucent brimming flood
Washed lovely, from the Tweed (pure parent-stream,
Whose pastoral banks first heard my Doric reed,
With sylvan Jed, thy tributary brook)
To where orca's or Betubium's highest peak –
Nurse of a people, in misfortune's school
Trained up to hardy deeds, soon visited
By Learning, when before the Gothic rage
She took her western flight; a manly race
Of unsubmitting spirit, wise and brave,
Who still through bleeding ages struggled hard
(As well unhappy Wallace can attest,
Great patriot-hero! ill requited chief!)[8]

These are familiar ideas. Thomson offered a brand of patriotism through natural resource already mentioned (Scotland's 'watery wealth'). We should be aware too of the beginnings of an idea of grandeur in wild terrain, one that is not fully theorised until

Edmund Burke's idea of 'the sublime' in the 1750s. Thomson urges us to 'see Caledonia in romantic view' when all too often previously and since Scotland's wildness (yoked to the idea of scarcity) is mocked by English observers. Thomson is quite rightly credited with minute natural observation in many places in his *The Seasons*, though in this passage we notice a mode of description that is frowned upon by those who like their Scottish literature directly realistic. The poem adopts the terminology attributed to the ancient world's most important geographer, Ptolemy, 'Orca' and 'Betubium' for the two northernmost promontories of Scotland. In this classicised landscape, where 'Caledonia' is also part of a suitably venerable vocabulary, we find a 'hardy' people, whose independence, or 'unsubmitting spirit', is celebrated, including even William Wallace, so far as standard English historiography had been concerned a terrorist. A nation too that can boast 'learning', originally from the Romans but, on their retreat in the face of the Germanic Gothic tribes, derived also in a deeply Christian sense from Columba and other Celtic saints. This is very powerful writing in favour of Scotland as a worthwhile place, somewhere that ought to be historically appreciated. This is what Thomson is urging on his British-wide audience. He is the first Scottish writer to argue, post-1707, that the different bits of the new United Kingdom must understand one another, must admire one another's attributes, not least in this equation those of Scotland.

Thomson's 'Scottishness' has been persistently called into question, and yet in the passage just considered he proudly talks of the birth of his writing near the Tweed in Roxburghshire. His career also demonstrates, we might say, that there is more than one way of being a Scottish writer in the eighteenth century. Along with others, notably James Arbuckle (1700–34) and Robert Blair (1699–1746), he contributes to the little-noticed anthology the *Edinburgh Miscellany* (1720), which generally shares the view with the circle of Pitcairne, Ruddiman and Ramsay and with the wider Augustan age that a new cultural injection is required, that more poetry ought to be produced. For many Presbyterians and 'Whigs' like Thomson (who was training for the ministry of the Church of Scotland at the time), in favour of the Union of Parliaments and of the Hanoverian dynasty that had replaced the Stuarts in 1689, literature is somewhat lacking in, and to be restored to, Scotland. Arbuckle's offering to the anthology of some Horatian satires and Thomson's of some amorous verse give the lie to the Presbyterians being entirely puritanical, even if some of them were. Arbuckle was an Irish Presbyterian who, like many of his compeers, studied at the University of Glasgow where, unlike the great universities of England, an oath of allegiance to the Church of England did not disbar them. His own fascinating literary career in Glasgow and Dublin remains inadequately documented and adds another complication to the notion of restricted 'Scottish' literature, as does Arbuckle's championing of Ramsay's vernacular Scots poetry (the two also address verse-epistles to one another) which one might assume he ought ideologically to frown upon. What has been almost unnoticed, in fact, is a cross-ideological conversation in early eighteenth-century Scottish poetry. As part of this dialogue, Thomson himself had briefly attempted work in the 'habbie' stanza in his youth, but chose a different literary direction.[9] This was probably not so much because Thomson rejected the Scots language *per se*, but the anti-Unionist, Jacobite ideological associations of the Scots verse revival. Another way for Thomson to be Scottish, as argued by several critics, was to bring to his landscape writing an apprehension of the sometimes sinister (as well as productive) hand of humanity in the landscape. This facet was one in which Thomson influenced Burns; for instance, in expressing distaste for the hunting of animals for sport. Thomson's sensibility here can be argued to be born of Calvinist-tinctured mistrust of the fallen world.[10]

In his own century the kind of poet he was certainly did not prevent him being appreciated by Robert Fergusson, who along with his colleagues in the Cape Club of Edinburgh in the 1770s would commemorate Thomson's birthday. Burns's 'The Vision' (1786) is also an attempt in Scots-English at the mode of *The Seasons*, where Scottish military prowess, learning and poetry are all celebrated in a journey through the Ayrshire landscape. Again on the supposedly negative side, Thomson has also been berated as the joint author of 'Rule Britannia' (1740), with another Scottish émigré, David Malloch (c.1705–65). This appeared in the play *Alfred, A Masque*, about King Alfred, in iconography not unlike William Wallace as a liberator of English people in the face of foreign incursions. 'Rule Britannia' has allowed lazy readings of Thomson as a cheerleader for the British empire, when actually he is writing well before the imperial heyday and his rhetoric of fortress Britannia is actually set up in opposition to what he perceives to be the more insidious expansionist powers of France and Spain, the former capable of invading Britain well into the eighteenth century. It is also the case that during the revolutionary 1790s Thomson enjoyed new popularity as a champion of 'liberty', a watchword in his poetic vocabulary. He even succeeded in being partly responsible for William Wallace, as mentioned in the passage above, becoming something of an icon against tyranny for English as well as Scottish radicals during this decade.

Like Thomson, a villain of the eighteenth-century Scottish literary and cultural scene for some critics, is David Hume (1711–76), notwithstanding that he is arguably the greatest philosopher ever produced in the British Isles. One of a number of Enlightenment intellectuals who compile 'Scotticisms' to be avoided in writing in the eighteenth century, he puts together his list in 1752. Hume is seen, therefore, as a cultural traitor. One might reply, however, that by the time Hume was writing, Scots as a language for prose at any rate might well sensibly be seen as dead, since there had existed no widely used or available written Scots prose tradition for a century or more. Hume was intent on perfecting his English, as an essayist and historian, his eye practically on the wider British marketplace, including Scotland, which had for many decades produced and consumed published prose that conformed increasingly to an English 'standard'. In this regard we might also turn to one of Hume's most notorious cultural comments made in 1757:

> Is it not strange that at a time when we have lost our princes, our parliaments, our independent government, even the presence of our chief nobility, are unhappy in our accent and pronunciation, speak a very corrupt dialect of the tongue of which we make use of; is it not strange, I say, that, in these circumstances, we should really be the people most distinguished for literature in Europe?[11]

Clearly, Hume here believes that brilliant creativity in a nation can thrive without the main institutions of the state and even in a situation of language instability. Here is an apprehension similar to David Daiches's notion of the paradox of eighteenth-century Scottish culture, but without the inevitably negative consequences that the twentieth-century critic reads as pertaining to this situation. Hume's conclusions here might look rather reasonable to postmodern eyes sceptical about the notion of rooted or natural culture. Hume's words are still somewhat adduced, though, as part of a prevailing orthodoxy that sees the Scottish Enlightenment as culturally synthetic. And a number of literary texts are included in a kind of Enlightenment anti-canon which seemingly attests to this false literary aesthetic.

Before we discuss some of these texts however, we should be aware of not reading Hume's pride in 'distinguished' Scottish 'literature' in the rather limited sense in which it is sometimes taken. What Hume had in mind was not simply 'creative' writing, but the burgeoning canon of philosophical and historical works which he and other Scots were producing, at the cutting edge of thought in the Western world at this time. Hume was himself one of the most popular essayists and historians in the British Isles during the eighteenth century, writing with a panache and range of interests unmatched by any English essayist. A large question is why his English essayist contemporaries are more readily accepted as worthy of study on courses in eighteenth-century literature, when these courses tend to ignore Hume's essays. He is not entirely acceptable within the canon, clearly, because of his relationship to English and his supposed disregard for the Scots language, even though his 'Scotticisms' are part of an understandable response to the course of written linguistic history in Scotland, and even though Hume, according to many contemporary accounts, spoke throughout his life in a broad Scots language with no hint of inferiority.

Sometimes read also as morally conservative, a familiar charge levelled at the moral philosophers of the Scottish Enlightenment by twentieth-century Scottish literary critics who wish to cement their version of it as *unimaginative*, Hume, in fact, is fearless as an essayist. He coolly analyses, for instance, suicide at a time when Christianity deemed it a taboo subject and a mortal sin. His explicit atheism also marks him out as a thinker not merely interested in the status quo, and this stance played a large part in his failure ever to attain an academic job such as would have suited his talents. Hume, in fact, became librarian to the Faculty of Advocates from 1751 in succession to Thomas Ruddiman, this change marking an ideological shift at the heart of an important national institution from anti-Unionism to Unionism. Hume, in this Unionism, like many of the thinkers of the Scottish Enlightenment, again raises suspicion in traditional Scottish literary criticism. Already mentioned is the cultural centre of Glasgow University for Irish Presbyterians and another philosopher, Francis Hutcheson (1694–1746), occupying the Chair of Moral Philosophy from 1729 is one such. Hutcheson is often credited with being the 'father' of the Scottish Enlightenment. He was a 'new licht' Presbyterian ushering in an age of moderatism in eighteenth-century Scotland away from a harsher Calvinist climate, though this moderatism is also frowned upon in some accounts of the Enlightenment imagination as though it was synonymous with insipidity. Hutcheson came into conflict with the Presbytery of Glasgow for proclaiming the possibility of salvation even for those who had not been exposed to Christian scripture. The fact that Hutcheson fended off this attack is testimony to an emerging age of greater religious freedom, not only in Scotland but in the British Isles as a whole. Hutcheson, like Hume and also Adam Smith (1723–90), was interested in rhetoric and belles-lettres, or polite and elegant literature. Smith, perhaps, especially can be seen historically as a pioneer of the study of vernacular literature in the university system, including an early form of what was later to be called 'practical criticism', but his predilection for 'politeness', or neoclassicism, tends to have his efforts viewed with suspicion by twentieth-century Scottish criticism.[12] Notoriously, Smith believed the gravediggers' scene in *Hamlet* to be out of place in its humour with the predominantly tragic mode of Shakespeare's play. Scottish critics have adduced this as evidence of Smith's lack of imagination, his insularity from 'earthiness' even. His judgements, if askew however, are no more so than many others in the age of neoclassicism and are typical of the academic outlook on literature until the new age of Romanticism begins to suggest a more 'democratic' interaction between literary modes and moods.

Where Scottish Enlightenment thinkers take an active interest in imaginative literature, two exemplars (both of which

Hume was to be counted as a supporter) are usually cited in testimony to their execrable judgement. Among a number of now largely forgotten plays, John Home (1722–1808) produced his *Douglas* (1757). Home's drama caused a furore when performed in Edinburgh, the Church of Scotland even disciplining ministers who attended its performance. It provides an interesting episode in the ongoing Calvinist hostility to the theatre in mid-eighteenth-century Scotland, and also the efforts of the Enlightenment *literati*, a number of whom helped Home refine his work, to promote the arts. It should be noted that these included men of the church such as the minister Alexander Carlyle (1722–1805), whose autobiography is interesting both in its style and humane perspective, as an example of the Presbyterian man of letters of the eighteenth century, a type that in more modern times has found little critical attention or favour.

Hume's *Douglas* had the unfortunate distinction of having a Scotsman proudly shout out at a London performance, 'Whaur's yer Wullie Shakespeare noo?' but the fact remains that it was a huge hit in England, and to an even greater extent than in Scotland. It is seen today as somewhat staid in its absolute observation of the classical unities and its neoclassical diction. However, it features more adventurous elements, including drawing upon the old ballad 'Gil Morrice' for plot-element that looks towards the emerging gothic sensibility. In presenting the ancient Scottish martial hero Douglas, the prologue to the play for London performances compared him to the English warrior Percy, thus making the point that both nations had come from a rough-hewn, but heroic past. This Scottish literature of equivalence, especially prevalent after the recent Jacobite Rebellion (1745–6) in which Home had fought on the government side, had as part of its agenda the projection of cultural parity between Scotland and England. It has been suggested that Home here, like James Thomson before him, is trying too hard. Equally, though, we might ask, what is wrong given the post-1707, indeed post-Jacobite, reality (where Scotland is seen witheringly by some English critics as a place of irredeemable backwardness) with a Scottish writer mounting some even-handed comparative analysis pointing out that England as well as Scotland has had something of a bloody, even primitive past?

An even more notorious literary case concerning precisely the issue of 'primitivism' revolves around the poetry of 'Ossian', a pre-Christian Gaelic poet, whose work James Macpherson (1736–96) claimed he had extensively translated. Macpherson published *Fragments of Ancient Poetry Collected in the Highlands of Scotland and Translated from the Gallic or Erse Language* in 1760. As with Home's *Douglas* prominent members of the Edinburgh *literati* were eager to promote the text. Keen among initial champions was another pioneer of the teaching of rhetoric and belles lettres in the university, Hugh Blair (1718–1800), which again in traditional Scottish criticism is adduced as evidence of an insincere compact among the Enlightenment *literati* from their sophisticated vantage point to produce to order a primitive text. 'Ossian' came to be a cross-border *cause célèbre* as Samuel Johnson lambasted the claims to authenticity for the material, and again this hostility is seen as expert testimony to the Scots trying too hard. However, the international reach of the Ossian material pertained for many years, as it influenced the Romantic Movement (many English poets included) in its communing with an alternative, more rough-hewn world very different from that of the eighteenth century. It inspired Napoleon with its martial nobility, and it underwrote the rediscovery of 'Celticism' over the next century.

At bottom, the truth seems to be that Macpherson had access to some original material but was creative in his stitching together and appropriating of materials (including Ulster legend) as he went on to produce two further Ossianic epics, *Fingal: an Ancient Epic Poem* (1761) and *Temora* (1763). 'Ossian' was so controversial that Henry Mackenzie chaired an investigation into the phenomenon for the Highland Society in 1805, which largely reached the balanced conclusion just outlined. Inauthentic in some elements Macpherson's creation may have been, but it helped create a useful, very anti-modern literary world, which inspired such poets as Goethe and Tennyson, and provided a mood that eventually undoubtedly fed into the fictional creations of J. R. R. Tolkien. Later Scottish critics than those of the Enlightenment have frowned upon 'Ossian' as representing the invention of a culture, while the Enlightenment ignored genuine Gaelic culture, including a very fine flowering of Scottish Gaelic poetry in the eighteenth century. However, the Scottish Enlightenment might have ignored the undoubtedly brilliant Alexander MacDonald (c.1695–c.1770) or Duncan Ban MacIntrye (1724–1812), but these poets did not fit the bill for Macpherson and others of like mind for some rather good reasons. For a start, MacDonald was avowedly a Jacobite representing proscribed politics and he, like MacIntyre, was, for all his Gaelic language, heavily influenced by the nature painting of James Thomson. That is to say these poets, contrary to a popular belief that lingers into the present in Scottish culture, did not simply have easy access to nature by dint of their Highlands upbringing, but were as influenced by written *literature* as other poets were (as with the Scots poets of the eighteenth century, Gaelic poetry suffers sometimes from the 'natural' stereotype). Rightly or wrongly, Macpherson in 'Ossian' was in search of something pre-eighteenth century, including eighteenth-century Gaelic poetry.[13]

The substantial critical industry surrounding 'Ossian' in recent years testifies not so much to an interest in the question of authenticity, but in the historical need the texts register for other things. These include valorising the Highlands (indeed, we have yet another inflection of the martial Scottish myth in Ossian) in the wake of the brutal putting down of the clans after the Jacobite rebellion. Also, there is the perhaps healthy reaction that the poems represent against modernity. Along with the emergent gothic tendency and the later new medievalism of the nineteenth century, the Ossian texts represent an alienated voice that make them, arguably, not so much aberrant as part of the mainstream trajectory of literary history.[14] The appeal of the Ossian poems lies in a lyrical, transient, even nebulous voice that is not merely the displacement of some Scottish 'authenticity', but is in keeping with the longing for something other than progress and civilisation, as championed by Enlightenment. In other words, paradoxically, it represents an anti-Enlightenment strain:

> What voice is that I hear? that voice like the summer-wind. – I sit not by the nodding rushes; I hear not the fount of the rock. Afar, Vinela, afar I go to the wars of Fingal. My dogs attend me no more. No more I tread the hill. No more from on high I see thee, fair-moving by the stream of the plain; bright as the bow of heaven; as the moon on the western wave.[15]

It is very evident from such a passage that we have here a harbinger of the Romantic voice that was to dominate the late eighteenth and much of the late nineteenth centuries in Western literary history. One might suggest that too much attention to Anglo-Scottish cultural tension in the eighteenth century has dominated much past discussion of *Douglas* and Ossian. Though such tension may well be a factor in the generation of these texts, the danger is that what is underplayed is their wider contribution to the emergent ages of sensibility and Romanticism. In other words, read for their paradoxes, these are odd, awkward and even inauthentic texts. Read in another way they speak of Scottish texts, as their reception histories clearly show, sitting in the mainstream of international literary history.

Another text which most certainly and explicitly deals with cultural tension in the nations of the British Isles of the eighteenth century is *The Expedition of Humphry Clinker* (1771). Its author was Tobias Smollett (1721–71), someone else whose contribution – to the novel in England and internationally as a key developer of the picaresque tradition of the eighteenth century – is perhaps undervalued in Scotland. Smollett is another writer who does not sit entirely comfortably in the canon if his patchy presence on university courses in Scottish literature is anything to go by, perhaps because only two of his novels are set (and then only partly) in his native land. *Humphry Clinker* is, as Robert Crawford especially has highlighted, a novel about prejudice.[16] The immediate context to this prejudice is hostility towards Scots in England in the 1760s. Since the time of the parliamentary Union, English resentment had frequently flared up over the supposedly unfair predominance of Scots in high political office in London. One such moment came in 1762 when Lord Bute replaced William Pitt the elder as prime minister. Bute was especially loathed by John Wilkes, whose popular periodical *The New Briton* alleged that the new administration was deeply corrupt and in this climate Scots, Bute and others around his ministry were particularly enjoying having their snouts in the trough. Among other Scots Wilkes disliked was Smollett, who throughout the 1750s had been editing the successful and often acerbic *Critical Review* from Chelsea in the English capital, so that he was seen in some quarters as yet another example of the 'Scot on the make' in England. As well as an onslaught of ridicule from the pages of *The New Briton*, Scots suffered from much caricature in word and in pictorial form in these years. A good example where both are seen is to be found in a poem by Wilkes's ally Charles Churchill, *The Prophecy of Famine* (1763), which quickly went through four editions in its year of publication. Not a very subtle work, the poem projects the Scots as a plague of locusts in England, largely because their own land is so unpromising. Wilkes's text had prefaced to it an illustration whose iconic power lived on long after the poem was largely forgotten. This depicted a sly-looking but emaciated, dirty, louse-infested Scot in a Highland plaid, which was ragged and barely sufficient to cover his modesty. Such stuff shows the one-brush, impoverished and brutal, but somehow also devious, Highlandry, with which all Scots were easily tarred in the years following the Jacobite rebellions.

It was against the crude, prejudiced image, which had easily penetrated popular consciousness in England, that *Humphry Clinker* was constructed as the most subtle of ripostes. The novel features the Bramble family from Wales (although the principal males of the family have been educated at Oxford and so they represent what we might now label 'middle England'). These Welsh folk, suitably neutral, then, in their national background, are able, largely, to travel objectively through England and Scotland, the message being, as in the case of Home's *Douglas*, that the new British nation ought to appreciate and understand its different historic parts. *Humphry Clinker* proffers a documentary realism, as it has characters complain about unsanitary public health conditions – as much at the spa town of Bath as at Edinburgh. The negative effects of urbanisation and luxury are also observed, more especially in England, with, for instance, the artificially whitened bread then becoming popular in London and elsewhere taken as an indicator of false, indeed unhealthy, taste. Mob-driven opinion and petty cruelty are particularly remarked upon by the main character, Matthew Bramble, amidst his fact-finding mission as to the state of eighteenth-century Britain. He rescues the eponymous Clinker, whom he finds living in abject poverty having become unemployed through no fault of his own in the English countryside. Echoing the illustration accompanying *The Prophecy of Famine*, Clinker has scarcely enough personal garments left to protect his modesty.

Clinker, in one of several deliberately hackneyed plot-lines in the novel, turns out to be Bramble's natural son, and is a canting, religious dissenter. England, just like Calvinist Scotland, has its theological fanatics. A very humane message of kinship, of 'Unionism', is writ large in the novel: we are all more alike than we think, all bonded together (or ought to be) and all responsible for one another in common social interest.

Finding much false community in the English countryside as well as happy versions of the same (in each of Wales, England and Scotland), Smollett's fiction bids us beware of facile stereotypes of identity. *Humphry Clinker* is a novel about misapprehension. One character is fearful of the sea journey that she believes necessary to reach Scotland; similarly, one has heard there is nothing to eat there but sheep's heads, oblivious to the logic that where there are heads there must be bodies. Smollett has his characters witness that rural poverty is greater in Scotland than in England. Bramble also notices that the formerly busy towns of Fife have lost out amidst new international trade patterns following the Union of 1707, even though Smollett himself was in favour of the Union overall. Bramble's nephew Jery Melford is very taken with both the beauty of the ladies and the Scots dialect and literature he encounters at Edinburgh. Matt himself is so impressed by the learning of the Enlightenment intellectuals in Scotland's capital that he calls it, in a phrase that has become famous, a 'hotbed of genius'. The message of the novel is be open, objective, and not simply believe other people's lazy, chauvinistic stories.

Humphry Clinker is, of course, a novel and an artfully constructed one. Not simply travel-writing in its appearance, it narrates the perspectives of its five central characters through their letters. It is an especially complex epistolary novel where sometimes the same event is reported by more than one character and the reader has to put these varying accounts side by side to work out the truth. It is also, alongside its documentary realism, a hugely funny, even farcical novel, the comedic element also serving to highlight the central theme of the subjectivity, the partiality, even the plain stupidity on occasion of the human point of view.

One episode highlights this aspect. The Bramble party enjoys hospitality at a country estate on Loch Lomond and their maid and another servant girl go bathing nude. Unfortunately, they are surprised by the resident squire out for a walk, and extricate themselves from their predicament by running past him covering their own eyes while leaving their nakedness in full view. This seemingly trivial, ludic incident demonstrates Smollett's theme of perception, that our eyes are often mistakenly, even unreasonably, blinkered. *Humphry Clinker* is a brilliantly illuminating novel formed quite precisely out of the Anglo-Scottish tension of the eighteenth century.

James Boswell (1740–95) is another of eighteenth-century Britain's great literary figures from Scotland, whose native country looks at him somewhat askance. He is for some Scottish critics one of the 'Anglos', like Thomson and Smollett, not entirely trusted for forging his career furth of Scotland. Boswell is also sometimes analysed according to a fraught personal identity, product of a harsh Calvinist father against whom he is seen rebelling, and this is supposed to explain why he seeks alternative paternal figures from other cultures – the Irishman Edmund Burke and, most famously, the Englishman Samuel Johnson. Boswell is sometimes read as a man in search of a solidity in identity that Scotland cannot provide, so that, for instance, the impracticality of patriotic action in eighteenth-century Scotland is transferred to his involvement in the Corsican liberation movement, which features in his best-selling book *An Account of Corsica* (1768). His life of Johnson published in 1791 – perhaps the major definer of the modern genre of biography – is one of two texts that celebrate a great Anglo-Scottish literary relationship. The other is Boswell's *The Journal of a Tour to the Hebrides*, documenting travels which the pair undertook in 1773, though the text was only partially published in 1785, and not fully known until 1936. Much of Boswell's writings in diary and in letter form were only discovered and retrieved during the twentieth century with the increasingly secure critical conclusion that he is one of the major writers of literary, non-fictional prose in the English language. Here we have yet another success to be chalked up to eighteenth-century Scottish culture.

Boswell is perhaps not entirely trusted in Scotland because of his friendship with Johnson, who is interested almost always negatively in the Scotland of the eighteenth century. Scourge of James

Macpherson, sometimes sceptical as to the genius of the Scottish Enlightenment and in his withering remarks about Scotland, such as the famous entry in his pioneering dictionary of the English language defining oats as fit for horses and Scotsmen, Johnson sometimes peddles a contempt for Scotland that is not all that far removed from the language of the Wilkesites. As well as genuine affection for Johnson, however, Boswell has tremendous fun baiting, indeed exposing, his Scotophobia. One exemplar of many he narrates from the *Tour to the Hebrides* shows very well the stage-managing Boswell, as in the Highlands Lady Lochbuy suggests breakfast for Johnson:

> She proposed that he should have some cold sheep's head for breakfast. Sir Allan seemed displeased at his sister's vulgarity, and wondered how such a thought should come into her head. From a mischievous love of sport, I took the lady's part; and very gravely said, 'I think it but fair to give him the offer of it. If he does not choose it, he may let it alone.' 'I think so,' said the lady, looking at her brother with an air of victory. Sir Allan finding the matter desperate, strutted around the room, and took snuff. When Dr Johnson came in, she called to him, 'Do you choose any cold sheep's head, sir?' 'No, Madam,' said he with a tone of surprise and anger. 'It is here, sir,' said she, supposing he had refused it to save the trouble of bringing it in. They thus went on at cross purposes, till he confirmed his refusal in a manner not to be misunderstood; while I sat by, and enjoyed my success.[17]

Here we have Boswell the man who enjoys the clash of cultures, who rightly extolled himself as a cosmopolitan citizen of the world. His notorious remark that any man tired of London was tired of life should not be taken as the ultimate Anglocentricity, but as an avowal of his love of the variety, indeed the constantly changing novelty, which England's capital then as now represented.

If Boswell was over time accepted into the canon of English literature for his contribution to biography, for his wit and humour as a journalist, a more instant Scottish success was Henry Mackenzie (1745–1831), who produced his novel *The Man of Feeling* in 1771.

It was such a palpable hit Britain-wide that an English clergyman fraudulently attempted to claim the authorship and Robert Burns was to claim that it was the book he most loved after the Bible. By the later nineteenth century it was usually thought to be unreadable, a testimony to the false refinement of the age of sensibility. Its central character, Harley, is a man so touched by the misfortunes of others that he frequently bursts into tears and the novel has often been read as, on Mackenzie's part, entirely sincere. The fact that Mackenzie was a hard-bitten lawyer and the cool adjudicator of the status of the Ossian poems has led critics to identify in the author the supposedly typical Scottish 'crisis of identity'. Mackenzie's novel is also used all too lazily to exemplify (*à la* Edwin Muir) the Scottish mismanagement of 'thought' and 'feeling', *The Man of Feeling* clearly exuding wrongful excess of the latter quality. However, there is more irony in the text than is usually noticed. One chapter in the rather fragmentary, episodically structured book is 'The Man of Feeling in a Brothel', where Harley weeps over the tragic tale of how a woman has fallen into prostitution. The reader may well wonder over the never explained occurrence of Harley's presence in this place to begin with. In another section, 'The Man of Feeling talks of what he does not understand', Harley proceeds to talk of the difficulty of behaving with individual morality when one is part of the colonising party, *à propos* contemporary British rule in India. Undoubtedly a strange text, Mackenzie's novel practises large-scale irony on a world which espouses moral feeling by making the reader witness unrealistic amounts of this – in Harley's emotional plenitude – but is actually hard-hearted. The unreality resides not so much with the often comical Harley, we might suggest, but ultimately with the pretence of wider human society to be feeling, a claim that Harley all too naively believes in as the licence for his own behaviour.

THE 'AGE OF SCOTT' AND THE 'BLACKWOODIANS'

More acceptable to traditionalist Scottish critics than the English-language Scottish literature of the eighteenth century, early nineteenth-century Scottish literature nonetheless shares with it some of the same problems of canonisation, or acceptance as either authentically Scottish, or even authentically literary product. There is the critical problem of 'Scotland and Romanticism' going back at least as far as G. Gregory Smith, where Scotland whether out of its thrawn, dour Calvinist culture, or through a supposedly culturally conservative Enlightenment, lingering into the early nineteenth century, is resistant to the Romantic creative strain. We have already learned to be suspicious of such generalisation from commentators and we might suggest that Ossian, Home's *Douglas* and even Mackenzie's *The Man of Feeling* are proto-Romantic texts, with their attention to primitivism, which in the case of each of these means bringing emotion to the fore as a motor in human culture as strong as rationality. Other Scottish signposts and contributions to the Romantic age would include a poem which meditates on literary creativity, 'The Minstrel' (in two parts, 1771 and 1774) by the Enlightenment philosopher James Beattie (1735–1803), another British-wide hit in its day, which influenced both Burns and Wordsworth. It also helped prompt the re-emergence of folk ballads in the later eighteenth century in printed form, as well as in performance provided by the likes of Anna Gordon Brown (1747–1810), whose father was an Aberdeen academic and whose husband was a Church of Scotland minister. The promotion of the renewed interest in folk culture, so often seen to be part of Romanticism, was clearly far from entirely absent in bourgeois Enlightenment Presbyterian households. It is only very recently that acceptance of Scotland as having a 'mainstream' Romantic culture has begun to spread – the work of Katie Trumpener, especially, and more recently Murray Pittock is important here.[18]

'Romantic' is, like so many labels of cultural periodisation, problematic, since it is one applied retrospectively, a description that would not necessarily have been recognised by those so-called in their own time. In Scotland until recently, a more usual period descriptor for early nineteenth-century literature in was the 'Age of Scott'. The epithet registers Walter Scott's capturing of the world's imagination with his poetry and prose about the history of Scotland and, even more generally, his bringing to life in fiction the historical past of England or Europe, found, for instance, in his *Ivanhoe* (1820) or in his *Tales of the Crusaders* (1825). However, Scott's imaginative rendering of Scottish history, in some ways a project continuous with the antiquarian labours of Burns, is seen by some to have too much of a vested, ideological view of Scotland and of the world. Politically conservative, his friend James Hogg claimed that the Reform Bill of 1832, which doubled the number of individuals entitled to vote in Britain, had killed him. Even more fancifully, Mark Twain, half in humour and wholly in earnest, blamed Scott as a cause of the American Civil War. His logic, more or less, was that Scott's irresponsible, romantic tales of derring-do had inspired the Southern states in their wrong-headed, 'chivalric' rebellion against progress. Scott, the Sheriff-Depute at Selkirkshire, opposed to the political reformers inspired by the French Revolution during the 1790s, the man who built his fantasy of a medieval baronial dwelling at Abbotsford during the 1810s and 1820s, and knighted for stage-managing the visit of King George IV to Edinburgh in 1822, where he brought to bear his imagination on the king's tartan-bedecked outfit for the occasion so that the monarch was reinvented as a deposed Stuart king, is a man much blamed by some commentators. He is condemned as backward-looking and fabricating bad fantasy as he wilfully evades the modern world.[19] Leaving aside such criticisms in the particular for the moment, these also attest to Scott's huge cultural significance in Scotland and far beyond in his own day.

Scott's literary career began with his translation of German poetry and ballads in the 1790s, in this manoeuvre contributing, we might suggest, to the mining of exotic, even supernatural material for which Germany suddenly became famous in Britain at this time. This taste also represented an interest in the fearful or unknown as a displaced reaction to the real political terror of France. Inspired by the example of German culture, as well as an eighteenth-century tradition of antiquarian collecting, Scott compiled his *The Minstrelsy of the Scottish Border* (1802–3). Scott's extensive annotation of this collection of border ballads, largely garnered from the oral tradition, brought renewed attention to the violent, supernaturally interpreted, legendary history of the Scottish (and indeed English) borders of more ancient times. His undoubted interference, or 'improvements' as he would have seen it, in these texts represent a level of editorial intervention unacceptable to modern scholarly eyes, though Scott was no more licentious in his treatment of 'traditional' material than Ramsay or Burns had been. *The Minstrelsy* was of a piece with the new cultural impetus towards folk and regional culture which informed the Romantic Movement. Out of his work on the ballads emerged Scott's original, narrative poetry, which combined gripping historical narrative with tales of love and other, sometimes darker passions, *The Lay of the Last Minstrel* was published in 1805, *Marmion*, centred on the Battle of Flodden, in 1808, and *The Lady of the Lake*, an epic love story, which opened up the trossachs and the Highlands as never before as a site of glamour and grandeur, in 1810. Scott's poetry was hugely popular at this time and contributed strongly to the medieval and gothic tendencies inflecting Romantic literature. According to Scott the emergence of Byron, who proffered an altogether racier and more ironically slanted, mock-heroic kind of narrative poetry, caused him to change tack and turn to fiction. However, Scott's increasingly large collection of prose chapbooks at this time, which demonstrates yet again that Scott was a pioneering collector of popular culture, whose stories so inform many of his novels, perhaps suggest that he was naturally inclining in the direction of writing imaginative prose.

The novel *Waverley* (1814) appeared anonymously, though its authorship was an open secret among the *literati* of Edinburgh, probably since such fiction was not seen to be a respectable pursuit for a lawyer and a gentleman. Edward Waverley, an English officer en route in 1745 to join his British army regiment in Dundee, is tricked into spending extensive time among the Jacobites, not yet in open rebellion, who intercept letters to him from his commanding officer demanding his immediate presence as civil war looms. Waverley, in ignorance of all this, is seduced by the beauty of the Highlands and the attractive tales, songs and chivalrous manner of the Jacobites, not least by the charms of Lady Flora Mac-Ivor who is part of the honey-trap. He is eventually assumed by his regiment to be a rebel and, outlawed, he does for a time throw in his lot with Charles Edward Stuart, who parades him in Edinburgh for propaganda purposes as a supposed indicator of the support for his cause among southerners. Edwin Muir reads Waverley and characters like him in Scott's fiction as lacking in commitment, indicating Scott's own compromised ambivalence, attracted to Scotland's history, especially its wilder, more 'independent' aspects, though believing as a Unionist that this dangerous past had been rightly superseded. The name of Scott's central character belongs, obviously, more to the eighteenth-century tradition of the novel where characters' names reflect very transparently their natures or motivations. It is possible to read in this detail Scott's partial ironicising of his central character, of a generally admirable but naïve and romantic young man who has spent too much time reading fiction (Scott is a much more playful writer than some critics have realised). The rugged landscape in the novel is majestic and dangerous, emblematic, clearly, of the clans who inhabit it. Waverley is traduced and seduced, in fact, by men not simply of exotic culture, but of clear and ruthless political ambition who wish to change the dynasty on the British throne. In other words, what we have in Scott's novel is a warning about the romantic perspective and a lesson in the *realpolitik* of history.

Throughout his *oeuvre*, Scott shows ambivalence to the real world and the romantic imagination, the problem being, as he was well aware, that humans create grand illusory fictions of the past (and of the present). This fabric has been inadequately appreciated by critics, especially following Muir, as they see Scott rather exclusively peddling romance at the expense of reality, creating 'Scottland' rather than conveying Scotland. Muir's point that Scott lacks commitment might actually be seen as commendable in an imaginative artist. The novelist's undoubted Unionism in real life was tempered in his creative life by an awareness of the harsh reality that some past aspects of Scottish life and culture, even somewhat attractive, were victims of history's progress. Scott's choice of a 'half-way' hero, temporarily Jacobite but ultimately emerging unscathed as the plot against him is revealed and understood, is perhaps not hugely credible, but this machination allowed the author a way inside both camps at a time when more modern, cross-cutting techniques which allow, say, a novel plotting both a Jacobite and a government loyalist caught up in the conflagration were not available. Nor really was the kind of unsatisfying, unjust ending that alternatively might have seen Waverley hanged as a rebel. Later in the nineteenth century unhappy endings became much more the norm. In other words, it is possible to suggest that Muir's critique of the kind of scenario found in *Waverley* over-reads, and in anachronistic fashion, the supposed artistic compromise of a Unionist Scot.[20]

Among Scott's other Scottish novels especial mention might be made of *The Tale of Old Mortality* (1816) and *The Heart of Mid-Lothian* (1818). The first of these texts looks to the religious wars of seventeenth-century Scotland. Where Scott had previously dealt with the Jacobites, now he went to a different historical place on the ideological spectrum to bring to fictional life the Covenanters. As in *Waverley*, it is clear here that 'moderates' are to be approved of. The central character, Henry Morton, is a sincere Presbyterian but disapproving of fanaticism, such as he finds in some of the Covenanters with whom he associates. His involvement with these is cemented after he has witnessed similar brutality towards ordinary (largely non-fanatical) folk associated with the Covenanting side from opposing royalist troops. Scott's portrait of thrawn, courageous Covenanters and gung-ho royalists who are dedicated, respectively to a God-ordained mission before principles of common humanity or a somewhat distant ruling monarch, shows precisely the lack of commitment, or the moderatism that has been identified in Scott. Absolute commitment or belief is a dangerous thing, as Scott shows, since it is not always in conformity to reason and the quiet, ordinary lives that most people wish to live.

A series of 'minor' characters in *Old Mortality* are caught up in the grand schemes of people more important than they are, both on the Covenanting and the Royalist side. Here and elsewhere, Scott is essaying a kind of historical fiction that shows the little person being dragged along on the tides of large affairs of state, and here he is a pioneer, a democratising literary influence even. If history in big terms has often tended to be about kings and queens, the small person is reflected upon in Scott's fiction with intensity as never before. *The Heart of Mid-Lothian* even more so deals with the 'minor' individual, in particular a milkmaid, Jeanie Deans, who goes on foot to London to win a reprieve for her sister wrongly convicted of infanticide in 1730s Edinburgh. With many coincidences and other as pieces of less than credible plot manipulation (though none of these is all that exceptional by nineteenth- or even twentieth-century standards), this novel nonetheless might be argued to be Scott's finest piece of fiction. It interweaves the incidents surrounding the presumed infanticide of Effie Deans, who has concealed her pregnancy so that the absence ultimately of any baby leads the authorities to this conclusion, and her sister's quest to clear her name, with the Porteous Riots of 1736.

Both of these scenarios revolve around the concept of justice. Porteous was the real-life Captain of the Edinburgh city-guard who had ordered his men to fire on a rioting crowd. Sentenced to death for his murderously precipitate action, Porteous was granted a royal pardon, specifically by Queen Caroline. While still imprisoned in the Tolbooth prison, however, he was seized upon by a section of the angry citizenry and summarily executed. Ugly and brutal though Porteous's end is, it is the result of remote and inadequate legal writ running from the centre of Unionist Britain. Jeanie Deans's eventual winning of an audience with Queen Caroline (her husband King George II is not absent from this scenario out of regal remoteness but because of his distracted, dissolute lifestyle) and the pardoning of Effie, in a very bald sense, balances the injustice emanating from the centre over the Porteous case. Jeanie believes her sister's impassioned plea of innocence but will not lie for her in court; she could have the charge of 'concealment' against Effie dismissed by saying she knew her sister was pregnant. Jeanie also refuses to trade in Effie's lover, an outlawed smuggler, in exchange for her sister's freedom. Instead, she sets off on a kind of pilgrim's progress through Britain, finding at one point a baying, murderous mob in England (counter-pointing the Porteous mob in Scotland), as well as other good and bad people on both sides of the border. She is guided only by her strong (as it transpires accurate) sense that Effie is innocent as part of her generally conscience-informed, courageous behaviour.

That Jeanie should win the pardon for her sister is, in one sense, satisfying, but in another it emphasises, as does Caroline's earlier action in the Porteous case, how arbitrary and even whimsical executive behaviour can be. As Caroline is aware in part of her motivation for her anger when Porteous was lynched, there was a strong element of 'national' outrage and defiance being expressed. The queen's pardoning of Effie might seemingly make reparation for her earlier mishandling of a Scottish case, but this would be a facile reading. Neither of Caroline's actions is hugely well informed, though she does begin to sense something of Jeanie's integrity, which helps lead her to a decision she is at first reluctant to make in favour of one of those rebellious Scots. We have the situation too, where the pardoned Effie does not lead an altogether happy life afterwards and where her illegitimate son leads an adventurous, godless life, as it appears to Jeanie, going off in the end perhaps to live among the American Indians. The moral then might appear to be, in douce, Christian moral terms, such as those to which Jeanie subscribes, that badness comes from badness. The possible conclusion is that Jeanie's labours on behalf of her sister and her family have been of little avail. This, however, would be to miss the point. The individual has pursued justice honestly and, in a way, the outcome does not matter. Life is messy, Scott is telling us, and we must strive to be conscientious amidst the emotionally-led dispensing of justice from various capricious places, whether the mob or royalty. Jeanie the good Presbyterian contrasted with her canting Presbyterian father and her flighty, hot-blooded sister, who eventually becomes a Catholic, another blow to Jeanie, is a figure of sincere virtue in a society, a nation and world where such is in short supply. In line with more recent readings of Scott's sensibility, rather than the purveyor of insipid romance, we might here infer a darker, more sceptical Walter Scott, who divines a world of chaos and contingency.

Scott is the most influential of a group of writers who write fiction in English, but who frequently feature the language of Scots in their character-dialogue in the first part of the nineteenth century. These writers contribute to *Blackwood's Magazine* founded in 1817 by Tory sympathisers who wished for an organ to counter the Whig *Edinburgh Review*, which had been founded in 1802. Editorship was taken over by John Wilson (1785–1854) and John Gibson Lockhart (1794–1854), who became Scott's son-in-law in 1820. Both of these individuals are today seen as rather elitist when their careers are taken in the round, but both were also highly talented, as a complicated and very funny satire, written with the help of James Hogg, which they published in their magazine, showed.[21] The 'Chaldee Manuscript' scandalised cultured society in Edinburgh and beyond with its attack, in mock Old Testament cadences, on the *Edinburgh Review*. *Blackwood's* also attacked the leading English Romantic poets of the day such as Wordsworth and Coleridge, even as it championed elements of the new Romantic culture such as the Gothic fiction strain. Indeed, it can even be claimed that *Blackwood's* plays an important part in the invention of the short-story form. A medium very much satisfying the new, increasingly urbanised, taste for the exotic, for supernatural and country tales from an audience in many ways distanced from the old ways of the countryside as the Industrial Revolution proceeds, short fiction of very high quality was published in *Blackwood's*. Contributing to the magazine were, for instance, not only Scots such as Scott, Hogg and John Galt but others also, as the nineteenth century stretched out, including Thomas De Quincey, Edgar Allan Poe, Charles Dickens and Joseph Conrad. To state the obvious, *Blackwood's* was an important site not only in Scottish literature, but also in literature in English more generally.[22]

Yet again, we find an interesting 'Scottish' institution, whose national boundaries are soon breached. In spite of the 'Maga's encouragement to the gothic strain, most certainly a genre of the Romantic period, this periodical, along with its erstwhile rival, the *Edinburgh Review*, also contributed, rather unfortunately perhaps, to Scotland's reputation as a place not amenable to Romanticism (the *Edinburgh Review* also attacked the likes of Wordsworth and Byron). However, in 1819 Lockhart, in his very well-written cultural portrait of the age, *Peter's Letters to his Kinfolk*, breaks ranks somewhat with his *Blackwood's* colleagues and defends Wordsworth against what he rather partially identifies as the crassness of the *Review* in failing to understand the literary spirit of the age. Lockhart's text, somewhat modelled on Smollett's *Humphry Clinker*, as a fictional Welsh visitor observes the colourful culture of early nineteenth-century Scotland, sees the *Review* as representing the continuation of the Scottish Enlightenment, an arid, over-intellectual, sceptical, (Humean) outlook, supposedly ill-equipped to be receptive to the new finer feeling and nature-delighting Romantic poets. Nonetheless, it can be suggested that Lockhart too contributes to a highly limited notion of native Scottish Romanticism, in his production of two hugely popular biographies of Burns (1828) and Scott (1837–8). When taken together it is quite clear that Lockhart's definition of the good Romantic artist, such as he reads his father-in-law, is that of the cultured gentleman, while Burns, though possessed of inspirational genius, is altogether too excitable and not a gentleman, as is shown in his more scatological productions and in his occasional political radicalism. (Lockhart also attempts to draw on testimony, however, that suggests that Burns was essentially a Tory.)[23] At this point, we might reflect upon the way in which the usages of 'Tory' and 'Whig', as historically received ideological labels which recur in Scottish culture, are played out in the early nineteenth century. With the satirical, obscurantist, religious language of the 'Chaldee Manuscript' Lockhart and his colleagues attempt to smear the Edinburgh reviewers with the old Calvinist, or at least Presbyterian hostility to profane or secular culture. At issue was the modern-day liberalism of many of those who described themselves as Whigs, including openness to political reform after the French Revolution. Tories such as Lockhart, clinging to rather elitist ideals of a settled and hierarchical society, saw the Revolution as antithetical to the idea of the individual of rarefied culture, of whom, in this mindset, there could be relatively few.

Associated with the *Blackwood's* grouping also is James Hogg (1770–1835), the 'Ettrick Shepherd'. He came from Covenanting stock, and so might well be thought naturally to belong, if anywhere, to the Whigs. Hogg's background, however, exemplifies the fact that descent in Covenanting Calvinism did not imply absolute Puritanism as propaganda against this identity sometimes suggested. His mother was something of a tradition-bearer where folksongs and ballads were concerned, resorted to by Scott when he was collecting the *Minstrelsy of the Scottish Border*, though opining to him that his efforts to fix this material in print, so much based on traditionally mutability, would actually kill it as living performance. Hogg, whom we have mentioned as a good poet in Scots, showed his versatility in also collecting, writing and publishing Jacobite songs, being a great satirical parodist in English, including writing pastiches of Wordsworth which have also done much to cement the idea, as mentioned above, of Scotland's supposed antipathy to Romanticism, to say nothing of his status as one of the greatest novelists produced by Scotland. There has been critical temptation also to read Hogg, steeped in the oral tradition but attracted to the Tory literary-set around *Blackwood's*, this Presbyterian purveyor of Stuart-loyal sentiment, as yet another exemplar of a 'crisis of identity'. However, we see in Hogg someone who very precisely gives the lie to this facile, identity-essentialist concept, as he draws with great panache on a range of literary and cultural materials and attitudes for aesthetic and, also commercial success.

Let us home in a bit more on the longstanding idea of the Scottish literary artist as a fatally divided individual in relation to what today tends to be seen as Hogg's greatest work, the novel, *The Private Memoirs and Confessions of a Justified Sinner* (1824). Hogg's text represents a conundrum in being largely critically unsung until the twentieth century. It is a telling fact that G. Gregory Smith, who knows Hogg's poetry, seems never to have read the novel. As Cairns Craig has suggested, and as we shall see especially later, Hogg's book is more of a twentieth- than a nineteenth-century work in its influence.[24] It has a very interesting reception history, being thought rather vulgar by the literary world of its day (including John Gibson Lockhart), the work of a man, perhaps, whose background might well lead him to lapses in taste, and only widely appreciated after an edition by André Gide in 1947. We might suggest that Hogg's *Confessions* is a very pertinent book after the Nazi death camps, Gide identifying the novel as one of the greatest fictional accounts of fanaticism and megalomania.[25] Deriving inspiration from Burns's 'Holy Willie's Prayer', the novel features Robert Wringhim, an extreme Calvinist of the early eighteenth century who believes that his predestined salvation means he can commit sin, including rape and murder, with moral impunity. Wringhim, though, deep down does not believe this inhuman state of affairs, as his conscience or, in a formulation which had been influentially inscribed by Francis Hutcheson, his 'moral sense' collides with his immoral actions so that his personality disintegrates. As a consequence of this state of affairs he attributes some of his nefariousness (or externalises it) to the figure of Gil-Martin, whom he at first attempts to rationalise as a force for good, perhaps even his guardian angel, though ultimately Wringhim sees this individual as the Devil, and is driven to suicide. A very humane book, one of the great psychological novels of the Romantic period, Hogg's book is also a disturbing, dark fiction even at the level of its textual fabric.

It is comprised principally of two parts, one narrated by the sinner himself, the other by an editor who comes across this first manuscript and attempts to explain it in psychological terms rather than in the supernatural terms in which Wringhim has couched his story. Very cunningly, however, this method of parallel or double narration itself represents a kind of demonic texture, as it is multi-voiced and so potentially leads the reader back to Wringhim's apprehension of a diabolically informed world. The key biblical text here, found in the Gospels, is Christ's encountering of a demonically possessed man, who responds to interrogation as to his identity, 'My name is legion, for we are many.' As well as the text in its literal duplicity to some extent corroborating the Calvinist view that the world is an untrustworthy place, neither the sinner's nor the editor's account can be taken as completely reliable. The sinner sometimes in his narration points to a psychological explanation for the many strange events in the plot, the editor sometimes slips towards a supernatural account. What we have, then, is a rather uncomfortable reading experience, where Hogg will not allow easy certitude. He provides ambivalence between an older (seemingly superseded) supernatural view of the world and a rational, enlightened version, something that marks Hogg out as a Romantic artist. As with other writers at this time, Hogg seems aware of the taste, somewhat paradoxical (in *Blackwood's Magazine* and elsewhere) for supernatural material for older, exotic mindsets and is warning the reader against smugness, asking, 'are you entirely sure that you are superior in your modernity and in what you believe?' It is something of a critical oddity that such an assured text (precisely because it is so masterly in its ambiguity) should sometimes be read in Scotland as demonstrating once again the trope of divided culture in national terms. Hogg's novel does, of course, exhibit division, but not as a Scottish neurosis. Rather, it is a quite brilliant fiction exploring a number of fault-lines – between belief and unbelief, between rationality and irrationality – common in the western mindset, then and now.

John Galt (1779–1839), like Hogg, was a sincere Presbyterian believer, interested therefore in the notion of God's plan for humanity, or providence, but far from entirely convinced that humans did not shape this for themselves and are not much more disruptive in their actions than are any 'acts of God'. In his novels he employed what he termed 'theoretical histories' or the charting of fictional individuals through the generations and in small communities with real history in the background. *Annals of the Parish* (1821) features the Reverend Micah Balwhidder through long years as a parish minister corresponding to the reign of George III (1760–1820). In the first-person narration Balwhidder reveals himself to be a man of both decency and self-importance. There is something immediately reductive in his self-conscious measuring his own tenure of a small parish in Ayrshire against that of the king; nonetheless, lest we laugh too precipitously at Balwhidder, we should be aware as readers that much information about a period of tumultuous change is recorded in Balwhidder's journal. Balwhidder is certainly ironicised, but the point is also being made that this is a time of American, French, Agrarian and Industrial revolutions when large-scale, disorienting historical change and displacement do register in every community and in the life of every individual.

Galt's *The Entail* (1823) is a Glasgow family saga in which the eponymous legal device is something to ensure that a landed estate belonging to the Walkinshaw family will remain intact, secure from being divided among a number of inheritors. The entail in Scots law was designed to protect economic stability, though sometimes in real life, and certainly in Galt's fiction, it causes division, corruption and tragedy as human emotions and infighting are inflamed by an instrument that is too mechanical. This is where Galt is at his most brilliant as a novelist, in showing inflexible rules and humanity in collision. His *Ringan Gilhaize* (1823) is another regionally-rooted historical novel which charts the progress of a committed Protestant family from the Reformation to the time of the Covenanters. Through the generations the Gilhaize family has a sure vision of its religious mission but its triumphs and sufferings, which weigh out as just about equal to one another, might be read as being as much about the elements of chance and contingency as about the guiding hand of God's providence. As with James Hogg in *Confessions*, Galt in this and other fictions asks the modern reader to consider their belief, or lack of it, in an ordered world, guided by some overarching plan, meaning or purpose, whether religious or not.

Another of the *Blackwood's* group who should be noted is Susan Ferrier (1782–1854), sometimes in the past referred to as the 'Scottish Jane Austen'. This epithet, as in the case of some other

Scottish writers compared to those of England, might make us pause to wonder whether it is genuine or insecure as an attempted measurement. As with the 'whaur's yer Wullie Shakespeare noo?' jibe with which the Scotsman heralded Home's *Douglas*, we notice a writer hugely popular in her own time, also south of the border, being comparatively vaunted rather than simply enjoyed for her own sake. If we have been questioning the supposed Anglocentric anxiety of the Scottish writer, there sometimes seems to be less reason to query this with regard to the Anglocentric Scottish critics and consumers of Scottish literature. One can say that, while lacking the stylistic panache of Austen, Ferrier is a writer of considerable ironic wit who, in her novel *Marriage* (1818) especially, is another very shrewd fictional commentator on human nature amidst Scottish mores and culture. Ferrier, along with Scott, Hogg and Galt, provides a confident wielding of Scottish subject-matter as never before for a wide and appreciative early nineteenth-century audience. This is, in a sense, a statement of the obvious verging on the platitudinous, but it perhaps needs to be highlighted in the face of pervasive critical pronouncement about the lack of sureness or even inadequacy of Scottish literature. Scotland at this time, as in most other ages, has its fair share of accomplished literary artists.

THE VICTORIAN PERIOD

A standard critical narrative is that Scottish literature goes into sharp decline after the 1830s (Scott, Hogg and Galt all died in this decade) and, as we have seen, poetry in Scots is seen to stand very palely in comparison to its creativity of the eighteenth century. Another convenient point of reference for critics is the anthology the *Whistle-binkie . . . Songs for the Social Circle*, from 1832, providing a safely mawkish and conservative home for work in Scots. It is, so the theory goes, a suitable depository for an antiquated, superseded form of expression as Britain heads towards the Victorian age. This over-neat narrative, however, fails to take account, for instance, of the publication in the *Whistle-binkie* of a newly discovered radical poem in the 1830s attributed to Burns, 'The Tree of Liberty', and, indeed, the fact that a number of poets, including

Alexander Rodger (1784–1846) and William Thom (1798–1848), both of these gifted in political and social satire, found an outlet here. Plainly, in the face of its rather one-dimensional part in the standard critical narrative, the *Whistle-binkie* is an area of Scottish literature that needs some proper, modern investigation.

Another factor in the supposed recession of Scottish literature in the early decades of the nineteenth century is the pull of the south. Thomas Carlyle (1795–1881) is seen here as emblematic. Finding school teaching and study for both the religious ministry and the law unsatisfactory, facts which are read by some of his biographers as indicating a telling restiveness with areas of traditional national pride, Carlyle also comes under the strong influence of German thinking and so is sometimes seen to mark the end of the dominance of indigenous Enlightenment philosophy in Scotland.[26] His essay 'Signs of the Times' (1829) appeared in the *Edinburgh Review* and proclaimed much of the thinking of the Scottish Enlightenment as 'mechanistic' (for instance, in its straightforward concern with identifying between moral good and evil). His critique of contemporary society in this essay harped on the materialism and the rationalism that were predominating as the dominant attitudes of the new age of rampant industry and capitalism. Old-fashioned moral philosophy, which might at its worst simply serve as a set of codes of behaviour useful as a form of social control to the new affluent middle class, was redundant. Carlyle advocated that human culture ought to be more meditative, thinking upon the whole person rather than upon his or her utilitarian or specialised part, as was too much the emphasis in the new 'machine age'. Carlyle here reveals himself to be something of the Romantic 'sage', as he is often described, concerned with a more mystical, imaginative purpose for humanity in tune with transcendental ideas pioneered by Immanuel Kant, where human experience is not to be limited by its reliance upon reason. In the 1830s Carlyle settled in London, taking up a career not only as a full-time writer but as a crowd-pulling public lecturer. His *The French Revolution* (1837) was famously described by John Stuart Mill as 'not so much a history as an epic poem' and is a vast rhetorical performance which, for instance, dwells on the horrors of the guillotine, as it essays the powerful emotional human volition of the Revolution as much as any economic or social circumstances underpinning the rationale of this perturbation. So, we have a Scottish writer who is writing from England, and imbued with German philosophical Romanticism (and so concerned to catch the zeitgeist or spirit of the age), about a defining moment not only in French but in world history. This is, indeed, a very international kind of Scottish literature.

Carlyle's *Sartor Resartus* (1833–4), or the 'tailor, re-tailored' has the fictional Professor Teufelsdröckh expounding the view that human clothes are the basis for human values, and that both are similarly transient in their fashionableness. Coming to a conclusion, ultimately, however, that is to be equated with the view of Carlyle himself, Teufelsdröckh sees a deeper spiritual reality running through history, the world and the universe. *Sartor* is a text that says in the final analysis that we should not mistake the present as the essence of reality, when significant meaning in the world takes time to roll out. Again, then, we see Carlyle's anti-mechanical agenda, a warning against the crass 'presentism' of modernity. Not without some justification, perhaps, claims are sometimes made that Carlyle's declamatory prose style owes something to the tradition of the Scottish pulpit; if this is true, it is one element among a number of 'national' as well as 'international' strands drawn upon not any more oddly or licentiously than William Dunbar or Robert Burns had done, or Hugh MacDiarmid was to. Perhaps part of the reason that Carlyle is often thought of as more of a 'British' writer than a Scottish one is not only to do with his predominant professional locus in the south, but also concerns his politics, as in succeeding work he moves towards advocating the idea of government by a strong (though just) leader, not bound by the rules of democracy. This attitude did not sit easily with the strong Scottish myth of people power.

As Scotland and the rest of Britain and its burgeoning empire seemingly settled from 1837 into the Victorian age, national distinctiveness among the different countries of the British Isles was clearly submerged to some extent. It is possible to argue that from the 1830s until the early twentieth century, Scotland, like its British sister-nations, assumed something of a 'regional' political and cultural identity (though to some extent this might well be argued from at least as far back as 1707 or even 1603). However, the Victorian age in Scottish literature is, arguably, the least overtly 'national'. We see something of this in a poet such as Thomas Aird (1802–76), part of the *Blackwood's Magazine* grouping overlapping slightly with and following Scott's generation. His long short story, *The Old Bachelor in the Old Scottish Village* (1845) is a typical Scottish product of its time in casting sentimental light upon the countryside. This 'retreat' to the rural is sometimes argued to represent the disengagement of Scottish literature in the nineteenth century from more important matters and to look towards the 'Kailyard' movement, though if this is true it owes much to the influence of Wordsworth. (Aird also wrote poetry very much in the Wordsworthian idiom.) If the recoiling from the urban, industrial nineteenth century is to be diagnosed in Scottish literature, it is perhaps no less prevalent in England and elsewhere, as many novels of country life are produced in the British Isles providing a context that in England was to give rise to Thomas Hardy.

If Scotland cannot boast such a figure, there are writers whose rural subject-matter is well written and informed by an awareness of new ideas in philosophy, religion and other spheres now abroad in the countryside. William Alexander (1826–94) produces his novel *Johnny Gibb of Gushetneuk* (1869–70) in English, but with a vigorous north-east dialogue, featuring a community-minded but independent-thinking protagonist who perpetuates the popular image of Robert Burns, of humble birth and large intelligence.[27] A different kind of 'evasion' of nineteenth-century reality, realism being a commodity upon which an undue premium has been placed in Scottish criticism, we might argue, is George MacDonald (1824–1905), whose novels *Phantastes: A Faery Romance for Men and Women* (1858) and *Lilith* (1895) represent fantasies with strong Christian allegorical keys. MacDonald is a later nineteenth-century Romantic whose work has been increasingly appreciated in the light of C. S. Lewis (towards whom Macdonald might be said to look), and has begun to garner serious critical attention from the closing decades of the twentieth century as he is understood as a writer who has serious things to say about human nature through the mode of fantasy.[28]

Other Scottish writers of the Victorian era have been slow to receive their critical due (at least in Scotland). James (B. V.)

Thomson (1834–82) (the B. V. standing for 'Bysshe' in tribute to Shelley, the 'Vanolis' an anagram of 'Novalis', another Romantic poet from Germany) is someone who is very much 'reclaimed' by Scottish literary studies in the later twentieth century.[29] Although born in Port Glasgow, he moved with his family to London when he was seven. After joining the army he was posted around England and Ireland, and on leaving became a business administrator in the United States and a journalist in London and in Spain, dying due to alcoholism before the age of fifty. His most famous literary work is the well-crafted long poem *The City of Dreadful Night* (1874), which is a paean to the death of God, a deeply-felt and horrifying meditation upon the absence of meaning in human life and in the universe. It is a text, however, not without some grim wit as its very elaborate structure and neat, numerically ordered cantos ironically counterpoint, even draw attention to, the thesis of purposelessness. In recent years, Thomson tends to be assumed into the Scottish canon on the basis of his Calvinist upbringing, which, it is supposed, provides bite to his pained expression of atheism.

Another 'émigré' Scottish writer, in London from 1888, is John Davidson (1857–1909), an acknowledged influence on T. S. Eliot and Hugh MacDiarmid in their attempts, respectively, to pick up on urban colloquial speech and to bring to bear upon poetry the language of science. It is clear that as something of a pre-Modernist, finding poetic material in the 'unpoetic' sites just mentioned, Davidson is regarded by MacDiarmid as one of the very few worthwhile Scottish writers of the nineteenth century. Davidson also witheringly joined in the attack on the 'Kailyard' school of fiction in *Baptist Lake* (1894).

Arguably, the Scottish literary renaissance from the 1920s, with its explicit nationalism and its predilection for the Scots language, tended to over-portray the Victorian period, in its absence of these things, as a wasteland. Following this influence, the Victorian period has perhaps been *the* Scottish literary wasteland alongside the seventeenth century for many generalist Scottish critics. For these, a gift is William McGonagall (c.1825–1902), a man who had a sudden revelation in his fifties that he was a poet, but providing a glaring exemplar of bad literature. McGonagall is the one Scottish poet of the Victorian period whose work, especially his *Poetic Gems*

(1890), has remained more or less continuously in print ever since. He recited his work, with its scansion and literary language patently unfit for purpose, around the pubs and halls of Dundee, where he was enjoyed as an object of public ridicule. Perhaps sadly displaying a level of mental disturbance or, alternatively, being something of a confidence trickster, McGonagall down to the present day, as the frequent parodies in the magazine *Private Eye* show, associates over-ponderous, out-of-control verse with the Scottish Victorian mindset.

Altogether more worthy, and attracting some recent critical reappraisal, is James Young Geddes (1850–1913). An earlier generation of Scottish poets had been under the influence of Wordsworth, who had gradually supplanted the large exemplar of Burns. For Geddes and a plethora of others, the American Walt Whitman, especially in his free verse, was the direction now to be followed. Here we might point to another interesting phenomenon of the kind to be found in the literatures of many countries: the literary lead emanates sometimes from beyond Scotland, moving from a Scot to an Englishman to an American. Geddes's masterpiece is the long poem 'Glendale & Co.' (1891), which, in a Whitmanian-eyed survey of people and places in Dundee, applies a critique derived to some extent from Carlyle that modern society is over-materialistic and is losing sight of deeper cultural values. Another poet who bucks the traditional Scottish diagnosis of infantilised, evasive Scottish literature of the Victorian age is Robert Williams Buchanan (1841–1901), who gained notoriety for his attack on Pre-Raphaelite sensibilities in an article, 'The Fleshly School of Poetry' (1872). This essay gained Buchanan the reputation as a Scottish puritan, although he was really a pioneering socialist worried about the exploitation of women. Vocal as an anti-vivisectionist and against British imperialism, a hater too of Rudyard Kipling, whom he took to be its cheerleader, Buchanan's *The New Rome* (1899), especially, highlights the work of the most politically dissenting Scottish poet of the nineteenth century.

The three most remarkable Scottish literary phenomena of the later nineteenth century are Margaret Oliphant (1828–97), Robert Louis Stevenson (1850–94) and the 'Kailyard' fiction of the 1880s and 1890s. Oliphant was a hugely prolific prose writer, including more than 200 essays for *Blackwood's Magazine*, and her two-volume *Annals of a Publishing House* (1897) is an excellent portrait of the publishing activities of William Blackwood's firm as one of the centres of the literary world. In this institutional sense, we might say then, that the Scottish literary world had internationalised itself during the nineteenth century. Nationally ambidextrous, Oliphant wrote novels chronicling English small-town life in the 1860s and 1870s, complementing the fictions of Scottish life she had been producing from the late 1840s. Among the former, *Miss Marjoribanks* (1866) features a central protagonist who sees (especially male-centred) society as hypocritical. Possessed of a kind of proto-feminist voice, Oliphant, in her greatest Scottish novel *Kirsteen* (1890), charts the peregrinations of a heroine through Scotland and London at the time of the Napoleonic Wars as she harvests an independent life and great loneliness. Widowed and left with three children before she was thirty, Oliphant knew at first hand the difficulties of the single and single-minded woman, and she is the first Scottish woman to make a long and full living as a professional writer.[30] We shall return to a reading of one of Oliphant's fine supernatural stories in Chapter 4.

Robert Louis Stevenson was Scotland's most successful writer since Walter Scott. His fame throughout Britain, America and in the South Seas, where he was eventually to settle for the final years of his life in Samoa, made him a truly international figure. For all that Stevenson has been consistently seen as one of the great prose stylists in English however, his critical reputation has waxed and waned, one apprehension of him as merely a writer of inconsequential romance or even of children's books. The latter reputation is largely down to his first novel, *Treasure Island* (1883), and *Kidnapped* (1885), in the twentieth century made into a Disney film and several cartoon versions, which are indeed, riveting boy's own yarns. What should not be ignored, however, is the much darker side to these novels, both of which feature a number of instances of what we would today call child abuse. This is something we find in a number of places in Stevenson's fiction; for instance, in *Kidnapped* where a cabin boy is beaten to death by a drunken First Mate.

Stevenson loved the work of Scott, and several of his novels revisit the Jacobite territory of *Waverley*. In one of these, *The Master of Ballantrae* (1889), we find the Dursideer family deciding expediently at the time of the 1745 rebellion that one son should go 'out' with Charles Edward Stuart while his brother remains loyal and at home on their estate so that whatever the outcome of the civil war the Dursideers are on the winning side. Yet in spite of its attempted expedience the Durisdeer family fails to thrive. Indeed their line dies out, largely because of a weak patriarch who indulges the favoured elder son, James, who has insisted unwisely on his Jacobite adventure, when it would have been better for his younger brother, Henry, to have followed the prince. When the Stuart cause fails, James is outlawed and with great petulance returns to persecute Henry for having ended up with the better fate, even though the latter had attempted to do his duty as cadet sibling, volunteering to be the one to be 'out', but overruled by James. James suggests that a toss of a coin should decide which of the brothers is 'out', but James may well have practised a sleight of hand to ensure the decision he wants. For the rest of the novel we see James full of tricks, including the fabrication of diabolic effects, to scare his brother's family. The only conclusion to be drawn is that James is an irresponsible freebooter who would have created drama and conflict whatever circumstances had surrounded his family or his country. This is where we see Stevenson develop Scott's fiction of historical conflict: he proposes that sometimes human nature is mysteriously motiveless, or might not make sense simply in historical context. In other words, human nature perhaps produces historical conflict as much as history produces human conflict.

Stevenson is a great purveyor of divided families and conflicted individuals, particularly in his earlier novel *The Strange Case of Dr Jekyll and Mr Hyde* (1886). This book's apprehension of sinister human nature ought to point us towards a reading of the later *The Master of Ballantrae* as a fiction of dark psychology, rather than as an historical romance or as being essentially about a divided Scotland. This book, from which the phrase 'polar twins' is taken and utilised by G. Gregory Smith, is also often wrongly appropriated as evidence for the essentially antisyzigical mindset of Scotland. In fact, as its London or non-Scottish setting should tell us, it is concerned with a more universal idea of human nature, which contains within it the urge to moral degeneracy, or evil, as fully as it does towards virtue, or good. Stevenson's novel is a very appropriate one for the age of

Darwinian doubt in which it was produced. Indeed, it features a version of Darwin's idea of the evolution, or increasing perfection of the human animal. The atheist Stevenson asks the question, what if evolution involved for humans the removal of spiritual values and the honing of physical animal powers? The contemporary bankruptcy of traditional notions of God after the discoveries of Darwin and other scientists of the nineteenth century set the scene here for Stevenson's fantasy of a man who discovers a way to tap into a nature unfettered by traditional moral constraints, which, in part, also draws superhuman strength from this lack of inhibition (as much, perhaps, as from the famous potion which Jekyll concocts to allow him to become Hyde). Stevenson's novel is a fable for the late nineteenth century, asking deep questions about what makes us human and whether society is a rightful constraint on the most indulgent excesses of human behaviour or whether its repressiveness causes the desire for this excess. Although Stevenson almost certainly had no direct awareness of the early work of Sigmund Freud (whose published work began to appear in the 1890s), it is symptomatic of the times that the novelist was asking very similar questions to the pioneer of psychoanalysis in Central Europe.

If Stevenson has sometimes been read as principally a peddler of adventure stories rather than as a purveyor of more vital fictions, then the 'Kailyard' (or cabbage-patch) movement is seen as *par excellence* an abuse of literature in nineteenth-century Scotland. 'Kailyard' was coined by the critic J. H. Millar in 1895 in *The New Review* as a pejorative term for the writings of J. M. Barrie (1860–1937), S. R. Crockett (1859–1914) and Ian Maclaren, the pseudonym of John Watson (1850–1907). Millar crystallised what a number of commentators had increasingly frowned upon in the last decade or so of the nineteenth century – the propensity for Scots to write couthy (that is, comfortably smug) tales of the Scottish countryside. Maclaren's *Beside the Bonnie Briar Bush* (1894) is a series of humorous and sentimental sketches ('idylls' as Maclaren himself termed them), centred on the fictional parish of Drumtochy, and like other works of its kind hugely popular in the 1890s, perhaps especially with expatriate Scots, including both those near at hand in England and further afield in the likes of Canada. Maclaren's book utilised a quotation from Burns, which provided both his title and the derogatory term coined by Millar: 'There grows a bonie brier-bush in our kail-yard'. For Millar and many subsequent critics 'Kailyard' came to signify not merely the indulging of mawkish sentiment and trivial parish affairs, but these things in place of more outward-looking concerns. Scotland in the 1890s was one of the fastest industrialising countries in the world. Alongside this fact was a consequent condition of urban poverty, even slums. As well as such material conditions, new revolutionary political and scientific ideas had been raging for at least thirty years. All of this seemed precisely to militate against the parish as a unit that made any sense in this modern world, and made it an anachronism as a literary setting. In *Beside the Bonnie Briar Bush* there is intellectual conversation among the peasants, though largely over fairly abstruse theological issues. Critics of kailyard fiction saw it as precisely a denial of modernity and social reality. It was seen to stand for diminution and escapism, as an *ersatz* creativity that projected a false image of the Scot as essentially a virtuous, stolid, stay-at-home peasant at a time when the British colonies were full of Scots exploiting other lands and peoples. After a hard day lording it over the natives, the Scots could relax with soothing tales about their own simple, parochial souls. In both its origins and in its reception, kailyard writing smacked to commentators of inauthenticity. Maclaren himself wrote from Liverpool, where he spent most of his adult life, and undertook tours of America where he was a very successful public speaker (with some solid reputation as a theologian).

If Maclaren was lachrymose and pietistic in his fiction in a way that seems to confirm the derogatory kailyard epithet, Crockett and Barrie are perhaps unfairly tarred with the same brush. Crockett explicitly deals with the poverty of the city in one novel, *Cleg Kelly, Arab of the City* (1896), and *The Men of the Moss Haggs* (1895) is a gripping historical novel on that recurrent Scottish theme, the Covenanters. Crockett was warmly admired by Robert Louis Stevenson, and J. M. Barrie was hailed by Patrick Geddes (as we saw in Chapter 1, where he praises Barrie's fictional setting of Thrums) as part of a sharp, new regional writing. Barrie's highly successful novel (which also became a play and a highly popular Hollywood film in 1934) *The Little Minister* (1891) to some extent conforms to the supposed kailyard mode with its diminutive subject-matter.

It features a minister who is literally 'little' and the rather small concerns of his parish are to the fore, including the immorality that emanates from drunkenness. On the other hand, this novel also depicts agrarian rioting as the authorities fail to control the price of food, the most pressing concern throughout the nineteenth century in Britain. Barrie's most famous work, the play *Peter Pan* (1904), about a boy who never grows up is also brought to bear, with a certain sleight of hand, to confirm the definition of kailyard as representing the unrealistically infantilised. We shall return to test a kailyard text in Chapter 4, but for the moment we might simply emphasise what one of its more recent and most sensitive analysers has suggested: that the kailyard 'school' is largely an invention of literary criticism rather than emanating in any identifiable way from those writers who have been associated with the label.[31]

EARLY TWENTIETH CENTURY

The notion of the kailyard provided one of the most potent reactions in early twentieth-century Scottish literature. Apart from Millar's usage, one literary text does most to cement the concept and that is the novel *The House with the Green Shutters* (1901) by George Douglas Brown (1869–1902). Deeply interested in Scottish literature and culture, Brown wrote literary criticism on Burns and compiled a glossary for the republication of Galt's novels by Blackwood's. Brown shares the Ayrshire origins of these writers and also a similar satirical ferocity with Burns and a critique of the small-town mentality which is influenced by Galt.

The House with the Green Shutters takes to the satiric extreme the idea of the diminutive perspective of the kailyard mentality: the title focuses not simply on a parish, not simply on one house, but on a close-focus detail of a house, the 'shutters', which carry, fairly obviously, the idea of being blinkered. The shutters in question are part of the paraphernalia of a house built by the businessman John Gourlay in the fictional Ayrshire town of Barbie, a name that suggests the 'barbed' nature of social relations among the townsfolk. Gourlay's pride in his physical house and his supposedly well-engendered family shows in fact his materialism and his aspirational conformity rather than any real prettiness or love in the station and makeup of the Gourlay family. In another sense his house, which points to Gourlay's sense of personal grandeur, carries one of several literary genres mockingly utilised in the novel. The idea of 'a house' stands for a (royal) family in the genre of tragic drama (Brown was a classical scholar at Glasgow and Oxford universities). The downfall of the house of Gourlay is one deeply mocked in the novel, and there is a constantly reductive, even cartoon element to the scenario of the text (as is apparent in such a throwaway name as 'Barbie'), while the local shopkeepers, tradesmen and councillors of the village act the part of a debased 'chorus' as found in Greek tragedy. Unlike the classical chorus, these bodies do not provide further illumination upon the action, but merely add to the sly and snide gossip that is so current in Barbie. Jealous of Gourlay's pre-eminence which is built upon his initial business success and also his large physical stature, the bodies are pettily delighted as things begin to unravel for him. This happens as a more modern operator in the field of haulage arrives and bests him, and as Gourlay's son, another John, goes to Edinburgh University but returns home having failed, much to the shame of his father. Although he wins a prize for descriptive writing at the outset of his studies, it is made clear that young Gourlay lacks the discipline required for more intellectual university study. Brown quite explicitly ties his critique of the Gourlay family to the plight of Scottish culture. He suggests that Scots, especially through the nineteenth century but in a manner stemming from the individualistic and puritanical trends within Scotland's Reformation, applied their imaginations to commerce and understood little of anything aesthetic. For Edwin Muir, Brown's book seemed to confirm his diagnosis of a disastrous Scottish split between 'feeling' and 'thought'. As Muir sees it, Gourlay Senior is, to a large extent, all practicality and Gourlay Junior stands for emotion, and never the twain shall meet.

Brown provides a somewhat grim picture of Scottish country life, quite clearly in an attempted antidote to the supposedly cosy, parish depiction of the kailyard at its worst. *The House with the Green Shutters* is a work of some frustration with regards to life in Scotland, but Brown's own biography might be borne in mind here. Brown was the illegitimate son of a remote and seemingly unloving farmer; after great academic success at Glasgow, he was deemed something of a failure at Oxford. To draw attention to this is not to call into question the undoubted craft and brilliance of his novel, but potentially to wonder how objective a view of Ayrshire or Scotland it can be taken to be. Clearly, to some extent, Brown projects the situation in his novel, with its echoes of his own life history, as representing Scotland. Arguably, however, it is no more truly accurate than the stereotypical kailyard scenario against which it reacts. We might suggest that commentators, including Edwin Muir, have taken Brown's novel too seriously as engaging with actual Scottish life. The farcical cartoon element in the book extends even to Gourlay Senior. As his son's drunken nature and university failure become apparent, he feels the urge to pick his heir up and use him, literally, as a club on the bodies. This mode of grim humour should be taken into account: for instance, when Gourlay Junior murders his father with that most domestic (or kailyard) of objects, a fireside poker. In other words, Brown, arguably, is visiting upon kailyard an extreme, or has been already suggested, an antidote-like reversal of its supposedly couthy portrait of life in small-town Scotland. We shall return to Brown's iconic anti-text in Chapter 4, as we consider its construction as a kind of literary game, rather than a straightforward 'condition of Scotland' novel.

Brown's novel, if anything, had a more powerful impact thirty years after it was published. Brown's text was taken to be a vision of a very real Scotland, a nation massively denying its actual historical nature, including its industrial and also imperial dynamics, and the novel was to form part of the foundational vision of the Scottish literary renaissance of the 1920s and 1930s. It is interesting that the critic John Speirs saw *The House with the Green Shutters*, in his *The Scots Literary Tradition* (1940), as one of the few authentic nineteenth- or twentieth-century 'Scots' texts. Even though Brown's novel is narrated in English and contains much excellent dialogue in Scots, however, it is no more superlative than a Scott or a Stevenson, or even, one might dare say, a Barrie, before him in regard to language use. Brown, seemingly, has passed an authenticity test in a way that is denied to these predecessors.

Of Brown's contemporaries there are very significant figures that are also, from the period of the literary renaissance until recent times, deemed less canonical. Arthur Conan Doyle (1859–1930), of Irish descent, was brought up and educated in Edinburgh, with much assertion in recent years that this formation – both the environment of the Scottish capital and its intellectual training in medicine – forms the deep roots of the character of Doyle's Sherlock Holmes, and the scenarios in which he becomes involved. However this may be, Doyle's politics were British imperialist and one might suggest that he erases much of his own early identity, both as a Catholic educated by Jesuits and as a Scot in any distinctive sense, which seems to matter little to him. Doyle's Holmes adventure *The Hound of the Baskervilles* (1902), with its supposedly supernatural hound portending the deaths of the heads of an English West Country family across the centuries, might be read as a kind of displacement of actually 'Celtic' (both Irish and Scottish) legends of this kind. Holmes's eventual puncturing of this scenario, by revealing a common criminal scheme, may be read as a comprehensive turning away by Doyle from own his Irish-Scottish heritage. As with most critical readings, however, this kind of psychological diagnosis of author from his fiction will appeal to some readers and not to others.

Almost as widely enjoyed as Doyle furth of Scotland as a great writer of adventure stories is John Buchan (1875–1940). His career in the colonial service in South Africa and Canada (of which he became Governor-General in 1935) and his patriotic hero, scourge of international plots against Britain, Richard Hannay (featuring most notably in *The Thirty-Nine Steps* (1915)), have seen Buchan dismissed, like Doyle, as a British imperialist. Buchan was, however, deeply interested in Scottish history and culture and was author in 1932 of a fine biography of Walter Scott, which confirms Buchan's dubious status in the eyes of those suspicious of Scott in the first place. His *Witch Wood* (1927) an historical tale of Scottish religion in the seventeenth century, suggests a critique of Calvinism at its most puritanical which produces an opposite cultural reaction against it (as douce Presbyterian peasants gather in the woods for pagan festivities). Here and throughout his finely crafted supernatural tales, Buchan shows himself to stand in a tradition of Scottish literature going back through Hogg to Burns. Here he is even something of a modernist writer projecting peripheral or underground cultural currents in a way that has affinities with MacDiarmid or Grassic Gibbon.

A third writer of immense reach in his own day, popular in Scotland and beyond, is Neil Munro (1864–1930), whose historical fiction (he is yet another writer heavily impacted by his early reading of Scott and Stevenson) was characterised by MacDiarmid as parochial escapism. Among a number of novels that have been reappraised in recent years, we might draw attention to just one, *The New Road* (1914), which utilises the very physical symbolism of the old drovers' road and the new road built by the British state as a means to suppress the Jacobites. This tale of the eighteenth century is no mere historical romance as it casts a sceptical eye on the idea of 'progress' and suggests that culture and tradition in the Lowlands as well as the Highlands is always uncertain, always in flux.[32] It is interesting to note the way in which Doyle, Buchan and Munro, all very 'mainstream' writers in their own day and in whom Scotland took great pride, were increasingly de-canonised during the twentieth century as dissenting readings of Scottish literary culture, which we might label broadly 'MacDiarmidism', came to predominate.

Even more than Grassic Gibbon, if the volume of critical treatment is to be taken as a signal, Neil Gunn (1891–1973) is *the* novelist of the twentieth-century literary renaissance. His best fiction is often concerned with the effects of the elements on the human environment, the cycle of life and how past memories, both personal and ancestral, affect the adult ordering of life. Gunn's *Butcher's Broom* (1934) brings a fictional treatment to bear on the brutal Highland Clearances (humans driven off the land to make way for more profitable sheep) and so counters the historical and imaginative amnesia that he and fellow nationalists such as MacDiarmid had diagnosed in Scottish history as the price to be paid for pursuing British 'progress'. Gunn's novel represented a watershed moment in Scottish culture as the Clearances were *felt* for the first time for many Anglophone Scots. *The Silver Darlings* (1941) follows the experiences of those cleared from the land and eking out a precarious existence on the margins during the nineteenth century as the great Scottish herring industry brought huge life-style change and eventual wealth (for some) to the coastal fringes of the countryside.

Gunn's historical fiction, with its attempts to understand the intimate lives of the common people more than any Scottish fiction writer previously, perhaps, is informed by complex symbolic and psychological patterns that reveal a modernist writer. These aspects are seen at their most abstruse in his *Highland River* (1937) as its main protagonist charts his course from boy to adulthood through his meditations upon the lifecycle of a salmon river.

Even more bleakly than Gunn, the documenter of Scotland's lamentable history is Fionn MacColla (pseudonym of Thomas Macdonald) (1906–75) whose *The Albannach* (1932) is a searing portrait of Highland life marred by both Puritanism and alcoholism and whose *And the Cock Crew* (1945) is an exquisitely appalling portrait of a Presbyterian minister scrupulously examining his conscience to find that the Clearances visited upon his flock are the providence of God. Along with Edwin Muir's travel-book *Scottish Journey* (1935), MacColla's writing represents the vision of the literary renaissance at its most nationally indicting. Where Muir glimpses Catholicism in *Scottish Journey* as offering a little to Scotland in the way of cultural goodness but never himself resorts to institutionalised religion, MacColla (who had been a Church of Scotland missionary in Palestine during the 1920s) converts to Roman Catholicism. His novels, although quite brilliantly observant of life in the Highlands and in Glasgow, carry in them rather too heavy an ideological apparatus based upon his religious predilections. At the other extreme, in a sense, is Eric Linklater (1899–1974) whose close cultural observation of Scotland is frequently comical. One of many Scottish writers who write interesting fiction about abroad, such as his riotously funny *Private Angelo* (1946), he also satirises the Scottish literary renaissance in a way that is both affectionate and sceptical in *Magnus Merriman* (1934). Unlike MacDiarmid or MacColla, Linklater is one of those writers who is interested in his own national context, but does not believe that it is absolutely central to his life and art any more than universal human and cultural mores.

For all his despair over the predicament of the Scottish writer, Edwin Muir is arguably the greatest Scottish poet in English in the first half of the twentieth century. When not penning poems or prose lamenting the impossibility of Scottish culture, he produced verse that shows him to be very much a modernist in his Jungian symbolism, which owes something also to the influence of T. S. Eliot. He was especially interested in such traditional problems as the meaning of human destiny and eternity. Two of his collections particularly stand out both in their prosodic facility and in thematic sensitivity. *Journeys and Places* (1937) is a welter of contemporary social and cultural comment with frequent mythical interventions; *The Labyrinth* (1949) contains some of the most tender poems of religious meditation ever produced in Scotland, and a number of texts that are subtly rousing and uplifting as Muir protests against political and cultural tyranny of all kinds.

It is not without some irony that the raised male voices in the debates during the literary renaissance (MacDiarmid versus Muir, for example) over how to produce a more literary Scotland have, until fairly recently, obscured the contribution of women. Muir's wife Willa (*née* Anderson) (1890–1970) produced much more accomplished fiction than her husband. The novel *Imagined Corners* (1931) is a technically ambitious novel where stifling, small-town life is analysed through multiple female perspectives, and gender is seen as an issue to an extent that one might well see, by contrast, the extended sexual symbolism of *A Drunk Man Looks at the Thistle* as so much frivolity. Catherine Carswell (1879–1946) in *Open the Door!* (1920), Nan Shepherd (1893–1981) in *The Quarry Wood* (1928), Nancy Brysson Morrison (1907–86) in *The Gowk Storm* (1933) and Naomi Mitchison (1897–1999) in *The Bull Calves* (1947) all produce highly complex novels of female experience that are ill served by discussion merely of literature in the 'national' context.[33]

LATER TWENTIETH CENTURY

Since the eighteenth century the bulk of Scottish literature has been written in English, and this is especially true of the later twentieth century. In poetry, most prominently of the generation immediately following MacDiarmid and Muir, are Norman MacCaig (1910–96), Sorley McLean (1911–96), Edwin Morgan (b.1920), George Mackay Brown (1921–96) and Iain Crichton

Smith (1928–98). This is a constellation of talent about whom there has been much critical writing.[34] Mackay Brown, equally good as a writer of fiction as a poet, was taught by Muir and converted to Catholicism. All his work is shot through by moments of grace suggesting that Scotland's Reformation is far from an all-consuming cultural disaster and cannot prevail. McLean and Smith (to both of whom we shall return) are writers in Gaelic, translating or overseeing their own work into English. Both demonstrate throughout their work, even as they contemplate the progressions of Scottish history that have not entirely been propitious for the Gaeltachd, that literary creativity is as vibrant there as elsewhere in Scotland. MacCaig is a poet of both huge personal candour and cool existentialist description, as modern a mind and polished craftsman as any in poet writing in English. Morgan, a hugely prolific poet (as well as playwright and critic), is now the Scottish 'Makar', appointed by the Scottish Executive, essentially a poet laureate for Scotland. A sharp observer of (especially Glaswegian) everyday life as well as an experimenter in concrete poetry and sound poetry, Morgan also writes a large body of sonnets. Intensely interested in Scotland, as well as East Europe, America and elsewhere (including the wider cosmos as he writes poetry about outer space), Morgan, who 'came out' as gay only when he reached his seventies, is a writer of appropriately diverse identity as an 'official' writer for twenty-first-century Scotland.[35] Alongside Tom Leonard, Liz Lochhead's poetry represents the most established corpus of work in the generation following Morgan. Of poets in any language (in the case of these three, largely this means English) the most critically acclaimed going into the twenty-first century are Carol Ann Duffy (b.1955), Kathleen Jamie (b.1962) and Don Paterson (b.1963).

In fiction, as well as George Mackay Brown's work, Robin Jenkins (1912–2005) and Muriel Spark (1918–2006) loom large. It is interesting that Jenkins opined towards the end of his life that Spark could not be thought of as a Scottish writer because of her predominant concerns beyond Scotland. Yet Jenkins is one of the finest Scottish practitioners of the novel furth of Scotland. His *Dust on the Paw* (1961) is a superb treatment of Western imperial ambitions in Afghanistan and *The Sardana Dancers* (1964) deals with the separatist cultural aspirations of Catalonia. Jenkins's

Scottish-located work includes *The Cone-Gatherers* (1955) and *The Changeling* (1958), as well as numerous very fine short stories. The first of these revisits James Hogg's 'justified sinner' theme as Duror, a gamekeeper during the Second World War on an Argyllshire estate, persecutes a disabled man doing home-front forestry work, appalled as he is by the imperfection that this individual, Calum, brings to a previously supposed paradise. A multi-layered work that reprises to some extent John Steinbeck's *Of Mice and Men*, the legend of Galahad and the folk-tale of the Green Man (to which we shall make reference again in Chapter 4 in a consideration of *The House with the Green Shutters*), it can be read as another work in the canon of the 'fearful' Calvinist imagination which sees the world as full of alluring and duplicitous stories.[36] In *The Changeling* a well-meaning school-teacher takes a delinquent Glasgow slum boy on holiday with his family, hoping to show him a different life, but things are made even worse for the boy and tragic consequences ensue. One of the preoccupations of the text is the fantasy version of the world humans construct for themselves which is so frequently shattered by brute reality. Albeit from a different (Catholic) background, George Friel (1910–75) is a novelist as adept as Jenkins is in cataloguing the squalid spaces, both social and cultural, of modern life, while similarly essaying (although without the Calvinist tincture) the imaginative urge that people in such limiting situations constantly display. His *Mr Alfred MA* (1972) traverses this terrain with a stylistic exuberance that makes it one of the greatest Scottish novels of the twentieth century.

The superlatively successful Scottish writer since Robert Louis Stevenson is Muriel Spark. Her most obviously Scottish novels are *The Ballad of Peckham Rye* (1960) and *The Prime of Miss Jean Brodie* (1961). In the first text, a supernatural visitor (he claims to be demonic) and also a 'Jock on the make' character, Dougal Douglas, wreaks havoc on the lives of people in a mundane London suburb. The character of Dougal pays homage to Hogg's Wringhim/Gil-Martin in featuring a duplicitous identity. To stage-manage his shape-changing propensity he reverses his name, becoming Douglas Dougal, so as to work fraudulently for two firms at the same time. He also enters into a *ménage à trois* with a man and a woman whose adulterous affair is, paradoxically, lacking in excitement.

With his interference new emotion is injected and the man murders the woman. In the latter example here, Dougal obeys the diabolic folk-rules. He can crank up badness or immorality where it already exists but cannot engender evil out of nothing. Is Dougal a small-time crook or a genuine agent of the supernatural? This is the question Spark poses to her readership and, whatever the answer, beyond this she also asks us to consider the possibility that there is another world beyond the materialistic (both consumerist and unimaginatively empirical) modern one. Spark herself was a practising Roman Catholic, something that along with her cosmopolitan subject matter has perhaps brought her disfavour from the Scottish literary establishment. Her novel *The Prime of Miss Jean Brodie* is, to some extent, a critique of Calvinism in featuring a teacher who attempts to play God and predestine the futures of her chosen pupils. Brodie is, on one level, a complex character representing the idea of imaginative plenitude compared explicitly to Mary, Queen of Scots, Catholic and with a great fondness for aesthetic beauty, and also to John Knox, the founding father of Scottish Calvinism. As well as symbolically standing for the divided Scotland, seemingly, Brodie is also a beleaguered, sometimes heroic, sometimes pathetic woman struggling to assert her own identity in the face of predominantly male-centred institutions in the inter-war period. We might, then, feel some sympathy for her. Brodie's plans are thwarted at every turn as the narrator/author-character intrudes flash-forwards into the narrative to give the plot away and so mocks the idea of predestination, her star pupil Sandy Stranger and Brodie all struggle for control of the story, both of herself and of her pupils. One of the earliest experimental, even postmodern, Scottish novels, *The Prime of Miss Jean Brodie* might also be read according to the Catholic predilections of its author who can be seen to warn against human beings' feeling that they have full control of the story. Final judgement, or how the story ends, is reserved in Spark's outlook for God alone.

Along with Jenkins, Spark and James Kelman, four other living writers of fiction might be mentioned who are of similar stature and of similar canonicity if college and university courses in Scottish literature are any indicator. They are Alasdair Gray (b.1934), William McIlvanney (b.1936), Janice Galloway (b.1955) and A. L. Kennedy (b. 1965). Gray's *Lanark* (1981) is his most famous book, a huge novel that took more than twenty-five years to write. It contains the dystopian tale of the eponymous character who might also be, as revealed in other parts of the text, Duncan Thaw, a tortured artist struggling to create art in an unpropitious, even hostile, Glaswegian and Scottish context. These spheres of fantasy and reality might be read as the continuance of the 'Caledonian Antisyzygy', but are better counted as representing a predominant mode of the Western postmodern novel, where uncertainty and scepticism about both personal and social worlds are writ large in the late twentieth century. We shall return to another of Gray's texts in Chapter 5. McIlvanney is a flamboyant stylist who has chronicled as well as anyone in fiction the changing trajectories of Scottish, and indeed class-mobile, post-industrial, post-Thatcherite British society. His *The Kiln* (1996) sums up such concerns particularly well, and is a meditation also on the difficulty (though no more of a hardship than elsewhere) of becoming a writer in Scotland. Such self-reflexive consideration of creativity predominates in the work of both Janice Galloway and A. L. Kennedy. Galloway's *The Trick is to Keep Breathing* (1989), to which we shall return, is a *tour-de-force* feminist and postmodernist work, a parodic revisiting of previous Scottish fictional terrain, including education with a nod towards *The Prime of Miss Jean Brodie*. A. L. Kennedy, like Galloway, has produced a highly consistent corpus of intensely engaged, pyrotechnical fiction, including *So I Am Glad* (1995), a postmodern fairy tale where the legend of Cyrano de Bergerac is relocated to Scotland. Kennedy is the most critically recognised among two dozen Scottish writers of fiction in the early twenty-first century, whose idioms, themes and formal variety are as vibrant as anywhere else.[37]

SUMMARY OF KEY POINTS

- Scottish literature in English remains significantly under-researched in the seventeenth, eighteenth and later nineteenth centuries, even though, especially in the earlier centuries, writers engaged directly with national concerns.

- In eighteenth-century Scottish Literature in English we find complex debates about the primitivism and civilisation of the Scottish nation. Much of this writing has been read as anti-Scottish according to rather narrow definitions of Scottish cultural authenticity. The same can be said for much nineteenth-century Scottish writing in English.
- The era of the Edinburgh periodical press and the nineteenth-century novel in Scotland is one that is intensely interested in Scottish culture and history, while also containing a wide British and international reach.
- Twentieth-century Scottish Literature in English, as well as more generally, is as diverse and in keeping with the trends of Western culture as anywhere else.

NOTES

1. Alexander Craig, *Poems of Alexander Craig* (Glasgow: Hunterian Club, 1873), p. 18.
2. *The Mercat Anthology of Early Scottish Literature*, p. 364.
3. As further reading in this area, see Michael Spiller, 'The Scottish Court and the Scottish Sonnet at the Union of Crowns', in *The Rose and the Thistle: Essays on the Culture of Late Medieval and Renaissance Scotland*, ed. Sally Mapstone (East Linton: Tuckwell, 1998), pp. 101–15; and Morna Fleming, 'Kin[g]es be the glas, the verie scole, the booke, / Where priuate men do learne, and read, and looke': The Translation of James VI to the Throne of England', in *Literature, Letters and the Canonical in Early Modern Scotland*, pp. 90–110.
4. *The Mercat Anthology of Early Scottish Literature*, p. xxix. See also in this area Sarah M. Dunnigan, 'A New Critical Cartography: Pre- and Post-Union Scottish Renaissance', in *Alba Literaria: A History of Scottish Literature*, ed. Marco Fazzini (Venezia: Amos Edizioni, 2005), pp. 99–119.
5. An interesting phenomenon here is the selection by Alexander Kinghorn and Alexander Law (eds), in *Poems by Allan Ramsay and Robert Fergusson* (Edinburgh: Scottish Academic Press, 1985), who were both involved in editing the six-volume

Scottish Text Society edition of Ramsay. In spite of this experience the editors are purblind to the excellence of some of Ramsay's work in English (or even Scots-English) and failed to select 'The Prospect of Plenty' or 'Wealth, or the Woody'. In their introduction, Kinghorn and Law even write of Ramsay inheriting 'the handicap of . . . a bilingual tradition' (p. xv).

6. *The Works of Allan Ramsay* Vol. II, p. 152.
7. Exemplary of the hostile attitude to Thomson from Scottish criticism of a traditional bent is to be found in Andrew Noble, 'Urbane Silence: Scottish Writing and the Nineteenth-Century City', in *Perspectives of the Scottish City*, ed. George Gordon (Aberdeen: Aberdeen University Press, 1985), pp. 64–70, which sees Thomson as a poet grasping with both hands a British future which is damaging to Scotland
8. James Thomson, *The Seasons* and *The Castle of Indolence*, ed. James Sambrook (Oxford: Oxford University Press, 1987), p. 113.
9. For details of this and of Thomson's contested Scottish context more generally, see Gerard Carruthers, 'James Thomson and Eighteenth-Century Scottish Literary Identity', in *James Thomson: Essays for the Tercentenary*, ed. Richard Terry (Liverpool: Liverpool University Press), pp. 165–90. See Terry's volume, generally, for essays that provide exciting, up-to-date scholarship on Thomson.
10. See especially Mary Jane Scott, *James Thomson, Anglo-Scot* (Athens, GA: University of Georgia Press, 1988). The volume that deals throughout with Thomson's Scottish Protestant identity, as well as making a strong case for numerous ways in which his Scottish culture shows.
11. *The Letters of David Hume*, Vol. 1, ed. J. Y. T. Greig (Oxford: Clarendon Press, 1969), p. 255.
12. See Chapter 1, n. 5, as well as Robert Crawford's 'Introduction' in his collection, *The Scottish Invention of English Literature* (Cambridge: Cambridge University Press, 1998), pp. 1–22, which suggests that Smith and other Scottish Enlightenment activists were, in cosmopolitan fashion, pioneers of the university study of rhetoric in a way that influences the eventual development of English Studies. See also in the same

collection Ian Duncan's 'Adam Smith, Samuel Johnson and the Institutions of English' (pp. 37–54), which argues for Smith as a foundational developer of the idea of 'character-study' in English studies.

13. As well as in its distinctive qualities, eighteenth-century Gaelic poetry in its 'mainstream' (including Thomsonian) idioms is well pointed up in Derick S. Thomson (ed.), *Gaelic Poetry in the Eighteenth Century* (Aberdeen: Association for Scottish Literary Studies, 1993).
14. Modern studies of the Ossian texts include Fiona Stafford, *The Sublime Savage* (Edinburgh: Edinburgh University Press, 1988), Howard Gaskill (ed.), *Ossian Revisited* (Edinburgh: Edinburgh University Press, 1991); and Dafydd Moore, *Enlightenment and Romance in James MacPherson's Poems of Ossian* (Aldershot: Ashgate, 2003).
15. *The Poems of Ossian*, ed. Howard Gaskill (Edinburgh: Edinburgh University Press, 1996), p. 7.
16. See Robert Crawford's very pertinent reading in *Devolving English Literature*, pp. 66–75.
17. Samuel Johnson and James Boswell, *A Journey to the Western Islands of Scotland* and *The Journal of A Tour to the Hebrides*, ed. Peter Levi (Harmondsworth: Penguin, 1984), p. 371.
18. Katie Trumpener, *Bardic Nationalism: The Romantic Novel and the British Empire* (Princeton, NJ: Princeton University Press, 1997); and Murray Pittock, *Scottish and Irish Romanticism* (Oxford: Oxford University Press, 2008).
19. There is a wealth of biographical material on Scott, taking various lines of argument in favour of or against Scott's influence in Scotland and beyond. As useful starting points, see John Sutherland, *The Life of Walter Scott: A Critical Biography* (Oxford: Blackwell, 1995); and A. N. Wilson, *A Life of Walter Scott* (Oxford: Oxford University Press, 1980). Especially judicious is the long entry on Scott by David Hewitt in the *New Dictionary of National Biography* (Oxford: Oxford University Press, 2004).
20. Some of the most excellent (often positive) criticism of Scott is to be found in J. H. Alexander and David Hewitt (eds), *Scott and His Influence* (Aberdeen: Association for Scottish Literary

Studies, 1983); Tom Crawford, *Walter Scott* (Edinburgh: Scottish Academic Press, 1982); and Jane Millgate, *Walter Scott: the Making of the Novelist* (Edinburgh: Edinburgh University Press, 1984).

21. See Andrew Noble, 'John Wilson (Christopher North) and the Tory Hegemony', in Douglas Gifford (ed.), *The History of Scottish Literature*, Vol. 3: *Nineteenth Century* (Aberdeen: Aberdeen University Press, 1988), pp. 125–52.
22. See the anthology *Tales of Terror from Blackwood's Magazine*, ed. Robert Morrison and Chris Baldick (Oxford: Oxford University Press, 1995).
23. See Gerard Carruthers, 'Remaking Romantic Scotland: Lockhart's Biographies of Burns and Scott', in *Romantic Biography*, ed. Arthur Bradley and Alan Rawes (Aldershot: Ashgate, 2003), pp. 93–108.
24. Cairns Craig, *The Modern Scottish Novel: Narrative and the National Imagination* (Edinburgh: Edinburgh University Press, 1999), p. 38.
25. See André Gide's introduction to Hogg's *Confessions* (London: Cresset Press, 1947).
26. See Ralph Jessop, *Carlyle and Scottish Thought* (Basingstoke: Macmillan, 1997) for a treatment that argues much more continuity between the Scottish Enlightenment and Carlyle than commentators usually allow.
27. See William Donaldson, *Popular Literature in Victorian Scotland* (Aberdeen: Aberdeen University Press, 1986) for the modern disinterment of Alexander and many suggestions about a much more interesting creative 'regional' literature in Victorian Scotland than Scottish criticism has traditionally seen.
28. See David S. Robb, *George MacDonald* (Edinburgh: Scottish Academic Press, 1987).
29. Although the Scottish poet Tom Leonard in his path-breaking study *Places of the Mind: The Life and Work of James Thomson ('B.V.')* (London: Jonathan Cape, 1993) does not care all that much about Thomson's Scottishness, the publisher highlights Thomson's nationality.
30. Oliphant and many other Scottish women writers are placed in particular context for the first time in Douglas Gifford

and Dorothy McMillan (eds), *A History of Scottish Women's Writing* (Edinburgh: Edinburgh University Press, 1997).

31. See Andrew Nash, *Kailyard and Scottish Literature* (Amsterdam and New York: Rodopi, 2007), especially pp. 11–47.
32. For the most recent re-readings of Munro and an appeal for him to be taken seriously as a literary artist, see Ronald W. Renton and Brian D. Osborne (eds), *Exploring New Roads: Essays on Neil Munro* (Colonsay: House of Lochar, 2003).
33. For the critical emergence of this terrain, see Carol Anderson and Aileen Christianson (eds), *Scottish Women's Fiction 1920s to 1960s: Journeys into Being* (East Linton: Tuckwell Press, 2000).
34. For the first proper history of Scottish poetry since the 1940s, see Christopher Whyte, *Modern Scottish Poetry* (Edinburgh: Edinburgh University Press, 2004).
35. For a fascinating glimpse of the more recent generation of Scottish poets, see Donny O' Rourke (ed.), *Dream State: The New Scottish Poets* (Edinburgh: Polygon, 1994; rev. edn. 2001), and for a further survey of Scottish poetry since the 1960s, see Gerard Carruthers, 'Scottish Literature: Second Renaissance', in *Twentieth-Century English Literature*, ed. Laura Marcus and Peter Nicholls (Cambridge: Cambridge University Press, 2004), pp. 668–84.
36. See Cairns Craig, *The Modern Scottish Novel: Narrative and the National Imagination* (Edinburgh: Edinburgh University Press, 1999), especially his chapter 'Fearful Selves' for the most modern reading of Calvinism in contemporary Scottish fiction.
37. For further summative consideration of contemporary Scottish fiction, see Gerard Carruthers, 'Fictions of Belonging: National Identity and the Novel in Ireland and Scotland', in *Companion to the British and Irish Novel*, 1945–2000, ed. Brian Shaffer (Oxford: Blackwell, 2005), pp. 112–27.

CHAPTER 4

Intimate Critical Spaces in Scottish Texts

In previous chapters we have considered Scottish literature through an historical continuum. Implicitly, one of our questions has been how important, and how much, continuity is necessary to define 'Scottish literature'. A sensible response might be that continuities exist and are important to observe through Scottish (or any other national or international) literary history, but that none of these is essential or nationally inevitable. As well as placing texts in literary history, we need to pay attention to texts in themselves, or to practise upon them more particular literary criticism, as we have been doing to some extent already. It might be fair to argue that sometimes in the criticism of Scottish literature there has been too much emphasis upon nationalism as an historical context at the expense of detailed analysis of other important contexts within these texts. For instance, the insistence upon national narrative has led to little work being done on the very interesting analysis of gender that might be carried out on John Home's *Douglas*, or of the treatment of women in Burns's work, or in any extended way, in Scotland at least, of Muriel Spark's Jewish or Catholic identities. Not only do texts and writers run the risk of being de-canonised in versions of literary history that are too narrow in their 'national' focus, but so too do different areas of critical interest.

A number of critical and theoretical areas in Scottish literature have arguably been examined rather more slowly and sporadically than in 'English Literature'. For example, it is only really since

1997 that a focused body of criticism on Scottish women's writing has begun to build up. Gender studies, including gay criticism or Queer Theory, more generally has registered even less so. This is no real surprise confirming what we might expect from the hierarchy of marginalisation in Scottish, British and Western society and culture.

We might do a little raw computation here. Three substantial volumes of criticism dedicated to Scottish women's writing have appeared since 1997, as well as a burgeoning number of essays in other books and journals. Useful but fewer, and perhaps patchier, volumes have appeared in the reading of gay formations and masculinity in Scottish literature since 1992.[1] Quite rightly, such new directions challenge the national-centric narratives of Scottish literature. For instance, Christopher Whyte edited a collection of critical essays by various hands entitled *Gendering the Nation* (1995) and subtitled 'Studies in Modern Scottish Literature', with the implicit barb (given that this is a book that includes treatment even of Robert Fergusson and Walter Scott) that the field of Scottish Literature has not been 'modern' enough in its slowness to attend to gender and sexuality. We might ask, as in the case of Edwin Morgan's treatment of Fergusson in Chapter 9 of Whyte's book speculating that the poet might have been gay, whether such treatment helps us appreciate a writer's work.[2] Two competing common-sense answers might be that a writer's work, if worth anything, ought to stand in its own right without the reader needing to know anything of his or her sexual preferences; or, on the other hand, that this is vital information about 'identity', in which Scottish literary studies, generally, has always been interested. We might suggest an interesting possible usage for Fergusson's posited gay orientation (if this could be proved) in countering what we have already observed in Chapter 1. This is the rather facile, long-standing critical view of eighteenth-century poetry in Scots as an unreserved, masculine, 'no-nonsense', implicitly, at least, heterosexual culture. In twenty-first-century Western culture the issue of identity seems to be infinitely contestable, so that the discipline of Scottish literature increasingly has to recognise this reality. In this chapter we shall consider a number of texts where we are less than centrally concerned to read 'Scottishness', where this might merely be one element among others, or where we might even practise some scepticism towards the importance of the nationality of the text. The poem 'The Freiris of Berwik' and Irvine Welsh's novel *Trainspotting* are read according to the very modern ideological concern with the body. William Dunbar's 'The Tretis of the Twa Mariit Wemen and the Wedo', Robert Burns's 'Tam o' Shanter', Margaret Oliphant's short story 'The Open Door' and Liz Lochhead's 'Rapunzstiltskin' are all read *à propos* gender relations, most especially feminism. Tom Leonard's poem 'A Summer's Day', George Douglas Brown's *The House with the Green Shutters*, J. M. Barrie's novella *Farewell Miss Julie Logan* and Janice Galloway's *The Trick is to Keep Breathing* are all read in terms of their well-marshalled literary materials. This leads us to some extent in each case to deconstruct the text, to reveal the rather self-contained system in which literature can be seen to operate rather than seeing these texts as automatically providing a window onto some kind of simple reality, Scottish or otherwise. Questions of the body, of gender, of literature's *raison d'être* being literature itself, being self-referential, rather than a simple window onto 'the real world' problematise the traditional concerns of reading a Scottish text. Scottish texts are as amenable as any others to being read according to modern theoretical and critical concerns. Might it be that Scottish literature as a discipline should increasingly be so unselfconscious as to practise an ever-widening set of reading practises in which 'Scottishness' is only one among many issues?

READING THE BODY

Let us begin applying, largely jargon-free, a range of critical and theoretical approaches to Scottish literature that are somewhat different in operation from the traditional pursuits of either nationality-spotting or gauging aesthetic excellence. We will consider the idea of the human body in two texts from very different periods. A number of sites of investigation practised in contemporary criticism apply a focus that is seen to be equally valid, whether dealing with a fifteenth- or a twentieth-century text. This is true in investigating the status of the body in literature, a long-standing human cultural concern, clearly, including in Christian theology, but one which takes on particularly accented forms in the light of feminist, gender and psychoanalytic criticism. It is also the case that focus upon such an intimate critical space owes something to the rise of New Historicism. Historicism in literary studies, generally, means analysing texts in their historical context, such as we have been attempting frequently in earlier chapters. New Historicism, among other things, studies supposedly less mainstream or central historical moments and contexts. It is less interested in the canonical in its historical considerations, and might include, for instance, the somewhat hidden history of gay culture through the ages. It is seemingly less respectful of history than 'Historicism', largely because it will often analyse literary and non-literary texts side by side, or blur the lines between major and minor texts or documents, and because it is less squeamish than traditional history in transgressing period boundaries. For instance, it might look at texts together from very different periods. It is probably the case in recent years, however, that historicist literary study has subtly and usefully incorporated many of the methods and insights of New Historicism, the latter becoming a more 'mainstream' critical methodology. Where the New Historicist mentality remains disjunctive to classic historicism is in its outlook as part of the poststructuralist family of theoretical approaches, where meaning is infinitely deferred and objective or unitary historical truth is largely unobtainable. New Historicists believe that texts or stories are all-encompassing in their power-motivated constructedness and that 'historical reality', something lying objectively beyond and seen through texts, is essentially unavailable. Generally, their critical project is to uncover competing, conflicting and contradictory 'stories' in texts often complicating received or accepted historical narratives. In pursuing such approaches, however, certain marginalised (usually political, social and cultural) 'truths' pertaining to power relations can be disinterred.

'The Freiris of Berwik' dates from around 1480 and was long attributed to William Dunbar, though for no very solid reason other than the canonical need, we might suggest, to attach the poem to a known 'makar', and perhaps also to anchor it certainly in a 'Scottish' context. It is entirely possible, in fact, that its author was from Berwick, the setting for the poem, which is a very uncertain Scottish or English town 'changing' national location a number of times between the fourteenth and the nineteenth centuries. The poem begins with an insistence upon the truth of the tale that we are about to be told:

> As it befell and happinnit in to deid [in fact]
> Upoun a rever, the quilk is callit Tweid [which] (ll. 1–2)[3]

The opening, however, is followed by a rather improbable and farcical tale that the readership, then and now, would be likely to conclude to be a comic fiction. How do we read this contradiction? One modern answer would be to regard the claim to truth and its rupturing as the story becomes apparent as part of the playfulness, the 'jouissance' in the phrase of Roland Barthes, of the text. Such a self-contained 'game' quality in the text would be much approved by those theoretical critics who wish literary texts to function in terms of their own disruptive literary system. Some critics approve of situations where contradiction in the text is embraced and consistent truth is laughed at so that the traditional claims of 'literary realism' are undermined. Literature in this theoretical mentality is a system which might reflect other social, cultural and political systems which tell us something of human power structures. However, it does not really offer a definitive picture of the world beyond the text.

We shall elucidate this 'reading against the text' as a straightforward window onto the world in our examination of 'The Freiris'. An answer to the puzzle of the claim to truth in 'The Freiris' might be that there is some masked truth, perhaps, a subversive truth even, other than the literal truth of the text that it seeks to impart. We shall consider such an option in the course of our exploration of the poem. The story is an artfully constructed but fairly straightforward anti-clerical tale in the mode of the Middle Ages *fabliau* (largely derived from French literature) where, in today's terms, the lower middle classes are satirised, often in their appetites and adultery. The plot of 'The Freiris' concerns an innkeeper's wife, Alison, who, while her husband is away, awaits her lover, the prior of the local Dominican friary. Her plans for a night of feasting and passion, however, are interrupted by the inconvenient arrival of two other Dominican friars and also, eventually, her husband. The attempts to disguise the situation lead to a broad and bawdy comedy that contrasts with the beginning of the poem:

> At Tweidis mowth, thair standis a nobill toun,
> Quhair mony lordis hes bene of grit renoune, [have lived]
> And mony worthy ladeis, fair of face,
> And mony ane fresche, lusty galland was [youthful; gallant]
> (ll.3–7)

The fineness of the town, which is also grandly fortified and has a plenitude of religious orders, marking out its importance and wealth, forms the contrasting background to the squalid story that soon emerges. We have the gradual establishment of an anti-romance mode as the worthy ladies and virulent young men are soon displaced by the lecherous Alison and the sly, supposedly holy friars. In orthodox enough satire, appearance is not to be trusted when it comes to the reality of human society and human nature. Humans gesture towards high ideals, but fall far short of these because, in Christian terms, we are sinful or, in more general terms, we are animals, though often hypocritical about our natural appetites.

The panoramic space, with its grand perspective of the town, which opens up at the outset of the poem is soon reduced. In various ways, space, which will be an important critical site for us to consider as we look at the treatment of the body in the text, is another area of new critical and theoretical investigation in recent years. Much new cultural, historical and critical commentary apprehends space inhabited by humans not merely as naturally or functionally ordered physical location, but as culturally constructed so that it says things about how humans 'write' their society, their towns, their homes, even the countryside. Two friars, Allane and Robert, are out in the country preaching, but fail to make their return before the town gate is closed for the night and so their friary is closed off to them. The text hints that this is deliberate on their part, providing them with an excuse to seek 'safety' (though actually they are removing themselves from their respectable priory space), in Alison's inn slightly beyond the town, much to the woman's chagrin as she is expecting Prior Johine. Alison is reluctantly persuaded to allow them to stay, but under pretence of modesty, as a woman home alone, insists that they spend the night in the loft. Slyly, of course, this mistrust also indicates scepticism towards the chastity of the two clerics. Allane and Robert, then, are confined to a constricted space, allowing Alison to prepare a sumptuous feast for her lover, Johine, which is lovingly catalogued by the narrator in all its luxury and variety. All in order, Alison retires to her chamber where:

> Scho pullit hir cunt and gaif hit buffettis tway [two slaps]
> Upon the cheikis, syne till it cowd scho say [labia; then addressed it thus]
> 'Ye sowld be blyth and glad at my requesit [invitation]
> Thir mullis of youris ar callit to ane feist' [lips; summoned] (ll.139–42)

We have here a very graphic moment. Does it represent an anti-feminist perspective in the notion of the private crudity of women, or is it part of a thematic fabric in the poem that views all humanity askance? We have moved in the poem from public spaces to an increasingly private domain, and eventually to the most private of female spaces, the sexual organs. We are also told earlier that Freir Johine 'had a prevy posterne [secret back entrance] of his own' (l.129) from the Dominican house, through which he was to leave and join his lover. The 'prevy posterne' clearly, however, is a *double entendre* referring too to his secret bodily access to Alison. Although bawdry is common in medieval literature, we might suggest in line with modern psychoanalytical apprehensions that this transgressive space is not mere salacious comedy but a bodily or material human reality. That is to say, a part of body space (most obviously the sexual organs) is not to be transgressed or explored, and is repressed by the normal Western codes of morality. A modern reading of the poem might highlight here not its seeming taste for 'bawdry', but the repression of desire.

When the lovers are together, Freir Robert in his loft is suspicious, as presumably he does not trust Alison's motivations, just as she does not trust his or Allane's. As a result he makes a slit in the floorboards with his dagger (a symbolic Freudian moment, perhaps) to view what is going on and sees the happy couple settling in for the night and their subsequent alarm as Alison's husband, Symon, returns home unexpectedly. In desperation Alison hurriedly hides the food she has laid on for the tryst and has Johine hide in a meal-chest. Here again, then, we have another constricted space. Alison puts on a show of great modesty as she at first pretends not to recognise Symon, seemingly regarding him as a potential customer at the inn and refusing him admission as she is a woman whose husband is away. When eventually admitted, Alison also points to the friars in the loft as yet more evidence of her female reserve, and Symon, probably secretly pleased but affecting mild annoyance that representatives of the church should be so treated, invites the friars to join him for a drink. Robert then unleashes his cunning plan, asking Symon if he would like fine food since he has magic powers to conjure up such things, and claiming also that he has a personal servant from the underworld that he can summon at will. First of all, and much to Symon's delighted amazement, he asks Alison to fetch him all the mouth-watering victuals she has hidden. She complies rather than have the actual situation revealed. Next, claiming that his supernatural attendant must keep his face hooded to hide its awful ugliness, he urges Johine to arise and do his bidding. Johine has little option but to go along with Robert's command using his cowl to hide his true identity, so that yet again we have human identity in confined space. Robert has Symon beat Johine, which he does and Johine is struck so hard he is propelled downstairs into a midden-heap. The poem ends:

> This is the story that hapnit of that frier;
> No more thair is, bot Chryst us help most deir. [precious]
> (ll.565–6)

This ending, imploring the help of the Christian saviour, might strike modern eyes as rather odd, a seemingly serious note coming on the back of a text, largely, of knockabout comedy. However, it might be read according to an orthodox medieval Christian mindset, where the lives of humans in the world are all rather ridiculous when compared to the afterlife in the presence of God.

This *contemptus mundi* outlook, then, is licensed to satirise human folly, even to enjoy it, when measured against the Creator's eternity. Human folly highlighted and laughed at, all that can be done is throw ourselves on the mercy of Christ.

Somewhat at odds with the Christian reading we have just suggested, the treatment of the body in the poem, whose details we have already observed, is a concern that only criticism from the later twentieth century would focus so seriously upon. Medieval thinkers often warned against sensuality and appetite, if not exactly as the enemy of reason in the way of subsequent, more puritanical Protestantism, but nevertheless as having the potential dangerously to cloud rationality. Sigmund Freud foregrounded more primal human urges, which erase to a large extent the old division between reason and feeling. Since his work in the early twentieth century, through the experience of the modernist and postmodernist periods and an increasingly secularised Western society, generally, the body has become a site for cultural enquiry. This site is less to be controlled morally than in previous eras and is to be seen as a reality to be understood with a lot less fear than previously. Let us, then, attempt to draw out a reading of 'The Freiris' which centres the body in this modern sense.

For a start this would begin to alter the mode in which we read the poem. We might register historically that the text is intended as a satire on those sinful desires that surface in humans, but the modern student of the body would suggest that this religious story of the body is an ideological construction. Bodily urges are natural, in fact, and not to be criticised so easily. Whatever the author's, perhaps anti-feminist, intentions for this scene, Alison might be read as she addresses her genitalia as instead rightly enjoying her body. This is a release, then, from the usual constraints of feminine modesty, a patriarchal marriage structure and of Christianity. Her adultery to some modern eyes might, then, appear justified. The true reality of the body is revealed in her most intimate scene, which ought to take human precedence over social and spiritual considerations. Clearly, the appetites of the three friars might be read similarly; they too are held in check, at least in public, by the conventions of religious holiness. They, like Alison, desire to indulge their bodily appetites, unnaturally suppressed. The fact that none of these characters demonstrates any guilt on this score might well confirm a reading of the claustrophobic world they long to escape. The hypocrisy we might say, rejecting a satirical reading, belongs to the culture and society of the human world rather than these characters *per se*.

The tricks with space in the poem form an essay on the way in which public and private spheres are somewhat muddled, the confined spaces being the psychoanalytically truer space and the larger spaces, such as the panoramic view of Berwick and institutions of church marriage, the rather falsely constructed ones. The cuckolded husband, Symon, without knowing it, practises revenge upon his wife's lover, Johine. Rather than this being seen to represent some kind of moral reckoning, however, we might suggest that the occasion when he beats Johine should be viewed as further confirmation of the way in which the characters in the poem are social automata, not actually engaged with a true moral order. Rather than dispensing moral justice, Symon, much less sly or intelligent than his wife but nonetheless in orthodox marital terms her 'master', thinks he is attacking a creature of the underworld. This scenario of rather nebulous engagement in fact might be seen to register in a deep way the real emptiness of the marriage. The bodily enactment and, indeed, abuse in the text point us ultimately towards not mere farce or Christian satire, it might be suggested, but to the body as a site of serious and sadly thwarted desire, surrounded by a whole series of false social conventions or 'stories'.

Let us turn to another Scottish text that deals with the body, Irvine Welsh's novel *Trainspotting* (1993). Like 'The Freiris of Berwik', *Trainspotting* is, in a sense, unproblematically Scottish in its narrative voices. This fact allows us, perhaps, to move easily to concerns other than those of any national sort when dealing with the two works. We might note, however, that just as we can raise a doubt about the original provenance of 'The Freiris', so we can suggest that the status of *Trainspotting* as a 'Scottish' text is not simple. 'The Freiris' is set in an historically liminal space between Scotland and England and might even have been written by an 'English' person, as the language of Northumberland when it was written would not have been all that different from the 'Scots' of the text. It appears in the canon of Scottish literature, however, because of a close kinship with the language of Dunbar, Henryson and other

Scottish writers. In contrast to the text's questionable national provenance, the traditional Christian satirical lens through which the text has been read and our modern reading of the treatment of the body, both represent more certain contexts within which to read it than any national context. Indeed, we might suggest that the solid location of the poem (heavily invested in Berwick, militarily and culturally) exists precisely because of the lack of national solidity, or the disputed ownership, of this town. We might even appropriate this fact to our modern reading of the poem in its theme of less to be trusted 'official' worlds, including national identity and its perhaps more real interior worlds of body and desire.

Trainspotting is also interesting as a more problematic Scottish text. For example, it is a novel that flies in the face of the one of the favoured modes of Scottish expression so far as traditional critics are concerned, realism. It may well be a gritty story of the drugs subculture of 1990s Edinburgh, but it is a book where its protagonists famously mock choosing 'life' and prefer instead to retreat into alternative worlds. It is also a novel where the group of young men, around whom the action revolves, express dislike for the culture of Glasgow. Like his main group of friends, a fan of Hibernian Football Club and of Irish-Scottish descent, another complicating fact of identity in the text, the character Renton encounters the Glasgow side of his family at the funeral of his brother. Ironically, he has been killed while serving in Ireland in the British Army. Renton thinks of his Glasgow family as typical Protestant 'weegies', even though Glasgow is a much more Catholic city than Edinburgh. Given his background, Renton is also enraged by the Union Flag on his brother's coffin even though it is entirely reasonable for his brother, Billy, as a serving British soldier, to be so honoured. Scottish, British, Irish and, indeed, regional identities are complex and entangled in myth and misapprehension, and this is what Welsh registers here and elsewhere in the novel. In fact, we might go so far as to say that nationality as such is not actually a crucial issue in *Trainspotting*. Renton registers the fact that Scotland has a far higher rate of HIV infection than elsewhere in Britain, and the implication, clearly, is that this and the higher rate of drug abuse is due to the greater social deprivation in Scotland during the 1980s and 1990s. However, it is not that there is some deliberate 'English' plot to look after itself more than Scotland (some of the English and Welsh regions in this period fare not much better than Scotland in terms of poverty and HIV). The issue, actually, is one of distance from the metropolis, London, which accrues for itself much of the national wealth. With ironic appropriateness, this is the locus to which Renton and his cronies resort at the end of the novel to do business with a major drug-dealer and extract a suitably handsome financial reward for illegal narcotics into which, through various quirks of fate, they have come into possession. One aspect that the novel certainly identifies is the failure of traditional ideas of community, and this *à propos* the economics of post-Thatcherite Britain, where everything has become business, everything a commodity.

At the purvey following his brother's funeral, Renton seduces his brother's pregnant partner in a scene where he narrates in minute detail the physical congress of his unhygienic body with the woman. This self-indulgence, so unattractively detailed, represents one of many hedonistic moments in the novel. We might suggest that these moments are not to be read simply in Freudian terms, where the life instinct in the presence of death leads to sex (in the case of the sex scene following the funeral, one can easily see how this reading might be made). Rather, life itself, where even the pleasures of the body have been turned into debased, selfish, consumerist appetites, is to be despised. We might understand this, as at one point Renton muses:

> Choose life. Choose mortgage payments; choose washing machines; choose cars; choose sitting oan a couch watching mind-numbing and spirit-crushing game shows, stuffing fuckin junk food intae yir mooth. Choose rotting away, pishing and shiteing yersel in a home, a total fuckin embarrassment tae the selfish, fucked-up brats ye've produced. Choose life.[4]

Registered here is Renton's view that normal, everyday consumer and leisure activities are no more constructive or even 'real' than the life of the junkie which he has chosen. Here and elsewhere in the novel he espouses with apposite brutality the idea that what passes for the meaningful is hollow. The body decays and becomes dys-functional anyway, whether in a retirement home or through drug abuse. We need to make sense of this thoughtful hedonism, and might begin by saying that for Renton the body is not any kind of sacred space, as it had been for much of Western Christian history. The moral prerogatives to keep it virtuous and healthy are undermined in the first instance with the decline of Christianity.

From the Modernist period, at least, we have the increasingly intense idea that the human body should be enjoyed and sometimes also the idea of living healthily so as to enjoy the body to the full. However, we might suggest that an increasingly disrespectful view of the body emerges in the twentieth century. Albeit that cruelty had always existed in human history, Auschwitz and the other Nazi death camps, as some thinkers have identified, define a moment after which there is a diminishing idea of taboos with regard to the treatment of the human body. This accounts for the sharp rise in the late twentieth century in things that might variously be thought of as progressive as well as repugnant in a list that would include greater supplies of pornography, more widespread drug-taking than ever before, abortion and genetic experimentation. We need to notice this general cultural background and the post-industrial Scotland that Renton and his friends inhabit. Homelessness on the streets of Edinburgh only began to occur in the 1980s and the public health, related to widespread unemployment, of the nation actually declined significantly in this decade, so what is there for Renton to believe in? He believes in neither the diseased body politic nor the usefulness of the individual body. In the case of the latter, Renton rebels against the rampant *individualism* that is espoused in the heightened consumerism and emphasised financial independence of the Thatcher government of the 1980s, which defines the mood of Britain arguably down to present times. Indeed, since Renton reads the body politic, or the nation, precisely as diseased, why should he have any hope of escaping personal disease? So we might interpret his sceptical mindset.

Where Renton is shown in a downward spiral of decreasing respect for his own body in the novel, the character Begbie loudly condemns the drug-taking of his associates and espouses supreme male healthiness, although he is also quite happy to profit from the drug deal that they all broker in London. Begbie is an urban hard-man type (another version of the 'fighting Jock'), whose masculinity is of interest to modern critics. His insistence upon his normative maleness, completely heterosexual and in no danger of ill health might cause suspicion and suggest, in fact, uncertainty in his identity. His revulsion at drugs, but not at his own vast consumption of alcohol or cigarettes, perhaps shows he is not so much scared of rampant HIV in itself, from which Renton and other 'users' are at risk, but from its association as the 'gay plague'. Whether or not this is the case and whether or not, as some critics might suggest, Begbie is himself a man of closet homosexual urges, he is most certainly full of male anxiety. This is revealed in the novel when he accidentally meets his father, an utterly dissolute alcoholic living rough. Immediately following this encounter, and shamed in front of Renton who witnesses it, he beats up an entirely innocent male passer-by. This individual, clearly, stands as a surrogate for the rage he feels towards his parent. This sequence of events, including a brief moment of vulnerability responded to very rapidly with utterly repulsive action, is quite clever in that it allows the reader no time to feel sorry for Begbie. His veneer is almost entirely constant and provides a rock-hard maleness that stands in contrast to Renton's dissolute maleness. Taken together, this pairing paints a picture where the alternatives are both unattractive and confirm the utter ugliness of male life in the novel. In so far as *Trainspotting* is a 'condition of Scotland' novel in the 1990s, it is a very bleak portrait, critiquing various working and under-classes as well as official government and cultural attitudes. That it has absolutely nothing positive to recommend of life in Scotland, either individually or culturally, and that it is sceptical towards the notion of a 'real Scotland' or a 'real Britain' or a 'real world' marks perhaps either the bleakest or most liberated points in the literature of the nation.

PRACTISING FEMINISM AND GENDER CRITIQUE

As suggested earlier, an urgent feminist question concerns the exclusion of female writers from a central place in the Scottish canon. This would be true of Muriel Spark, whose femininity is one of the parcel of non-mainstream attributes she displays and which have brought her only rather grudging acceptance in Scotland. It may be true too of Naomi Mitchison (perhaps even in this book's all too brief mention of this author in Chapter 3), an immensely prolific writer about whom doctoral dissertations have begun to be produced over the past decade or so. An interesting exercise is to compare Scottish anthologies of fiction and poetry, where it will be found that even the 'major' women writers tend to warrant less space individually than 'major' male authors. What we are concerned about in the next section, however, is practising feminist criticism in a range of Scottish texts.

We begin with William Dunbar's poem 'The Tretis of the Twa Mariit Wemen and the Wedo', from the early 1500s, which can be read as an anti-feminist or misogynistic text. One aspect of feminist criticism is to consider and critique anti-feminism, which might be generated by female as well as male writers since both inhabit the same institutionally sexist culture and society.[5] In 'The Tretis' there are a number of elements that might be labelled anti-feminist, and these include the setting of the poem, the position of the narrator and the characters of the women in the text. At the opening of the text, it is midsummer evening and three women foregather in a lovely garden. We might note a huge amount of 'the feminine' brought together in the poem, where this represents 'alterity' and in two different ways. First of all, midsummer night is associated in folk culture with enchantment and with the supernatural and so establishes the suggestion that these women are unnatural or have something of the night about them. As if this was not enough, they are, at the same time, associated in their *locus amoenus* with a very stereotypical kind of femininity: with nature. This duplicitous signal in the text, where the women are both supernatural and natural at the same time is of importance in our feminist reading. We ought to consider next the position of the narrator, who is a voyeur: he overhears the women as he spies upon them. His is the illicit male gaze, regarding what he is not entitled to view, and we might label him a 'Peeping Tom', a pervert even. Given this potentially unreliable status we might also call into question his commentary on the women. However, if we do so then we begin to suggest that Dunbar himself is deliberately mounting a kind of feminist critique. A very basic reading strategy that feminists have to decide upon is whether they are 'reading against the text', extracting from it unknown prejudices that are inherent in its author and society, or whether a writer is more or less knowingly contributing to a feminist analysis. The third major area for discussion in our text is the selfish, cruel and 'man-eating' parlance found as the female protagonists discuss relations between the sexes.

That these women might be sinister fairy folk is not only attested to by the time of the calendar, but also by the imagery which is to be found enveloping them. Nature in the garden in which they are found is particularly lush and fertile, almost claustrophobically so (so as to become sinister). Also, they are near a holly tree, associated with magical druidic rites. We have too the repetition of the colour green, which is the colour of enchantment and of fairyland. Likewise there is the fact that we have three women gathered together, their number being a traditional one for a group of witches. It is also the case that the widow in the poem is passing on advice, instructing the other two women in the 'dark art' of manipulating men. What is clear enough for the feminist critic here is the simultaneous fear of, and attraction to, women on the part of the narrator (and also of the author?) which might be thought to sum up a characteristically contradictory male attitude to women. It might be suggested that the simultaneously natural and supernatural couching of these women also sums up male confusion, or the inability of the male to conceive the female realistically as simply human beings equal to men.

The narrator is arguably somewhat afraid of the women, which manifests itself in his staying hidden to observe them and this, it could be claimed, generates his confused, even over-excited language in the opening description. Again, we come back to the vexed question of how much the author and narrator are to be equated as sharing the same view and, alternatively, of the extent that there might be ironic distance between the author and his character-creation, the narrator. The narrator is perhaps himself sexually inadequate. The only way he can deal with women is by spying on them, framing them in a situation that amounts to a private fantasy. His senses are in overdrive as he observes not only the women and the garden but also a private feast the women are about to consume. All of these elements blend into one as he registers that collectively these are 'Fragrant, all full of fresche odour, finest of smell' (l.34). Just as he is unsure whether these women are natural or unnatural, the narrator yet again lacks precise discrimination. We can ask: is this sensory overload a quality that pertains to the author of the text, or merely one of its characters, the over-exuberant narrator?

The women when they speak confirm the sensuality of their pretty appearance and their appetite as shown in their fine food, but in a way now deeply horrible. Women, then, might appear pleasing, but underneath and closer up there is something darker. In cultural terms, the feminist would suggest that this configuration is symptomatic of an attitude that derives from orthodox, archetypal Christianity where Eve is the attractive tempter of Adam to evil, thus revealing her interior propensity to sin and untrustworthiness generally. The widow asks the two married women to comment on marriage and whether they might choose differently given the opportunity. The first woman replies indicating that she has had little free choice in the matter. In the medieval period women of the better class, as these are, would have often been used to marriages more or less arranged out of financial interest, the power of her family then coming before her personal happiness. She also goes on to cast her husband in the light of a stupid, unattractive, sexually incapable individual, of which the following is only a small sample:

> I have ane wallidrag, ane worm, ane auld wobat carle; [worthless man]
> hairy caterpillar of a churl
> A waistit wolroun na worth bot wourdis to clatter [wasted wild boar; gibber]
> Ane bumbart, ane dronbee, ane bag full of flewme, [lazy fellow; drone; phlegm]
> Ane scabbard skarth, ane scorpioun, ane scutarde behind. [scabby monster; bum shitter] (ll.89–93)

Is this, and the explicit sexual talk throughout the poem, something that the narrator (and by extension the male readership) might be said to be shuddering at? Alternatively, do such scenes actually reveal male enjoyment in a fictional fantasy of physically energetic, sexually voracious femininity?

We should note too the mode of flyting, alliterative, highly descriptive abuse exchanged in medieval public contests (sometimes at the Royal Court) in Scotland between male poets. In the lines quoted above and those of the text that immediately follow them we have female flyting (albeit at an absent protagonist) and in a (supposedly) non-public female space. Whether or not Dunbar intends to show it, a feminist critic might say that he is delineating the more limited forum and utterance vouchsafed to females in this world. The poem, for all its supposed comic intent, actually fulfils the serious purpose of revealing female empowerment as inferior in scope to that of the male.

In the interests of beginning to suggest more of the possibilities of a project (one that has never been undertaken in any extensive way) where feminist perspectives are applied to canonical Scottish texts (most especially, perhaps, those by male writers), let us follow on from our reading of 'The Tretis' by turning briefly to Robert Burns's 'Tam o' Shanter' (1790). Like the 'The Tretis' this is a poem that contains, centrally, an illicit male gaze. Tam the farmer is returning home from market-day drunk when he is attracted by noise coming from the ruined kirk (church) of Alloway. On stealthy, closer inspection he witnesses an orgy in full swing, with the devil playing the pipes. Around Satan are cavorting a coven of witches and warlocks attended by various other presences, including the dead in their upright coffins. At the climax of the poem, which a critic interested in sexuality might well interpret literally, Tam ejaculates, 'Weel done, Cutty-Sark' (l.189) in admiration of a pretty girl who is among the throng and whose sark (or chemise) is a 'cutty' so short as to fail to cover her modesty.[6] Following Tam's cry, 'in an instant all was dark' (l.190), a formulation that might be read by someone interested in the psychoanalysis of the text as representing the male orgasm (ejaculation) with simultaneous emptying oblivion (darkness or even death) with which this act has sometimes been associated.

The notion of Tam's orgasm, even metaphoric but perhaps actual, would have puzzled most readers or critics prior to the twentieth century (and is of an order of critical observation that might still appear odd to many modern eyes). However, the poem can be read, in feminist terms, supporting this sexual reality. Tam has been tarrying at the local inn, fancying the barmaid and loath to go out into the night after a day's drinking, not only because the weather is unpromising but because he does not wish to go home to face his 'nagging' wife, Kate. At home, Kate is thought of by Tam, 'nursing her wrath to keep it warm' (l.12), and here we have in a nutshell the double-edged identity of the female as seen by the male: a mother-figure ('nursing'), but also fearful in her spiteful anger. When Tam does leave the comfort of the hostelry he is assailed, we might say, by mother nature. The storm that assails him on the road parallels the outpouring of anger he has had from Kate in the past when he has been partying too long, and which he expects again when he returns home. Taking refuge from the storm, or from Kate, he espies or conjures up the fantasy of the orgy at Alloway kirk. This is an alternative, witch-like but sexy (and equally flawed) vision of femininity from that he is reluctant to return home to. We can read the poem, then, as a series of misunderstandings of womanhood by the immature male psyche of Tam.

The ending of the poem has been thought dissatisfying by many critics. Here Tam, fleeing for his life from the satanic hordes, has his mare, Maggie, leap across a burn, containing the sacred element of water over which his diabolic pursuers cannot follow, not before, however, a witch has caught and removed the largest part of Maggie's tail. In our feminist reading we might suggest here a (comical) castration metaphor and the poem ends with a plea against male roistering:

> Think, ye may buy the joys o'er dear,
> Remember Tam o' Shanter's mare. (ll.223–4)

If Maggie has had symbolic castration practised on *her*, this is somewhat ridiculous but operates as a warning to Tam about his future behaviour. However, given that neither Maggie nor Tam has come to serious harm, we might well see the narrator's couching of a moral lesson in these last lines as tongue-in-cheek, and therefore as imploding. Tam, we might well conclude, will behave irresponsibly again; male nature will not change all that easily. We might add here discussion of one final interesting moment from the early criticism of the poem, where John Gibson Lockhart in his biography of Burns claims that there is a superior version of the legend of 'Tam o' Shanter', the 'Galloway' version. He assumes Burns to have used this as a model, but claims the poet has produced an inferior ending to that of the folk-legend. In the 'Galloway' story, a woman is found in bed the next day with hairs from the horse's tail in her hand. She is revealed, then, to have been one of the witches participating in the orgy and chase, and so is executed as a result. However, this folk-tale, which probably did not actually exist prior to Burns's writing of his poem, maintains a misogynistic logic: that women are to be desired and feared with not much room for shades of reaction in between. Burns's poem in our reading above, however, actually runs against such simple misogyny. In this reading Burns's poem, in fact, reveals the immaturity of the male psyche. The rather inconsequential, comical ending of 'Tam o' Shanter' conspires to be dismissive of Tam. What he has been experiencing in the text has been his own fear of femininity rather than the actually supernatural.

Another text where the feminist perspective might be applied is Margaret Oliphant's short-story 'The Open Door' (1882). Often read as simply a tale of the supernatural, it might be said to concern a more natural 'mystery' which has to do with gender relations. The text is narrated by Colonel Henry Mortimer, who is in conventional terms in a position of trust since as readers we usually expect a narrator to be largely reliable. Mortimer has returned from military service in India to late Victorian Midlothian in search of a peaceful life for his family. All is not restful for the Mortimers in their new life however, as his only son Roland is disturbed by feverish illness in which he claims to be witnessing paranormal phenomena, especially hearing voices. As a man of purposeful rationality, Mortimer seemingly sets out to explain away Roland's experiences as externalised versions of his illness, and, as readers, we are likely to be on his side. Mortimer is a man of action, who, unlike his butler (also a man of previous and brave military service), does not allow himself to be scared by and flee from their attempted investigations as they perceive the strange phenomenon of an unseen child's voice. This ghostly boy is heard to plead, 'Let me in mother!' Through this experience, then, unlike his friend the doctor who remains a determined sceptic, Mortimer reverses his initial conclusion, becoming open-minded about the supernatural visitation.

Mortimer's version of events is likely to carry the unaware reader with it through the text. This is unsurprising as he is a character who seems on the face of things to be commendably rational and also honest in admitting of things he cannot fully understand when he experiences them. However, if we re-read Oliphant's text, we begin to realise that the situation might not be as 'straightforward' as Mortimer has it. There are perhaps mysteries in the text other than the ghost. Among these is Mortimer telling us that Roland seems to become more ill when he is not around. Mortimer is sometimes absent, for unexplained reasons, in London. We might well overlook this 'gap' in the text, however, due to the fact that our first-person narrator is a patriarchal figure of authority, whose movements are not to be questioned, but to be seen as his own capable business. Reading against this, we might wonder if Mortimer when away from his family is indulging in an alternative life of private excess and other women (prostitutes even). Mortimer is, then, both an unreliable narrator and not so steady a respectable family man as he would like us to believe. Mortimer's absences in India, in the line of military duty presumably, and those unexplained ones when the family returns to Scotland, arguably speak of a male void that lies at the root of Roland's illness. A younger only son, surrounded by a mother and sisters at home, he is the heir that Mortimer has been delighted to sire at last. Roland, we can infer, has this huge weight of expectation thrust upon him. By dint of gender alone he, rather than any of the women in Mortimer's family, is thrust to the centre of hope and attention, and the psychological effect of this, it might be suggested, makes him ill. Constitutionally a gentler creature to begin with than his father would like, Roland suffers all kinds of implicit pressures from his father and the patriarchal standards of family and society more widely. In the story, disturbed maleness – and also displaced femininity – are registered by the ghostly boy. He is heard to plead pityingly for his mother to let him in, and this is explained by the local lore of a boy who had returned home to the family cottage (now ruined in the grounds of Mortimer's estate) to find his mother dead. Taken together, Roland's state of mind, which so often approaches hysteria and which is having an increasingly detrimental effect also on his mother's health (and the ghost-child with his mother), speaks of a situation where the gender categories, and also family categories, are causing pain and concern.

Relationships are not healthily completed in this story, and its ending where Mortimer seemingly accepts the supernatural possibility is, if we are alert, only falsely satisfying. He has found an easy solution in beginning to believe that the problem of his son is 'out there' and has nothing to do with Roland's inner state of mind, or with him or his family. That is to say Mortimer's mindset has not actually altered in any significant sense. Patriarchy remains unchallenged and intact, even as maleness has been subtly undermined throughout the story. Issues of gender, maleness and femaleness have not actually come to the centre of the text and remain unresolved.

Let us look very briefly at a final text here, Liz Lochhead's poem 'Rapunzstiltskin' (1981), a text that most definitely purveys a feminist perspective. It begins *in media res*:

> & just when our maiden had got
> good & used to her isolation,
> stopped daily expecting to be rescued,
> had come to almost love her tower,
> along comes This Prince
> with absolutely
> all the wrong answers.[7]

The very opening of the poem contributes thematically to the idea of a familiar story, one that has started long ago regarding the place of woman in society. Another inherited element is the fairytale of Rumplestiltskin (as collected by the Brothers Grimm in the early nineteenth century), a form which as often as not codifies rather conservative social values. Here the idea of the woman isolated, even endangered in 'her tower', is the excuse for heroic, female-saving, female-completing male behaviour.

The male's 'wrong answers' in the poem are not 'wrong' because they dissent from simply peddling the standard safe, virtuous ones indicating his honourable intentions. To begin with, he speaks to the maiden's supposedly liberated (post-feminist) desire, bringing her sex manuals. This is one of a number of 'riddles' of which Lochhead's poem is composed, and which her female protagonist's beau fails to solve:

She pulled her glasses off.
'All the better to see you with my dear?' he hazarded.
She screamed, cut off her hair.
'Why you're beautiful?' he guessed tentatively.
'No, No, No!' she
shrieked & stamped her foot so
hard it sank six cubits through the floorboards.
'I love you?' he came up with
as finally she tore herself in two.

What we have indicated here are the pre-programmed responses of the male, which, aptly, are cued by the most basic stories that children are told. The poem points to a deep, immoveable, infantilised cultural conditioning with regard to the male perspective on the female. The male cannot see the woman in straightforwardly realistic terms but attempts to impose upon her a range of stories, his desire for her and her aesthetic beauty, and his overwhelming emotion (love) for her. None of these resolves the situation for the woman with the result that she is depicted in the end tearing herself in two. In this way, the female character resists her 'wholeness': the master-key to her that the male character is desperately attempting to locate.

Lochhead's poem is a very clever use and jumbling up of materials deeply embedded in a culture that can imagine the female in various limited ways, but fails realistically to deal with a woman's individuality. Witty, comical and bitter, it invites us to consider how deeply so many stories in our culture are conservatively male-centred.

DECONSTRUCTING SCOTTISH LITERATURE

So far this chapter has been concerned to explore some theoretical approaches to Scottish literature, and what modern theoretical approaches have in common are two broad, overlapping methodologies. The first of these is to find off-centre narratives, such as is found in the feminist or gyno-critical project of placing concerns of femininity and gender relations at the forefront of discussion, so that issues of power and hierarchy in society and culture are interrogated.

Similarly, the second of these is also materialist (or concentrates on human constructedness). It refuses to accept at face value the idea of a world where things are more or less as they should be; that the ordering of the world is largely a matter of accidental nature (or perhaps of God's designing) rather than deeply constructed by human power structures. As a result the idea of traditional literary realism, where a text somehow neutrally reflects the reality of the world, and guides us to who and what is important in it or what lies at the 'centre' of the text as 'really important', is also called into question. Related to all of this is the resistance to 'meta-narrative': the cogent, unitary story in a text that the author, or society, might wish to direct us toward. Such a revisionist re-reading by definition will often come into conflict with the idea of a national literature, or the idea that literature easily reflects national reality.

In its most basic definition, the materialism to which we have just been referring points to the materials that make up or 'construct' the text: conventions of language, form, genre and so on. This 'conventionality', or prior usage, necessarily implies a level of artificiality or fabrication. In other words, literary texts in the first instance do not refer simply to the 'real world' but are dependent upon other stories, are formed from and react in relation to these pre-existing stories. Important here too is the intertextual dependency of stories and texts upon one another so that the absolute autonomy or integrity of any literary text is a rather simplistic idea.

Decentring major narratives and unpicking the various different materials in a text both represent strategies in 'deconstruction'. In Chapter 1 we attempted to deconstruct a fairly long tradition of Scottish literary criticism. We noticed the ideas and rhetoric of 'the Caledonian Antisyzygy' promulgated by critics, not out of straightforward literary historical observation but as tropes passed from one critic to another. In observing this process, we highlighted assumptions such as the organicist outlook where 'healthy' literature for many of these critics is taken necessarily to coincide with a healthy nation. Such assumptions do not necessarily stand up to historical scrutiny and underpin overarching meta-narratives that rely too much upon one central story. Literary theory in the early twenty-first century is resistant to such singular narratives, seeking to challenge these and to reveal instead a plethora of possible alternative stories that might be practised in relation to any literary text. It often also sees contradiction and lack of textual unity as the underlying status of literature.

In this section we shall look at some particular Scottish literary texts to highlight the modern theoretical dispensation of deconstruction. A very helpful place to begin here is Tom Leonard's poem 'A Summer's Day' (1975), since it comes ready-made as an act of literary dissent or deconstruction in itself. It is a work very explicitly parading its own textuality. Leonard's poem takes its title in an intertextuality (or a usage of pre-existing literary material) with William Shakespeare's sonnet 'Shall I compare thee to a summer's day'. It also stands, however, in opposition to Shakespeare's text, oppositions or binaries being the foundational logic in texts which often interest those who practise deconstruction. Leonard is not interested in the inherent value or aesthetic of Shakespeare's text. What he is observing is the way in which Shakespeare has been appropriated as an idea of 'high culture', particularly the way high culture is used to define and devalue cultural expression that is perceived to stand apart from or below high culture. Systematically, Leonard counters the values that attach to Shakespeare's poem and does this, among other ways, by disrupting its form. Leonard's poem in counterpoint to the sonnet form is a line short (thirteen rather than fourteen); it is an imperfect sonnet, eschewing also any of the sonnet's usual schemes of rhythm and rhyme. Unlike the sonnet also, which is intended usually as a showy, witty performance of virtuoso control, Leonard's text features a narrator, a working-class Glasgow male, who seems to be, certainly believes himself to be, inarticulate:

> yir eyes ur
> eh
> a mean yir
> pirrit this wey
> ah a thingk yir
> byewtifil like ehm[8]

The speaker lacks self-confidence in expression because, it is implied, his own Glasgow patois is not valued in the first place for its expressive possibilities. His language is not one that readily turns to poetry and, the text suggests, this has something to do with the fact that poetry stands outwith his experience, appropriated as this usually is within 'higher' dialects of English. 'A Summer's Day' is the metaphor the speaker cannot reach for or never attains here, lying beyond, as a title, the actual lived or spoken experience of the narrator. Leonard's 'A Summer's Day' is a kind of anti-poem, asking questions about access to literature.

In the case of Shakespeare, used in a certain way, this may be high art English literature, but Leonard's posing of the inaccessibility of this is far from exclusively a Scottish issue. 'Dialect' writing across England, Wales and Northern Ireland arguably enjoys an even less mainstream cultural place than Scots. Leonard is raising a problem in general for 'vernacular' (here meaning non-standard English) expression. Scots, a particular Glasgow, working-class Scots, is here the exemplar by which a much more universal situation is addressed. As already suggested in an earlier chapter, Leonard, the most successful poet in Scots of the later decades of the twentieth century, was never the 'poster-boy' of Scots language activism precisely because his work sought not to champion self-contained authenticity but to point to a wider set of linguistic and power relations. For Leonard, it is simply not possible to identify a 'true' (meaning both pure and capable) Scots literary tradition standing in splendid isolation. For one thing any such standardisation would be likely to be overbearing with regard to literature in certain Scots dialects, which would not all fit easily into any such unitary notion. For another, Scots (either 'high' literary Scots or 'common' Glaswegian Scots) used in literature cannot be divorced in its activities from awareness of (especially high) English literature, which is so prevalently present in Scottish culture, education and society. Leonard's 'A Summer's Day' is a clever act in the deconstruction of high art (rather than simply 'English Literature') from the point of view of, very imprecisely, 'Scottish Literature'. Indeed, as with Welsh's *Trainspotting*, it points to a register of local Scottish expression that is also often culturally frowned upon and disempowered in Scotland due to the predilections of class more than because of the 'national' situation.

The project of the deconstructionists and poststructuralists (the latter mode of criticism emerging from the former) attempted to show the fault-lines running through any kind of univocal, or organically complete, text. For a start, narratives are seen always to rely upon pre-existing materials. These are often ideologically constructed in an overt political fashion, although at their most basic rely upon deep, socially and psychologically conditioned categories. These would include ideas such as 'good' and 'bad', which are not so much moral absolutes speaking to some kind of transcendent reality lying above and beyond, but actually rather simplistic (though perhaps necessary) binary structures by which humans order their societies and their world. Structuralist analyses have their roots in the rise of anthropology from the late nineteenth century which saw a more basic material rather than a moral sense actually structuring both stories and societies.

Humans tell stories not through some singular sense of 'truth' or 'reality', but in a systematic way where concepts take on definition with regard to how these are used through traditions of story-telling. Most especially ideas are relative, are defined by their opposite, so that 'good' and 'bad' define one another through cultural usage rather than emanating from any pre-existing, transcendent moral universalism. The idea of oppositions or differences defining one another, relying upon one another, runs counter to the essentialist notion of a settled, self-contained 'Scottish' text. As a number of critics have argued, residual essentialism – the lingering desire for organically complete Scottish texts, or an organically complete Scottish literature more generally – has made the subject somewhat impervious to new theoretical disquisitions.[9] Apart from shifting the material centre of attention in their readings away from the national condition (to the body or gender or class) these new forms of criticism utilise notions of the construction of literary texts that are to be unwoven in their disparate, often contradictory, discourses. The idea of the 'Caledonian Antisyzygy' might look as though it belongs to this kind of critical reading. Leaving aside its own constructedness, which we have already examined, a number of critics have pretended that the concept is a kind of harbinger of the discursive plurality that modern literary theory is often interested in seeking out. In its anxiety over missing wholeness, the antisyzygy trope is nothing of the kind.

Let us round out this chapter by examining several other Scottish texts according to the idea of the materials, structures and differences that inform them. In doing so, we shall see where such basic deconstructive practices might lead us in terms of the definition of the 'Scottish' text and the idea that this provides us with access to some kind of essentially Scottish 'reality'.

We return to a very canonical text, *The House with the Green Shutters* (1901). The centrality of Brown's novel in the twentieth-century canon is not only because it is well written, but because it also subscribes to a set of values and observations that concur with those of twentieth-century Scottish literary criticism as it developed. *The House with the Green Shutters* finds approval with Scottish criticism because it was deeply sceptical of a dominant form of contemporary Scottish literature, the Kailyard, as this has been persistently read as representing a debasing of the 'reality' of Scotland.

We can do an interesting thing with Brown's novel, however, in a kind of poststructuralist reading that sees it not only as an anti-kailyard novel, but as a novel that is deeply sceptical of the project of literary realism more generally. That is to say, we might read the novel as one not merely corrosive in its view of kailyard, but in its view of the literary form of the novel itself. This kind of reading is also in line with recent trends in literary criticism that see literature pre-dating the postmodernist period as capable of being read in postmodernist fashion: in other words, containing texts that are much more playful, joyously unrooted and more semantically detached than they have previously been thought to be. To some extent our reading of 'Tam o' Shanter', with its myriad psychological uncertainty underneath a seemingly simple narrative-tale, represents this kind of criticism too.

As previously discussed, one of the structures of Brown's novel is to oppose the kailyard scenario it mimics and satirises with a generic opposition: the 'high literary art' of tragedy which is crushingly thrown against kailyard. We might here draw on Brown's own biography as a classical scholar steeped in the idea of a hierarchy of genres at which classical tragic drama stood at the apex, and suggest that he might not be entirely sure that the novel *per se* (and not only the kailyard form) is a respectable literary mode. Brown's text all too easily collapses its own central myth – that of the bourgeois family in small-town Scotland – under the grand conception of heroic deeds and great dynasties coming to ruin which are large structural points of reference drawn from Greek tragedy.

Added to this, there is a surfeit of other generic forms. One of these is gothic horror, as John Gourlay's house is often depicted as animate, staring down on the town. Not only this, it is described at various points as extracting the life from the Gourlay family, almost as though it were a bloodsucking entity such as a vampire. We have a certain folktale idiom too. John Gourlay Senior, it might be suggested, is a version of the Green Man (and the colour 'green' of course is writ large in the title of the text). This is a fairly ubiquitous folk figure in the West with many mutations, Robin Hood being one in England and Johnny Appleseed in the United States. Huge in stature, Gourlay is a force for life and destruction. The Green Man in folklore represents and can deal out both fertility and, to complete the cycle of life, destruction. One horrifying pointer of this is found as he thumps his wife's breast, which had suckled the children he has sired, and which leads to her developing cancer. Gourlay also strikes fear into the townsfolk of Barbie, who when negotiating with him wish to do so away from his house as though this is his lair from which he derives some strange power. The idea is that this man, bestial-like, derives primal energy from an environment that is peculiarly his own. Gourlay's prodigious strength and energy are evident throughout the novel and in a moment that is part cartoon, and not entirely incredible from the portrait we have of him, he feels like picking up his despised son and using him as a weapon with which to beat a business rival. This last example points also to a rather melodramatic aspect, perhaps intentionally comic, in the text. This novel is a text that shifts around in its mode, perhaps as has been suggested earlier, visiting upon the kailyard genre a shower of over-wrought literary modes: tragedy, gothic and folk supernatural, as well as melodrama. These materials render the novel rather more unstable than is usually noticed, however, and suggest potentially that it might be read as a kind of game, rather along the lines of the postmodern text constructed of various fictive strands and which eschews realism.

Given the various genre strands we have noticed, *The House with the Green Shutters* can be read as a self-contained literary text as much as that of kailyard fiction. Of course, this reading reacts against the strongly inscribed notion in Scottish criticism that we have noted already: that Scottish texts are down to earth and realistic and that Brown's text is to be taken as absolute testimony to the Scottish historical character and situation. *The House with the Green Shutters* punishes the unreal (kailyard) with the unreal in a kind of poetic justice, but it is, on this reading, a particularly artificial text. Teasing out the various genres and modes might lead us to conclude, in Roland Barthes's phrase, that Brown's text has a 'stereographic plurality', a number of competing voices that cannot be realistically reconciled, that it is in the final analysis an open-ended text which shows Brown making cleverly interesting literary patterns.[10] Can Gourlay be all of a man of 'kailyard' or parochial mentality, an important tragic protagonist and the Green Man who also outrages the kailyard location? Such shifting patterns in the text resist closure and reveal instead a writer manipulating bits of bricolage (or pre-existing stories) to create, in one sense, a fairly unique literary assemblage. We have a story that offers a number of primal alternatives about human behaviour for the reader to ponder (timid? noble? brutally primal?) rather than some definitive critique of Scottish character. It is interesting to realise that such a cornerstone of the modern Scottish literary canon, so strongly formed by the predilection for 'social realism', might be read as a rather slippery text. Is Brown's novel primarily important as a Scottish text, as a commentary on diseased Scottish literature? Is it ultimately much more about wider more primal human stories, or 'materials', other than those of the kailyard?

We might undertake a similar act of simple deconstruction and, at the same time, mount some revisionism with regard to the kailyard by turning to J. M. Barrie's novella *Farewell Miss Julie Logan* (1932). This is to cheat a little since it is a very late kailyard text (post-dating the supposed heyday of the genre from the 1880s–90s). In another way it is rather exemplary in that Barrie was by now fully aware of the criticism (which became particularly pronounced in the 1920s) of the kailyard mode and he quite deliberately revisits this replying to its critics.

Farewell Miss Julie Logan replays a number of scenarios from Scottish culture and literature. These include the romantic myth of Flora MacDonald who helped Charles Edward Stuart escape after the failed Jacobite rebellion of 1745. In Barrie's novel this is echoed by the eponymous character, seemingly a ghostly visitant to the nineteenth century who has in life helped 'the Pretender' across difficult rocky terrain, negotiating especially a precariously perched 'rocking stone'. Another familiar strand of Scottish culture essayed in the text is Scottish Calvinism. At the outset of the story Adam Yestreen, with the pointed symbolism of his name, is an elderly, reminiscing 'Auld Licht' Presbyterian minister who belongs to an older time rooted in sincerely held Bible values, where the Sabbath is kept sacred, and frivolity, such as musical expression, is banned on this day. Already, then, Barrie sets up an opposition between romantic and puritanical versions of Scottish culture, of the kind we have frequently encountered already. Another element was the arrival of southern outsiders, from the Lowlands of Scotland, but especially from England from the mid-nineteenth century to places such as Yestreen's Highland parish for recreational purposes, especially hunting. The English encourage Yestreen to keep a diary in his younger days during the 1860s, and it is this that Yestreen is contemplating in his old age at the beginning of the book. Clearly, Yestreen is a revisiting (though in more puritanical guise) of Galt's Micah Balwhidder in *Annals of the Parish*. The diary is a kind of joke suggestion from the incomers, with their notion that nothing actually happens in a community such as this. Indeed, the 'action' past and present in the novella occurs in a remote valley, frequently completely shut off for weeks at a time by the snows of winter. We should notice here both the enclosed status of the valley and of the text in the sense that this is largely a self-contained, subjective diary. In his journal, the young Yestreen believes the English he encounters to be frivolous, all action and no thought, in contrast to his own contemplation of everything before acting. Ironically, however, Yestreen is soon to do something on utter impulse, and this is to fall in love with Julie, who appears one day in the community, though she is perhaps apparent only to the minister. She is either a ghost or a figment of Yestreen's repressed feelings and imagination. The dénouement of the action occurs as Yestreen carries Julie across a stream and literally drops her, not for confessing that she is unreal but because she admits to being a Catholic.

In terms of the supposed parochial, inward-looking nature of the kailyard community, Yestreen's shocked reaction to Julie's revelation, so comical for the reader, is confirmation. In another sense, however, what the text points to are large religious and ideological battles of the past which perhaps have been somewhat slow to shift from Scotland but which were historically definitive and ought not simply to be dismissed as irrelevant. Change comes slowly to communities such as this, Barrie is indicating, and it also comes sometimes in very small but important ways. For instance, the postman in the village obtains a newfangled bicycle and the entire community rallies round when it needs repair. Life-changing innovation is not only about large-scale industrial processes, so notoriously absent from kailyard fiction. In a sense the English demanding the diary account from Yestreen for their enlightened amusement mirrors the huge audience for kailyard in its heyday. Kailyard is not simply a product from within but responds to demand from without. It might also supply a need for simpler, alternative values which had been demanded in reaction against itself by the industrialising, late nineteenth-century English-speaking world.

Barrie's text is one that sets up a whole series of indeterminacies. In the first instance, these revolve around the standard staples of Scottish culture: romantic Jacobitism, the supernatural, unbending Presbyterianism and country parish life. However, there is also the awkwardness of desire, repressed male and empty (if Julie is merely a figment of Yestreen's imagination), and a dialogue about the body and the mind. Longing for the absent feminine is encapsulated by a presence that is a ghost, is Catholic even. *Farewell Miss Julie Logan* speaks, perhaps, of elements that have sometimes been displaced from Scotland. Barrie's text is a palimpsest of identities, where later cultures have over-written previous ones. In his afterword to his edition of the novella, Alistair McCleery writes of how Barrie and the other writers of the kailyard came to be viewed by the 1930s as 'traitors to national consciousness', when, in fact, their empathetic elements, their sympathy for community and history (as opposed to the often angry, condemnatory 'condition of Scotland' novels which came to the fore at this time) were perhaps qualities too readily discarded.[11] Here we may notice another all too generalising reflex in Scottish literary criticism, where an entire genre is written off for being too regional, too feeling and not hard-headed enough. *Farewell Miss Julie Logan* is concerned with the intimate spaces of desire and community living, but it also registers large-scale Scottish cultural history, without assuming that the disparate elements of this can easily be summed up or closed off. It is intriguing that, like *The House with the Green Shutters*, the literary and cultural elements of Barrie's novella ultimately transcend merely Scottish interest to speak more universally of mysterious, or at least awkward, human nature. In its wielding of texts of various kinds, many strongly Scottish, it casts doubt on any grand project of seeing Scotland in large and easy to be comprehended unitary terms which sweep away awkward historical and discursive difference.

Let us turn to the later twentieth century to view a Scottish novel, which in a fully postmodern sense is self-reflexively aware of its own status as text. Janice Galloway's *The Trick is to Keep Breathing* (1989) is a tale of the breakdown of Joy Stone, whose lover, Michael, has left his wife for Joy. Unfortunately while overseas with Joy, Michael dies in a swimming accident and the novel charts the grief-stricken aftermath. In so far as we might suggest an overarching theme for the novel, this is functionality. The title itself is a nicely energised cliché, a popular saying that alludes with grim irony to the death of Joy's lover and also to her own minimalised rather than heroic existence following the trauma. Gender and sexuality are to the fore in the text. She has sexual encounters following the death with Tony her boss, and with David ten years her junior, to whom she has been a school-teacher. Is this female liberation or is it female subjugation, the act of someone who feels she needs a man to function, to complete her? Is it a desperate attempt to find the feeling she has lost in the tragedy? Her sense of loss and diminishment is mirrored not only in anorexia where she is starving (punishing?) her body, but also in the very fabric of the text. Throughout the novel we find 'o o o' which, coming where these signs do, before and after sections, look almost like an elegant, fine-book-decorative device. What we become aware of, however, is that these are best read as gasps for, or attempts at, breath. This is *not* a fine book, but a book about disintegration where the typography collaborates with the wantonness of the situation. For instance, on one profligate page we have the single word 'oops', signing a long moment of mental wobble where nothing is easily found to surround or to offset this experience.[12] The usual functioning of the novel, then, when we should expect a page to be filled for good economic reasons, is disrupted to convey in a very material rendition the helplessness, the alienation that Joy is feeling. Another instance of textual playfulness is found as elements from conventional women's magazines and daytime television programmes, of the kind which feature the likes of cooking tips, makeup advice and horoscopes, suddenly appear without explanation. Again, these form part of a puzzle for the reader, who has to work out that these bits of text represent conservative, normative wisdom about how a woman should behave. Such material bombards Joy, and the disconnected narrative (or unexplained intertextuality), its chaos, often leaves us little immediate context for these interventions. The result is that the reader is as perplexed as Joy herself. Joy is in a state of vulnerable detachment, perhaps clinically depressed, and everyday normality, as represented by TV and magazines, is frightening to her. In the light of her personal tragedy, she is experiencing the common reaction of shock that the world can continue as if nothing has happened and it now represents a mundane functionality to which she feels she cannot aspire. She is traumatised and this is exacerbated by guilt and stigma which attach to her from people who see her involvement with Michael as leading to his demise, which in the most prosaic sense it has.

Often a rather grim book, *The Trick is to Keep Breathing* is also, however, humorous. Among a number of pieces of Scottish pastiche, Joy thinks of herself as a Jean Brodie figure, she is a school-teacher and is suffering, albeit in a different way, from an overloaded (or perhaps overloading) imagination. Joy is also a reprise of the oxymoronic protagonist of Scottish literature (found pre-eminently in Hogg's 'justified sinner'). We see this from her name, with its contrasted metaphoric signals between pleasure and Puritanism. We have an entertainingly bad pun as Joy's physical disrepair leads to her failure to menstruate and so 'you cannot get blood from a stone.' Galloway, then, neatly brings together a kind of fictionality, previous Scottish literary history, adapting it for her modern purposes of charting a very individual female loneliness. Postmodern devices of textual trickery and recycling previously used materials are to the fore in this Scottish novel. As with the texts we have looked at by George Douglas Brown and J. M. Barrie, in Janice Galloway's novel, Scottish materials are part of the fabric of the text so that, although in some aspects all of these fictions may be said to be about the Scotland of their times, they are all books that in a sense are about the materials themselves, literary and cultural, that can be conjugated by the Scottish writer. Scottish materials are to be used rather subjectively. In Galloway's novel, these are appropriated to provide a portrait of an individual (and so nation is subservient to individual character). One of the large implicit questions in Galloway's text is this: can Joy be thought in any sense to be 'real' given that she is so 'constructed' from fragments of other literary stories? Is this fictionality a gambit which provides an overarching metaphor for the distance Joy feels from 'real life'? Or, in postmodern mode, is Galloway sceptical about the projects of literary description with regard to the individual or the community, foregrounding this scepticism in literary gaming?

If there is a real Scotland, we might read Brown, Barrie and Galloway as not so much rendering this (or not), but utilising and wielding its cultural narratives for purposes that in the end (and we might say this of all creative literature) are not really to do with documentary realism, but are more personal and also more open-ended. This is one of the conclusions that ought to be reached about Scottish literature: that 'its' texts might be engaged with nation or national literary culture but do not absolutely speak for, to or of only it. Might it be time to see nation as only a minor, or subsidiary, concern in Scottish literature? Might it be time to see the use of 'Scottish' literary materials as subsidiary to the very particular creative schemes of individual literary artists?

NOTES

1. These are Carolina Gonda (ed.), *Tea and Leg-Irons: New Feminist Readings from Scotland* (London: Open Letters, 1992); and Christopher Whyte (ed.), *Gendering the Nation* (Edinburgh: Edinburgh University Press, 1995).
2. See Edwin Morgan, 'A Scottish Trawl', in *Gendering the Nation*, ed. Whyte, pp. 205–22, especially, pp. 208–10.

3. The text of the poem followed is that provided by R. D. S. Jack and P. A. T. Rozendaal, in *The Mercat Anthology of Early Scottish Literature*, pp. 152–65.
4. Irvine Welsh, *Trainspotting* (London: Minerva, 1996), p. 187.
5. The text of the poem followed is that provided in *The Mercat Anthology of Early Scottish Literature*, pp. 136–51.
6. Robert Burns, *Burns: Poems & Songs*, ed. James Kinsley, pp. 443–9.
7. Liz Lochhead, *Dreaming Frankenstein & Collected Poems* (Edinburgh: Polygon, 2003), pp. 78–9.
8. Leonard, *Intimate Voices*, p. 41.
9. See the very interesting discussion of the Scottish resistance to theory in two articles: Alex Thomson, '"You can't there from here": Devolution and Scottish Literary History'; and Matthew Wickman, 'Scotland – the Event; or Theory After Muir' from the online *International Journal of Scottish Literature*, 3 (Autumn/Winter 2007); also Eleanor Bell and Gavin Miller (eds), *Scotland in Theory* (Amsterdam and New York: Rodopi, 2004).
10. See Roland Barthes, 'From Work to Text' (1971), reprinted in Niall Lucy (ed.), *Postmodern Literary Theory* (Oxford: Blackwell, 2000), pp. 285–92.
11. J. M. Barrie, *Farewell Miss Julie Logan*, afterword by Alistair McCleery (Edinburgh: Scottish Academic Press, 1989), p. 90.
12. Janice Galloway, *The Trick is to Keep Breathing* (London: Vintage, 1999), p. 189.

CHAPTER 5

Literary Relations: Scotland and Other Places

If the last chapter especially began to suggest approaches that did not necessarily see nation as the primary or most central concern in analysing Scottish literary texts, this chapter considers going beyond Scottish literature in the sense of examining what we might very broadly refer to as its international and intercultural literary relations.

To begin with, we might briefly sketch some further canonical problems for Scottish literature in this regard. So far in this book, we have not mentioned Allan Massie (b.1938), whose best work is as brilliantly plotted and structured as any Scottish fiction of the last thirty years. His work is sometimes of the Scottish locale, but the problem is that, arguably, his finest work is set elsewhere, notably in Ancient Rome. His most celebrated novel, *A Question of Loyalties* (1989), which might be said to deal as exquisitely in moral ambiguity as anything by Hogg or Stevenson, is set in Vichy France during the Second World War. In this text and elsewhere, Massie examines how large-scale historical events play out in the personal lives of 'unimportant' protagonists, and this focus is something that derives to a large extent from the fact that he is an expert disciple of Walter Scott. Massie, like Scott, has been an enthusiastic Unionist and Tory and so apart from his 'international' subject-matter, perhaps his face does not fit with the traditional ideological predilections of Scottish criticism towards nationalism and socialism.

Likewise, we have not discussed Alexander Trocchi (1925–84), memorably condemned in the early 1960s by Hugh MacDiarmid as 'cosmopolitan scum' for having more in common with American Beat writers than any sensibility more recognisably Scottish. Trocchi lived for a time in Paris where, among other things, he wrote pornography, and was long resident in New York where he was a drug addict who prostituted his wife to feed his addiction. His *Young Adam* (1954) is existentialist in outlook as it follows the life of a drifter, determinedly without any essential ties of identity, and who is involved in a tragic accident which is unjustly interpreted as murder. Joe (we are never given his second name) works on a boat along the Forth and Clyde canal, a great symbol of Scotland's post-Enlightenment industrial success. Joe's pointed detachment from such national or communal history represents the new, international culture of the 1950s and 1960s. This sees the world altogether more sceptically, in less confidently rational and historically progressive or connected terms. Only after his death did Scotland begin to take Trocchi seriously and, tellingly, Irvine Welsh during the 1990s identified him as an important inspiration. Unsurprisingly, then, new ways of tracing influence through Scottish writing continue to present themselves, which again should make us view the idea of settled tradition askance.

Even more problematic than expatriate writers like Trocchi, it might be thought, are writers who are descendants of the Scottish Diaspora, of whom there are a number in Australia, Canada, New Zealand and the United States. These tend to be little noticed in Scotland. One recent exception who brings this neglect into sharp focus is the Nova Scotian Alistair MacLeod (b.1936), whose *No Great Mischief* (1999) was nominated for literary awards in Canada, Ireland, the United States and Scotland. MacLeod's novel is a book full of stories about members of the MacDonald clan following the failure of the Jacobite rebellion and changes in the later eighteenth-century Highlands. It follows the family in its achievements and failures in war, industry and family also on the other side of the Atlantic. Often lyrical, it is a piece of fiction that, while not post-modernist, treats its historical action unsentimentally as myriad in possibility and not all-determined. It does not condemn or lament the loss of alternative histories, of a Scotland that might have been otherwise, and so does not place undue emphasis upon the supposedly catastrophic failure of a past Scotland. This is the kind of vision that is more easily sent back to a modern Scotland which is perhaps beginning to move away from a version of its cultural past that is all loss and (diseased) post-1707 gain. An interesting comparison presents itself with Irish literature, which seemingly accommodates its creative diaspora much more easily. This is perhaps because unlike the Scottish Clearances, from which it is possible to argue Scotland long suffered amnesia, the Irish potato famine of the nineteenth century resulted in the exodus of a much more culturally mainstream, albeit beset, part of the people. The famine became fairly immediately a strong central component in the Irish sense of historical identity, in a way that was only true with regards to the Clearances for Scotland not until more than a century after they had begun. Irish literature is seen easily to include frequent examples like Edward McCourt, who went to Canada as a young child and who in the 1940s and 1950s wrote fiction set in Canada (though sometimes featuring emigrant protagonists from Ulster); Edwin O'Connor, the Rhode Island-born and based writer, whose fiction deals with intrigues of the Irish American community; or Frank McCourt born in New York and remaining always a US citizen, though resident for part of his childhood in Limerick before returning to America. McCourt's *Angela's Ashes* (1996) is one of the most celebrated prose accounts of provincial Irish life in the decades following Independence. It might be argued that much of this book is, as much as anything, well-researched reconstruction and re-imagining by an 'outsider' (an American adult) recounting a child's Irish formation in the first part of the twentieth century.

Anthologies of Irish writing, including the 'Field Day' anthology series, are much more inclusive in their coverage than any historical Scottish literary anthology. An especially interesting case for Scotland is Bernard Mac Laverty (b.1942), born and brought up in Belfast but resident and writing in two Scottish locations, Glasgow and Islay, for more than thirty years. Fairly unproblematically claimed by Irish Literature (his fiction includes coverage of the post-1969 'Troubles' of Ulster and critique of Irish Catholic education), an interesting phenomenon has been Mac Laverty's recent inclusion in accounts of Scottish literature. This is especially so since the appearance of the novel *Grace Notes* (1997) featuring a Belfast Catholic musician in her sojourns in Ulster, Glasgow, the Scottish Highlands and Russia. Mac Laverty's inclusion in Scottish Literature makes sense here partly in terms of place, but it can be argued that his Scottish context has been important since the 1970s. He has been part of a vibrant Glasgow writing scene (Kelman, Gray, Leonard, Lochhead et al.), where his friendships and creative writing teaching have made him one of the most visible and admired writers and public readers in contemporary Scotland. If both Irish and Scottish writing claim Mac Laverty, then what does this mean? Perhaps such hybrid identity or plurality is more acceptable than any other kind in an increasingly multicultural world.[1] As we have noted, Scotland in the past certainly shared an east–west cultural axis with Ireland, an early historical reality remembered in the anthology *The Triumph Tree*. Also, the 'Ossian' poems of the eighteenth century are interesting in the controversy over their 'appropriation' of Ulster materials, which can be claimed to have also some rooted provenance in the Scottish Highlands. The offence taken at 'Ossian' in some Irish quarters was due to the fact that, with much justification, these were seen in their Anglophone versions to be associated with colonial Britain. Any real historical kinship between Irish and Scottish Gael as manifest in the texts was somewhat beside the point, overwritten as the poems were by the language of a conqueror. This less than simple relationship between two Celtic cousins is thrown into the spotlight also by Ulster-Scots poets of the eighteenth and nineteenth centuries, especially James Orr and Samuel Thomson, considerable talents who have only recently begun to receive extended literary appreciation. For too long these writers were wrongly thought to be mere imitators of Burns. Their placement was awkward too as they supported the radical politics of the culturally and religiously ecumenical United Irishmen of the 1790s. At the same time, they were largely to be associated (and in rather simplistic terms), from the nineteenth century onwards, with the culture of the colonising 'Settlement' of Ulster by Scots from the seventeenth century. It is only very recently that the 'Field Day' project in Irish Literature has begun to include such writing and that Scottish criticism of writing in Scots has begun to feel comfortable with the kinship between Ulster writers and Scottish writers. Again, we notice the new dispensation of hybrid identity in operation, though there are those in Ulster who are uneasy about the inclusion of these writers in a supposedly Irish canon, however loosely this is defined, when no Scottish anthology has yet included them. We return to the question: inclusiveness or annexation? We might also observe that if Orr or Thomson were to be included in a collection of 'Scottish' poetry, there would probably be fewer objections from many in Ulster who are uneasy with regard to the 'Field Day' attention to this poetry. We have here an obviously telling case of canonicity being not simply about territorial commonalities but also about certain ideological and 'national' perspectives. Even though Orr and Thomson were sympathetic to a united Ireland, the community from which they emerged, Ulster Protestantism, is presently against such an idea. Given the trammelled complexities of the situation in this example, it may be best, one might (still somewhat provocatively) propose, that Orr and Thomson be reserved for courses in and anthologies of Ulster Scots, rather than Irish or Scottish writing.

One other Irish/Ulster complication *à propos* Scottish literature might here be briefly mentioned, *Across the Water* (2000), an anthology which collects together Scottish writers who are of Irish ancestry. Such a book is, perhaps, in line with recent emphases on disinterring ethnic identities or on hybrid identity depending on how one accents these entangled roots. There are competing voices who read each of these identity formations as either culturally positive or unhealthy. Much work in the field of contemporary literary studies is increasingly devoted to its institutional (including publishing) history and dynamics. Next to no work has been done comparing the anthologising principles of Scottish, Irish and Welsh literary collections (and, of course, such comparison might well be extended to other English-speaking literatures). Might the comparison of, say, Irish and Scottish anthologies, of the kind which we have merely made passing reference to above reveal important ideological history where light is thrown upon differing self-conceptions in Irish and Scottish culture with regard to the respective relations of these with Britain? Work on such 'cultural materials' as anthologies is a good example of the kind of modern literary critical work that is not necessarily looking for the 'truth' of national or any other kind of identity, so much as focusing on how people and their institutions operate upon *assumptions* about nation and identity.

The historical Scottish Diaspora of writers to England, as we have seen in earlier chapters, has been a long-standing 'problem' for Scottish criticism until comparatively recently. Still today, though, James Thomson, James Boswell, Thomas Carlyle or Muriel Spark, all undoubtedly major writers, have less attention paid to them than the likes of William Dunbar, Robert Burns or Hugh MacDiarmid in university courses in Scottish literature. Another institutional question presents itself here. Is this state of affairs because of the insularity of the subject of Scottish literature, or (not necessarily a polar opposite alternative) because such authors are often covered in 'English Literature' and are therefore all too easily as well as happily conceded? Have these writers been 'colonised' by English literature? If so, does Scottish literature not have a duty to decolonise them? If the answer is yes, how is decolonisation to take place? To some extent we have shown in an earlier chapter how this might be begun with James Thomson, though reassignment of Thomson's Scottishness must be with regard to one of several alternative kinds of Scottish identity. Essentialist re-appropriation – Thomson as 'only' or in any sense 'exclusively' a Scottish writer – would be no better than simply leaving him to reside in English Literature where this southern-living, British-addressing author also surely belongs.

In some ways less certainly Scottish than Thomson or Trocchi, who, for what it is worth, were at least born in Scotland, are other writers who seem to show 'awareness' of their Scottish lineage. This is true of William Boyd (b.1952), born in Africa and whose novels are set very widely across the world and usually with no explicit connection to Scotland. Boyd is on record as 'feeling' Scottish to some extent, and it is interesting that the Scottish quality press review his books with a frequency and a placement that sees him certainly regarded as a Scot, while university courses in Scottish literature have tended not to teach his work. Elspeth Barker (b.1940), Candia McWilliam (b.1995), born in Edinburgh though southern-educated, and Emma Tennant (b.1937), are all very much intelligent observers of the culture of England (especially its south-eastern part), but are aware too of their Scottish ancestry and have wielded Scottish subject matter. Are they part of Scottish literature? What is to be done with Andrew O'Hagan (b.1968), brought up in Scotland, of strong Irish family origins, based now in London, a celebrated journalist and fiction-writer, whose Scottish subject-matter shows him often rather disenchanted with the cultural condition of Scotland? He sees his nation of birth as frequently small-minded and in his preferential option for English, or perhaps London, culture, might there be a case for saying that he is not a Scottish writer (indeed, that he is an 'English' writer), or is this to revert to the kind of essentialism that says only writers who have a more positively healthy relationship with the nation are part of Scottish literature? Such questions verge, perhaps, almost upon silliness, but they are begged by the very idea of national canons of literature in a Western world that actually, for many hundreds of years, has been porous in national boundaries.

One partial answer to the problem of national cultural formation for the subject of Scottish literature is to accept, as is the case in English literature, and increasingly in such areas as American or Irish Literature, that contradictions are to be rooted out honestly and left on the table rather than resolved according to the more traditional aspiration in the humanities of making cohesive sense of culture. Modern theory has taught us to unpack artifice and ideology, as well as a range of awkwardly, even repressively, situated elements such as class, gender and sexuality, which *cannot* be reassembled into any kind of cultural holism. Scottish literature ought perhaps to become Scottish *literatures* (and there are signs in the most recent university courses that this is happening already). The subject can accommodate courses with relatively easily canonised Scottish texts, such as Barbour's *The Brus*, say, which, for all its 'foreign' materials, as we have observed, has a fairly clear relationship to 'mainstream' Scottish dynastic history. However, this is not to say that more radical, theoretical approaches might not be applied to this text, its heavily masculinist construction being one under-examined area. The subject perhaps also ought to consider 'debatably' Scottish texts, not with the aim of pronouncing definitively one way or another on their final national identity, but rather to contribute to the project of describing cultural indeterminacy. In other words, Scottish literary studies, like other parts of literary studies, might have the entirely valid aim of shedding light on both what people have believed to be national cultural formation as well as places where the very paradigm of 'national culture' perhaps breaks down.

Another problem for Scottish Literature is that of the 'incomer', the writer who takes up residence in the country. As well as Bernard Mac Laverty, two other examples spring immediately to the fore: Margaret Elphinstone (b.1948), English but settled in Scotland and whose fiction is deeply engaged with Scottish history; and likewise Scottish resident, J. K. Rowling (b.1965), sometimes now claimed as a Scottish writer. Rowling is a writer whose phenomenal global success might well be seen as testimony to what an imaginatively amenable place modern Scotland is, as well as, quite properly, being a massive economic product of which the nation can be proud. Scotland's pride in Rowling also, again quite rightly, represents the new, more multicultural Scotland where belonging is about residence and contribution, rather than birthright. On this basis, however, we might ask, is Irvine Welsh resident in Ireland since the 1990s now an Irish writer? Is the work of one of the most considerable poets of the later twentieth century, W. S. Graham (1918–86), born in Scotland but resident in England for much of his life and who writes much more often about England than Scotland, an English writer? (The same question could be asked of Muriel Spark.) What if a writer, as a number in literary history have done, changes his or her nationality officially? Does the national affiliation of their work simply migrate with them? There are also short-term visitors to Scottish culture, even sometimes imaginatively if not actually (what about William Shakespeare's *Macbeth*, for instance?), who often reflect deeply on their engagement with Scotland. Might this be thought to be Scottish literature? In the eighteenth and nineteenth centuries, especially the Romantic period when Scotland is seen as a site of particular imaginative interest, in its natural beauty and in its supernatural legends, writers from outside comment on the country in ways that make for major creative interventions. This is true of such English examples as William Collins's 'Ode on the Popular Superstitions of the Highlands of Scotland' (1750), of journals of their travels by Dorothy and William Wordsworth, and of substantial amounts of poetry by William Wordsworth, John Keats and Arthur Hugh Clough.

Let us consider an instance of comparative literary relation, as well as beginning to make a little more extended consideration of the contemporary critical concern of postcolonialism, in the case of William Wordsworth's poem, 'The Solitary Reaper' (1807). Based on a real-life observation made by the poet, it might be seen, on one level, as a fairly straightforward piece of reportage:

> Behold her, single in the field,
> Yon solitary Highland Lass,
> Reaping and singing by herself;
> Stop here, or gently pass!
> Alone she cuts, and binds the grain,
> And sings a melancholy strain;
> O listen! for the Vale profound
> Is overflowing with the sound.[2]

A postcolonial reading of this poem would ignore, or perhaps turn on its head, the admiring objectification going on in this text. The speaker enjoys and imperatively commends the Highland girl as, clearly, a figure who can be easily, universally admired, and here is the first point which postcolonialism would begin to interrogate. The seeming empathy with the girl, as the rest of the poem confirms, does not in fact run very deeply. The narrator enjoins the reader to 'behold her' (which in itself might be read as a metaphor of male sexual possession) 'single', 'solitary' and 'alone', in other words apart from her culture, consumed by another culture, the Anglophone culture of the author/narrator and the reader. It may well be the case that this is how, factually, Wordsworth has actually encountered his real-life subject, but the situation is not therefore rendered simple. Both Wordsworth's real-life travel in the Highlands and the poem itself, it can be argued, show the footprints of cultural consumption. His romantic interaction with the exotic Highland scene is enabled by its subjugation, where through the eighteenth century with the modernisation of the Highlands by means of military roads, new maps and the crushing of the clans (their martial capability, their raiding and blackmail), the Highlands became increasingly a safe tourist destination. The romantic signifier of the girl can therefore be read as a remnant of a culture defeated by the culture to which Wordsworth fairly centrally belonged (in time he was to become poet laureate of Britain), and which is now being reprocessed.

The postcolonial critic Edward Said, in his pioneering *Orientalism* (1978), pointed out the way in which foreign, non-Western 'otherness' was created and consumed by Western commentators. These sought not so much to understand these cultures but to revel in the spectacle and sensation of their difference. In stanza 2 of 'The Solitary Reaper', the girl is compared to a nightingale and a cuckoo, pretty metaphors, but again arguably evading engagement with her humanity. Although in stanza 3 the narrator asks, 'Will no-one tell me what she sings?' and wonders if it is of ancient battles or personal troubles, by the end of the poem it is clear that he neither needs nor wishes to know:

> I listened till I had my fill:
> And, as I mounted up the hill,
> The music in my heart I bore,
> Long after it was heard no more.

The narrator has consumed the song and the singer in his own way, as romantic spectacle, and takes away his own experience of it. He has not enquired into what the girl's Gaelic words actually mean and is content with his generalised impression. What might be revealed, of course, is a song of a defeated people, or interference of some kind with her culture from outside. The general 'atmosphere' of such things is in the air (and enjoyed) but not actually analysed by the narrator. Instead, the girl is detached from such contexts: 'behold her single'.

'The Solitary Reaper' represents a famous moment in the depiction of Romantic Scotland, and a number of texts from within Scotland write back to it, either consciously or perhaps even unconsciously. We might turn to one of these, 'A Young Highland Girl Studying Poetry' (1961), to pursue some interesting work in the dialogue of English-Scottish, or at least Anglophone-Scottish Gaelic, culture. Again, a general point here might be made about the study of Scottish (as well as English) literature that, rather than assuming a single nationalist viewpoint, it might be best to aspire to become dialogic by examining *literary relations*. Generally, Smith's poem cleverly reverses the order of Wordsworth's text, as a Highland schoolgirl observes English poetry with some incomprehension:

> Poetry drives its lines into her forehead
> like an angled plough across a bare field.[3]

Here we have a clever conceit where the girl's crinkled forehead, as she strives to extract meaning from what she is reading, is compared to the furrow of the plough. What is also set up, however, is the contrast between the natural girl and unnatural poetry, even as she is poeticised by the opening metaphor. Here Smith acknowledges the way in which poetry (texts like 'The Solitary Reaper' and even here, albeit with self-reflexive acknowledgement, his own) consumes young girls, people of the Gaeltachd, and perhaps simply people generally. Poetry is an intrusion into her genuinely 'natural', everyday world where:

> The earth they lived from did not make them soulful.
> The foreign rose abated at their mouth.

Smith acknowledges the artificiality and vanity of literary expression. As a common theme observable across his *oeuvre*, this perhaps has something to do both with his early exposure to Calvinist culture and a strong sense that he has deserted his native western islands. Going to university to pursue a career as a school and university teacher in the Lowlands, Smith sometimes worries in his work that he has become separated from his roots. The people of the young Highland girl's community, he states, do not naturally become 'soulful' or transported away romantically by nature and the language of Romantic literature, and English, 'the foreign rose', did not, and perhaps still does not, come easily to them. 'A Young Highland Girl Studying Poetry' is about the imposition of written poetry (on a culture that had traditionally placed more stress upon oral expression), the English language, and the Romantic perspective generally, including in an arch way that of the narrator-poet here himself. Postcolonial commentary has in recent years celebrated dual identity or polyvalency, but here the narrator, if we reasonably infer him to be largely speaking for Smith himself, also feels himself somewhat colonised, shut out of his own culture, of which he retains an understanding but from which he is distanced in his own career as 'English' poet. There is wry humour, clearly, in the poem, but there is also real alienation on the part of the narrator.

We might briefly refer here to the work of Sorley MacLean, probably the greatest Gaelic poet of the twentieth century, whose poetry represents the most vocal anger against outside interference with indigenous culture (of the Gealtachd) in the whole of 'Scottish' literature. Might MacLean's anger point us to the fact that Scottish Gaelic culture has indeed been colonised by 'Britain' in a way that Anglophone Scottish culture has not? In 'A Highland Woman' (1943), MacLean provides a nice inversion of the 'colonial gaze', the appropriating, consuming depiction by a more powerful culture which we arguably witness in 'The Solitary Reaper':

> Has Thou seen her, great Jew,
> who art called the One Son of God?
> Hast Thou, on Thy Way, seen the like of her
> Labouring in the distant vineyard?
>
> The load of fruits on her back,
> a bitter sweat on brow and cheek;
> and the clay basin heavy on the back
> of her bent, poor, wretched head.[4]

MacLean's technique here is, in classic postcolonial sensibility, to reject the universalism of Christ, the defining centrality of 2,000 years of Western culture. Christ, the poem makes clear, has not seen the like of the Highland woman's grinding toil, 'labouring' as he has been in the pleasant-sounding 'distant vineyard'. Daringly, MacLean has the woman's depiction mimic a kind of Calvary, bent over, carrying seaweed for her children to eat across a time-span of twenty years, rather than Christ's single sacrifice, carrying the abstract sins of the world on his back. In orthodox Christianity, the *felix culpa* ('happy fault') of Original Sin brings about the need for the Saviour, Christ, the bitter-sweet incarnation. MacLean's Highland woman shows instead 'a bitter sweat'. There is nothing redemptive for her, or about her, except (implicitly) the love for her family. Even this, however, is constrained by the grim context of 'the castle' (the domineering landlord who also demands a share of her labours) and the 'gentle church', ironically anything but (and also in the service of the 'gentry'), as in its Calvinist inflexion it dwells upon the state of sinfulness. Unlike Christ's death, her death has no resonance, brings her no memorialisation:

> And her time has gone like a black slush
> seeping through the thatch of a poor dwelling:
> the hard black-labour was her inheritance;
> grey is her sleep tonight.

'A Highland Woman' both appropriates and resists one of the master-metaphors of Western culture, that Christ represents a pattern of suffering that might be replicated in, and so potentially glorifies, every human life. MacLean's poem is a pointedly blasphemous site of resistance. It deals with memories of the Clearances, in which the Scottish church was often complicit. The latter frequently told the people that God's will was in operation, so that they must make way on the land in order that profitable sheep might instead be reared. The woman in MacLean's poem is in every sense a marginal figure as she scrapes a living from the seashore and the universalising, valorising image of Christ, which might be applied to her is 'subverted' by her simple, grim reality.

In the case of Scotland it is possible to argue that a colonial project has gone on, which, often quite intentionally, has sought to extirpate Gaelic culture. The situation is complicated, however, by the fact that evangelical Protestantism, for instance, initially imposed upon the Gaeltachd as a 'civilising' mechanism intended to root out 'native' culture in some senses has actually supported the ongoing cultural distinctiveness. Cultural hybridity is in evidence as, for instance, attested by the haunting Gaelic-language psalm-singing of the Western Isles, or a burgeoning devotional literature since the nineteenth century that has actually aided the survival of the Gaelic language. In addition, the meditations on the effectiveness, or alternatively the vanity of poetry (in its 'universalising' project), and the partial rejection of the puritanical Calvinist vision that we have seen in Iain Crichton Smith, and which we can detect also in MacLean's 'Highland Woman', might themselves be seen as valuably dubious, hybrid modes of expression. If Calvinism and poetry have been, in some of their history, colonising forces, they are themselves often in conflict. These are part of a whole palimpsest of cultural identity, elements which are not so easy to undo, but might be juggled with, to point out the difficulty of identity in Gaelic culture no less so than elsewhere in the West. Out of unpropitious circumstances, as much as any more positive ones, emerges literary expression.

As we consider the situation of the Gaeltachd, we might glance at Walter Scott's short story 'The Two Drovers' (1827), where Robin Oig McCombich is a skilful cattle-drover driving huge herds to market in England. On his travels he has befriended an Englishman of the same trade as himself, Harry Wakefield, and, as it turns out, they are headed for the same resting-point in Cumbria with their droves. Due to a misunderstanding between a landowner and his factor, both have been promised the identical spot, and Robin reaching it first offers to share the pasture with his friend, but Harry takes umbrage and refuses to speak to the Highlander. Later meeting at an inn, in a fist-fight Harry bests Robin, who is otherwise defenceless, having left his dirk in the safe-keeping of a Lowland Scot. This disarmed state has come about after Robin's aunt had prophesied at the outset of the journey that she foresaw 'Saxon' blood upon it. Robin returns to the inn having retrieved his weapon, stabs Harry to death and is hanged for his crime.

We might notice first of all the purposes of Walter Scott, which are familiar with those of some eighteenth-century Scottish writers dealing with the aftermath of Union. Scott sets up an equivalence: just as Highland Scotland has its Robin Oig McCombich, man of ancient culture (though also of considerable modern ability, polyglot and economically astute in his cross-border trade), so too does England have its proudly traditional men of old-fashioned culture. Interestingly, in a reversal of the received stereotype, it is Harry, otherwise basically honest and honourable, who is somewhat hot-headed, rather than Robin. Harry is described as a 'yeoman', an independent-minded individual who has supposedly formed the backbone to the history of the English nation. This in an age since the eighteenth century of ever more complex diplomatic negotiations: Scott is writing at a time when Europe, following the recent Napoleonic Wars, has been settled through a range of complex treaty and territorial agreements. In other words, Harry's fists are somewhat outmoded, even ineffective, just as is Robin's clan culture, one historically instancing numerous examples of cold-blooded revenge. Scott is saying that the unsophisticated elements of each of their cultures must now be subsumed in a more progressive British age. The cosmopolitan Unionist sentiment here can be read as generously inclusive, but the story could be seen to demand, in the terminology of postcolonial theory, that the 'subaltern' cultures, of both Robin and Harry step into line. The story might in fact be read as Scott imagining the future imperial progress of Britain which is to demand that the commendable courage and economic savvy of both Robin and Harry be harnessed for the common good, as Britain not only develops its internal markets but expands, often by force, overseas ones.

Much has been written about the large part played by Scots in the British Empire of the nineteenth century, though it is only recently that Scottish literature in this context has begun to have some extended attention paid to it.[5] Robert Louis Stevenson is a complicated case here, in his body of 'South Seas' fiction. This was the result of his residence in Samoa in the Southern Pacific where he was withering in his view of Western imperialism in the area, at one point fearing with some justification that the British government might deport him for views unhelpful to the 'national interest'. Large questions might be posed about Stevenson's engagement with Polynesian culture, where he became a respected community leader and reworked a number of local folktales into short stories. Did he, then, 'go native' or did he act 'masterfully' in Samoa, appropriating position and cultural materials for himself? Certainly, in his fiction of the South Seas, Stevenson is sceptical both about the whites 'bringing civilisation' and the 'simple paradise' of Polynesia. As Stevenson makes plain in a number of texts and largely before Western history dealt much with the issue, Europeans brought disease to the South Seas (to which the local inhabitants had no resistance and so were decimated). He also plays upon another cultural prejudice, that 'primitive' cultures are fetishist and full of 'mumbo-jumbo'. Memorably, in his novella *The Beach of Falesá* (1892), it is the white man, Case, who constructs a series of contraptions and tricks to fool the local people into thinking that a part of the hinterland is possessed by a devil that only he can control. Through such intimidation Case hopes to control the area's natural resources for ultimate monetary gain. In the same text another character uses a ludicrous 'marriage certificate' to make a sexual conquest of the beautiful Uma. Uncomprehending, Uma is delighted with the document:

> This is to certify that Uma daughter of Fa'avao of Falesá island of ________, is legally married to Mr John Wiltshire for one night, and Mr John Wiltshire is at liberty to send her to hell next morning.
>
> John Blackamoor
> Extracted from the register Chaplain to the Hulks
> by William T. Randall
> Master Mariner.[6]

Clearly, Stevenson shows in these examples the shoddy and predatory nature of colonial power, economically and sexually acquisitive and giving little in exchange. Such details, certainly, were extremely shocking for Western readers when the story was serialised, as it originally was, in such a mainstream organ as the *Illustrated London News*. For all Stevenson's critique of corrupt behaviour, however, the question is, does he, as some postcolonial thinkers might suggest, nonetheless leave intact the master–servant, civilised–primitive paradigms of colonial conception?

One might suggest that, historically, Stevenson was depicting what he saw with some accuracy, which was the exploitation of the weak by the strong. Indeed, in *The Beach of Falesá*, he shows how the whites reflect and rapaciously exploit the 'otherness' of the natives through their possession of both diabolic magic and enticing written legal contracts. The distinction of the whites in the text is to have no beliefs, in contrast to the credulity of the Polynesians who are shown to have some sense of cultural solidity, albeit that this is routinely abused. Stevenson depicts in his text the empty-of-value, imperial consumption of locality. We see this in the opening of *The Beach of Falesá*, as Wiltshire narrates:

> I saw that island first when it was neither night nor morning. The moon was to the west, setting, but still broad and bright. To the east, and right amidships of the dawn, which was all pink, the daystar sparkled like a diamond. The land breeze blew in our faces, and smelt strong of wild lime and vanilla: other things besides, but these were the most plain; and the chill of it set me sneezing . . . Here was a fresh experience: even the tongue would be quite strange to me; and the look of these woods and mountains, and the rare smell of them, renewed my blood.[7]

Postcolonial interpretation, like many other theoretical approaches, reads 'against the text' to extract inadequacies and prejudices of which the author is unaware (in a manner we have suggested might be possible for 'The Two Drovers'). Here, however, we might suggest that Stevenson, though he would not have known the phrase, dissects the 'colonial gaze'. Wiltshire is heading towards the unknown, and the prettiness of the approaching vista and its natural surroundings are full of promise (according to standard romantic/adventure description). Wiltshire, of course, is no romantic voyager, one of the tropes which has historically placed a favourable gloss on overseas expedition, both in fiction and prose documentary accounts, and which Stevenson explodes). Naturally engaged as they would be, Wiltshire's senses speak ultimately (when we re-read the full extent of the story), not of innocent consumption but of commodities (some known, others unknown) in which he sees business opportunity. The strangeness of some things he is about to encounter, such as resources, land and language, cause him excitement, not as any simple 'tourist' but in a much creepier, almost vampiric fashion as the exploiter will have his 'blood renewed' by the appropriation of these. In a further bitterly ironic usage, Wiltshire will have his blood (line) renewed through his marriage to Uma, with whom he 'settles' on Falesá, and has many children after defeating, indeed killing, Case, his rival for mastery of the locale. This 'happy ending' is somewhat spoiled, however, as the text concludes with expressions of contempt by Wiltshire for his 'half-caste' children. 'But they're mine', he says, and the reader wonders for a moment if we have here parental affection before properly realising that this *possessiveness* is simply another example of acquisitive ownership by Wiltshire and other white characters in the text. Stevenson's considerable body of fiction of colonial oppression in the South Seas remains under-researched in comparison to his 'Scottish fiction', and until it becomes a more urgent site for investigation our estimation of this Scottish (and, indeed, British) author must remain perforce very partial and, it might be argued, rather unhelpfully inward-looking.

Alasdair Gray's short story 'Five Letters from an Eastern Empire' (1979) makes for one of the most interesting Scottish texts in the areas of 'Orientalism' and postcolonialism. Along with Tom Leonard and James Kelman, Gray has foregrounded in his fiction (as well as elsewhere) a great deal of discussion about the uses of literature, and this story arises to some extent from such concerns. 'Five Letters' deals with a state poet, Bohu, removed from a very young age and isolated in the emperor's palace to fulfil his literary function. Gray is, of course, playing on the reader's preconceptions of 'an eastern empire', China perhaps. The whole story is somewhat 'inscrutable', 'alien', 'chilling', 'ordered', 'exotic', 'fearful' even in the cultural mores it describes. This is the first manoeuvre of the text, to make the reader feel strange or alienated, though, of course, doing so by playing upon a set of Western preconceptions culled probably from cinema, books and a long tradition of 'Orientalism' which marvels at the adumbrated qualities just listed.

On his approach to the Emperor's vast, newly built palace by boat, Bohu, as part of the 'honoured-guest-class' (here Gray mimics awkward translation into English from some Sino-language), and his colleagues fear that a turn in the river is not taking them to the Emperor but into exile among the 'barbarians'. We are made aware, then, of an imperious dictator and nervousness among his subjects; one 'rumour' about the palace is that it is designed to control the flow of water around the empire and, therefore, can either provide irrigation or drought. The impression of ruthless control is confirmed as Bohu writes his first letter home to his parents and opines, 'A poet cannot know his theme until the emperor orders it'.[8] Even more icily (and in a nice piece of the 'inscrutable' offered to the reader), Bohu is allowed to think of the many millions losing their homes, their lives in labour and the severe punishment for tardiness in the building of the palace, so that 'a long act of intricately planned cruelty has given the empire this calm and solemn heart'.[9] What is mimicked here is again a kind of Eastern (perhaps 'ying' and 'yang') philosophy, supposedly very alien to the Western mindset. Among many other details, the oddest of them all occurs when Bohu discovers that the Emperor is not real, being made instead of papier mâché, and seems to be a puppet. Either mechanically, or through some act of voice-throwing from one of his many 'headmasters' who control all areas of life, or perhaps even magically (it is never actually determined), the Emperor speaks. He tells Bohu and his large assembly of 'headmasters' that he has destroyed the old capital, killing its many inhabitants, for fomenting rebellion. Bohu learns that his parents have also been killed, requests death for himself and is told he will be allowed to die after he has written a poem celebrating the Emperor's 'irrevocable justice'. His poem 'The Emperor's Injustice', which dwells upon the pathetic remnants of human life (buttons, kites and other detritus) in the city after it has been extinguished, concludes sardonically with the line that the people 'Are honoured guests of the emperor, underground'.[10] Surprisingly, in the final part of the story, Gigadib, 'Headmaster of modern and classical literature', reveals that the intended massacre had not, in fact, been carried out. Bohu's poem is to be sent out in advance of the great purge so as to extinguish any flickers of opposition with its great emotional prescience and sense of inevitability.

Gray's story shows that literature can be used and abused as propaganda, towards evil ends, but this is not really its central point. Bohu's poem is not straightforward propaganda; it is a rather romantic lament, entirely comprehensible to the Western sensibility. It might call to mind the aftermath of any number of battles or massacres in Europe or America. The poem may represent a reminder to the reader that the different society posited in Gray's short story is not, in fact, all that different from many Western societies. Eventual confluence in Gray's text is helped also by the way in which the poem in its outburst of passion and anger suddenly dissolves the stoical cod-Orientalism that the author has constructed. The reader has sought to make sense of this, in its own terms, asking what it all means, how it functions, as though this were a 'real' society, rather than a highly fictive composite of stereotypical features of the Orient. In fact, there is very little actual 'otherness' under this veneer. Instead, there is an allegory of how people everywhere are manipulated by those who set up hierarchy and control for their own sakes. Indeed, the eventual emptiness of the Emperor and the naked wielding of power around his empire are largely deficient of any real 'philosophy', such as the greater good of the nation or of the people, which have often been used as a central plank in Eastern (and many other) cultures. If anything, Gray's story owes much more to the (largely Western) Kafkaesque literary nightmare of bureaucracy/power for its own sake. Gray's story is one of the cleverest, most deceptive depictions of 'other places' in modern Scottish literature to say something ultimately about sameness rather than otherness.

We have been sketching in various ways something of the literary relations of Scottish literature. From the beginning of this book we have explored the dynamics of Anglo-Scottish literary and cultural relations. Other sites of comparison clearly present themselves, including, perhaps most pertinently, those of Irish and American literatures, not only because of a certain amount of cultural kinship with each of these, but also because all of Scottish, Irish and American literatures might be said to have been viewed and have perhaps viewed themselves, at various points in their cultural history, as provincial offshoots of metropolitan English culture.

This chapter has considered what might be argued to be the colonisation of Scottish Gaelic culture, and helps us towards the possible conclusion that any real culturally colonising story in the British Isles might actually involve the 'British' subjugation of Scottish Gaelic, Irish Gaelic and Welsh language (not to mention also Cornish and Manx language) cultures. There is not the space here to fully explore this proposition, but it is useful to hold it in mind as a possible counterweight against the notion that Scottish literature (especially literature in Scots) has ever truly been removed from the literary 'centre' to the 'periphery'. When we consider the profile of Scots, we can see it figuring prominently in all the 'mainstream' types and modes of eighteenth- and nineteenth-century British literature (in pastoral, in satire, in didacticism, during the Romantic period, in gothic, in the novel of psychological and cultural realism). The same is true of its prominence during the modernist period and in the fiction of the later twentieth century. James Kelman's *How Late it Was, How Late* even won the Booker Prize, something no Gaelic or Welsh novel has managed.

As we have seen, the 'Celtic' factor complicates the story of Scottish literature. In our analysis of Scottish criticism's convoluted appropriation of an idea of Scotland's Celtic inheritance even within its Anglophone (including Scots language) culture, we have charted a process similar to that charted by Linda Colley in *Britons: Forging the Nation* 1707–1837 (1992). Here Celticism is used as a recycled block in the construction of a pan-British cultural identity. In the case of Scottish criticism we might refer to a Scoto-Celtic culture. As we saw in Chapter 1, the Scoto-Celtic discourse sits, to begin with, as a (sub-Arnoldian) readjustment of Scotland's self-conception within the late Victorian British culture with which it shares, actually, a fear of deep cultural disruption. Later, Scoto-Celticism is used by the likes of Hugh MacDiarmid in an attempt at a more or less full-blown dissent from British culture. Ireland, in its actually dominant Anglophone culture, has a Celtic story perhaps not entirely dissimilar to that of Scotland, and so recent comparisons of Scottish and Irish literature in their Anglophone versions tend not so much to look for essential kinship (though other analogies in situation might be studied), in a way that one might still do with some basic degree of historical empiricism across Scottish and Irish Gaelic.

SCOTLAND AND IRELAND

The very interesting current trend with regard to the comparison of Anglophone Scottish and Irish literatures is the identification, especially in later twentieth-century literature, of texts that have commonality across the Irish Sea in their dissent from national myths. This has been all the more striking in Ireland, a nation that only rid itself of colonising British (including many Scottish) troops in 1921 (leaving aside the vexed issue of Northern Ireland). Ireland's Catholic identity, a powerful site of resistance to colonial rule prior to Irish independence, remained a strong, unifying presence in the culture thereafter but also formulated strong censorship laws which have put huge pressure on Irish writers. As recently as 1965 a very accomplished writer of fiction, John McGahern, was removed by the state from his position as a school-teacher for writing a novel that was sexually explicit, but by no means pornographic. Edna O'Brien has often come into conflict with Irish life and culture in its Catholic accents for her depiction in her fiction of the poor facilities for sexual health available to women in her country. What McGahern, O'Brien and many others have in common with Scottish writers of the later twentieth century is a frequently expressed scepticism towards 'belonging' to a uniformly 'healthy', often 'unhealthy' nation, where insecurities and overcompensations in 'native' identity sometimes contrast with a supposedly less judgemental, more cosmopolitan English culture.

The complicating difference for Scottish writers is that many elements that have been read as unpropitious to their culture, Protestantism most obviously, or the Enlightenment, have divided commentators as to whether these are indigenous Scottish cultural features, or aiders and abettors of colonial Britishness. The British cultural formation likewise might or might not be read as a colonial configuration in Scotland. The most fruitful comparative work regarding Scottish and Irish literatures, certainly with regard to twentieth-century writing, sees interesting comparisons between Scottish and Irish writers in their often common imaginative negotiations across contested (Anglo-Scottish, Anglo-Irish) spaces, and also with myths of history, family and individuality and many other 'conflicts in identity'.[11]

SCOTLAND AND AMERICA

Longer standing than the comparison of Scottish with Irish literature is the comparison of Scottish with American cultural expression. This has proceeded to some extent along the lines of foundational Scottish cultural influence in the United States from early on, in the work of many Scottish educators and politicians who played a part in the institutional foundations of the American republic. At the margins of this influence there are such interesting characters as James Thomson Callendar (1758–1803), who fled

Scotland in the 1790s after being convicted of political sedition. He is sometimes credited as the inventor of tabloid journalism in forcefully exposing political sleaze, both financial corruption and sexual misdemeanours, at the very top of American politics in the early 1800s. Another writer who fled Scotland during the same period for the same reasons, James Tytler (1745–1804) composed a poem, 'Rising of the Sun in the West' (1793), which contributed to the idea of a new, post-French revolutionary, republican freedom particularly to be found in the US. It is interesting the way in which Scots in both the American and French Revolutions play a role in America's re-imagining itself as a nation. Robert Burns, whose work was a favourite of Abraham Lincoln, played a strong part in the idea of the 'self-made' poet and indeed self-made 'man' in nineteenth-century American culture. Along with Walter Scott, whose novels were voraciously read across the Atlantic, and Robert Louis Stevenson, Burns makes up the three Scottish writers best known and most resonant in American culture. John Steinbeck's novel *Of Mice and Men* (1937) takes its title, of course, from a line in Burns's 'To a Mouse', and Robin Jenkins, with deliberate wittiness in completing a circle of Scottish-American textual exchange, produced *The Cone-Gatherers* (1955) to replay something of the basic scenario of the American novel in Argyllshire. Such instances are, perhaps, merely minor footnotes in literary history, but demonstrate once again the inter-(national)-textuality of all literatures. Less wholesome Scottish influence in American literature might be read in several black poets. For instance, we find the Jamaican-born Claud Mackay, a writer associated with the Harlem Renaissance movement in the early decades of the twentieth century, whose name bears testimony to the strong Scottish involvement in slavery on the other side of the Atlantic. Here, clearly, is a postcolonial legacy in which Scotland is implicated and which still awaits proper investigation.

Leaving aside such fascinating cultural history, it is the analogous relations between Scottish and American literatures that have most occupied commentators. A famous essay published in 1954 identified the problem of American and Scottish cultures as satellites of the English metropolis and saw much inadequate mimicking of the latter in each of the former so as to avoid their own inherent provinciality.[12] This influential essay reinforced an idea, familiar to us from Chapter 1, of falseness in imagination. It is interesting that America as well as Scotland should be so charged. More recently the work of Susan Manning has highlighted much less anxious, more self-confident 'provinciality' in each of Scottish and American literatures. The two countries are seen to be more relaxed about the necessity of tradition, partly due, she argues, to a common influence from innovative-loving Scottish Enlightenment philosophy. This helps explain the licentious creativity of the poems of 'Ossian' or of Emily Dickinson.[13] Manning has also been a pioneer of the idea that puritanical cultural formation in American and Scottish cultures has had interestingly positive effects on the literatures of the two nations.[14] In this regard, crucial literary texts emerge for Scotland and America, respectively, in Hogg's *Private Memoirs and Confessions of a Justified Sinner* (1824) and Nathaniel Hawthorne's *The Scarlet Letter* (1850). Both of these, while explicitly criticising the harsh Puritan vision in its effects on human relations, also suggest a duplicitous world (somewhat in line with the Puritan view that the world belongs to the Devil), which we should move through fearfully rather than confidently. Due to Puritan roots, and also, perhaps, less lengthy experiences of national independence, America and Scotland are cultures not so confident in their views of civilisation or the progress of the world than England might be said to be, given, until recently, its imperially dominant presence across the globe.

Both Hogg's and Hawthorne's texts have been replayed on numerous occasions by other writers in their respective cultures, testimony, it might be argued, to the capacity for Scottish and American literatures to reinvent and sustain their own particular traditions. Examples would be Spark's *The Prime of Miss Jean Brodie* and Toni Morrison's *Beloved* (1987), respectively. Fractured personality and experiences in books like those by Spark and Morrison are themes that are of perennial interest in literature: in discourses of uncertainty both reported upon and imagined, even embodied in the mode of narration. Literature is often considered at its best when peddling ambiguity, rather than supposed cultural certainty. In the later nineteenth century the three great anti-imperial writers in English are all provincially related to English culture, Robert

Louis Stevenson (who enjoys hugely popular literary tours of the United States), Herman Melville, whose South Seas and seafaring fiction precedes and is curiously analogous to Stevenson's work in the same vein (even though much of Melville's work was not widely known until after Stevenson's death) and the Polish exile in England, Joseph Conrad. The argument might go that Scottish and American literature, to some extent because of the conception of their own national condition, has been particularly interested in primitive, uncertain, marginal places and that this interest is seen to advantage in the literary creativity of these nations.

NOTES

1. For a very wide-ranging discussion of this issue, see Cairns Craig, 'Scotland and Hybridity', in *Beyond Scotland: New International Contexts for Twentieth-Century Scottish Literature*, ed. Gerard Carruthers, David Goldie and Alastair Renfrew (Amsterdam and New York: Rodopi, 2004), pp. 229–53.
2. *The Oxford Authors: William Wordsworth*, ed. Stephen Gill (Oxford: Oxford University Press, 1984), pp. 319–20.
3. Iain Crichton Smith, *Selected Poems* (Manchester: Carcanet, 1985), pp. 16–17.
4. *Nua-Bhardachd Ghaidhlig: Modern Scottish Gaelic Poems*, pp. 104–6.
5. See the first full-length study of this topic, Douglas Mack, *Scottish Fiction and the British Empire* (Edinburgh: Edinburgh University Press, 2006). See also Berthold Schoene (ed.), *The Edinburgh Companion to Contemporary Scottish Literature* (Edinburgh: Edinburgh University Press, 2007) for much on the relationship of Scotland to postcolonial theory.
6. Robert Louis Stevenson, *South Sea Tales* ed. Roslyn Jolly (Oxford: Oxford University Press, 1996), p. 11.
7. Ibid., p. 3.
8. Alasdair Gray, *Unlikely Stories Mostly* (London: Penguin, 1984), p. 93.
9. Ibid., p. 93.
10. Ibid., p. 127.

11. See, especially, Ray Ryan, *Ireland and Scotland: Literature and Culture, State and Nation,* 1966–2000 (Oxford: Oxford University Press, 2002).
12. John Clive and Bernard Bailyn, 'England's Cultural Provinces: Scotland and America', *William and Mary Quarterly*, 3rd series, No. 11 (1954), pp. 200–13.
13. Susan Manning, *Fragments of Union: Making Connections in Scottish and American Writing* (Basingstoke: Palgrave Macmillan, 2002).
14. Susan Manning, *The Puritan-Provincial Vision: Scottish and American Literature in the Nineteenth Century* (Cambridge: Cambridge University Press, 1990).

Conclusion

Rather than simply identifying what Scottish literature is, this book has raised problems with defining the 'subject' and also what constitutes Scottish literary texts. In so doing, however, the intention has been to open up Scottish literature to more possibilities than were sometimes allowed in the Scottish critical tradition which we surveyed in Chapter 1. Examining Scottish *literatures* rather than any singular tradition would seem to be the way forward in the twenty-first-century climate of multiculturalism and in an age when we are sceptical about claims to absolutely coherent national, or even personal, identity. As we have seen in our two chapters on Scottish literature in Scots and Scottish literature in English, these have been convenient but somewhat artificial ways of addressing the history of Scottish literature. Canonicity, or belonging to a tradition of literature defined by national or other cultural factors, is more a matter of humans (critics and commentators) choosing to find such coherence and overlook variegation. Scottish texts, whether in Scots or English (or Gaelic or any other language or that matter), are usually made up of both local and more international and cosmopolitan materials. For instance, can the sonnet, or the novel, or the short story be said to belong any more to one nation than others? These literary modes or forms are, of course, commonly shared across huge swathes of international human culture. Scotland, like many other places, has made significant contributions to the writing and development of all of these things. As a result we might argue that the most significant Scottish literature is, perhaps, to be most approvingly registered when it contributes to a wider, rather than just a 'local' culture. 'The Scottish contribution to literature', rather than merely 'Scottish Literature', is one way of looking at what counts. Of course, this also might be argued to be too prescriptive. No one should be prevented from arguing that the most significant Scottish literature is actually that which tells us about Scottish culture and history.

Much of this book has been precisely about the interaction between literature and the Scottish nation (as well as, to some extent, the British nation). At the same time, international concerns (wider than those pertaining solely to Anglo-Scottish relations) have frequently been signalled. Just as it might be argued there can be no singular Scottish literature, so too it might be proposed that there is no singular way of studying Scottish literature. If this book has argued that some writers are left out to suit certain vested critical narratives or practices, perhaps it too is guilty of something of the same. There are always gaps, or writers and concerns being excluded, in any work of criticism, most especially one that undertakes a long historical survey. In the case of the present book, one issue that might be raised, for instance, is its exclusion from the discussion of the best-selling mode of Scottish literature: crime fiction. Absent from the foregoing chapters have been the names of Christopher Brookmyre, Ian Rankin, Alexander MacColl Smith or Val McDermid. The present writer would claim that this is because of the main concerns of his book, but might the accusation of wrongly ignoring the most popular form of Scottish literature be levelled against me here?

Practical Criticism, Historicist, New Historicist, Feminist, Queer, Psychoanalytic and many other kinds of reading might all be applied to Scottish literature, and we have sampled a little of some of these kinds of criticism in this book. In the early twenty-first century, a healthy 'critical community' ought to comprise various and diverse critical voices. The future health of Scottish literary studies demands this, if it is to be in line with other areas of literary study and so as to be prevented from becoming merely a minor adjunct to the discipline of history. As the final part of Chapter 5 attempted to suggest, albeit raising more general questions than can be easily answered for the moment, a future direction for Scottish literary study should lie in the area of comparative literature. The study of Scottish literature has sometimes been looked on askance by those who take it to be a parochial or ghetto concern. It is, however, precisely in its openness to an international agenda, as well as a diversity of critical and theoretical practice, that the subject of Scottish literature will survive and thrive. No more than any other branch of literary study does the area of Scottish literature have anything to fear from the future.

Student Resources

QUESTIONS AND POINTS FOR DISCUSSION

What follows is a series of questions for further discussion arising out of the foregoing chapters. All the questions allow plenty of room for differing viewpoints according to varying political viewpoints and critical priorities of students and teachers.

Chapter 1

- What function does the 'Celtic' component have in the rise of Scottish Literature in the late nineteenth century?
- What does Edwin Muir mean by a 'homogeneous language', and how credible is this concept?
- To what extent might we accuse much twentieth-century Scottish criticism of being pessimistic and even 'defeatist' in being Anglocentric?
- How do we account for the changing place of 'Protestantism' in accounts of Scottish literary history?
- What does the vocabulary of 'antisyzygy', 'dissociation', 'reductive idiom' 'paradox' and 'crisis of identity' have in common?

Chapter 2

- Is the medieval period the first era of Scottish literature?
- How 'native' or 'cosmopolitan', respectively, is Scottish

Literature from the medieval period to the end of the sixteenth century?

- How antiquarian and how contemporary might eighteenth-century Scots poetry be said to be?
- Is the literature of the twentieth century in Scots as powerful as in any previous century?
- How useful is it to think of a 'tradition' or a history of literature in Scots?

Chapter 3

- What are the key factors that have seen some English language areas or periods of Scottish literature marginalised from the canon?
- Do seventeenth- and eighteenth-century Scottish literatures in English become too British?
- If, by the Victorian period, Scottish literature is less distinctively national, does this matter?
- In the twentieth century is Scottish Literature as vibrant as before?
- Is it less useful to think of a 'tradition' or a history of Scottish literature in English than in Scots?

Chapter 4

- Which reading of 'The Freiris of Berwik' is the more convincing: one that takes into account historical context and sees Christian morality castigating human sinfulness, or a newer reading that concentrates on the bodily rather than the spiritual sphere?
- How do other male characters in *Trainspotting* help corroborate the reading of maleness and the body in Chapter 4? Is Welsh's novel one of utter alienation and without anything positive to identify in modern Scotland/the world?
- Much more of the detail in Dunbar's 'The Tretis' might be adduced to support the feminist reading pursued in Chapter 4. Taken as a whole, is it a text that invites conspiratorial male laughter at female duplicity, or is there any sympathy for the plight of the female to be extracted from the poem?

- Sometimes 'Tam o' Shanter' has been read as a very male poem, in the sense of being about masculine cronyism. The narrator (perhaps also Burns himself), Tam and Tam's friend in the poem 'Souter (Cobbler) Johnny' are all complicit in a world of irresponsible, alcohol-fuelled brotherhood. This, if observed, might present an alternative feminist reading of the poem's actual 'anti-feminism'. Is this reading, or that mounted in Chapter 4, more credible?
- Some feminist critics, those who place an especial emphasis on psychoanalysis, might point to the title 'The Open Door' and equate this with the female genitalia. How credible do you find this reading, and if you do not find it so, how is its symbolic sense best comprehended?
- How well, or not, does the reading of *Farewell Miss Julie Logan* bring a justified revisionism to the idea of kailyard writing?
- Bearing in mind the foregoing discussion of *The Trick is to Keep Breathing* (and similar questions might be posed with regard to *The House with the Green Shutters*), might it be the case that contemporary Scottish writing has very little to do with the 'national' situation? Might it speak, in fact, of much larger, though also perhaps more personal human issues that transcend national boundaries?

Chapter 5

- There has been much debate about whether Scotland culturally, historically and politically has been colonised by England, or alternatively has been a more or less equal partner in the British colonial project both at home and abroad, building a super-state and an empire. Does the case of James Thomson, both the qualities of his writing (even in the brief sketch of these already provided in this book) and his place or lack of it in Scottish and English canons, throw any light on the question of colonisation?
- Might it be argued that the exemplar of postcolonial criticism attempted in Chapter 5 on Wordsworth's 'The Solitary Reaper' (on a text which is an example of Romantic poetry) is unfair in any ways?

- If Smith's 'A Young Highland Girl Studying Poetry' is taken as a whole – obviously we have only looked at a few of its thematic features – might there be a sense of resolution for the narrator-poet in the sense that he produces his poem anyway; this fact attesting to value in uncovering a culturally fraught situation? Given the text's clear awareness of cultural colonisation, is it any less culpable (might it perhaps be even more so) than Wordsworth's text in its consumption of 'the other'?
- In reading MacLean's 'A Highland Woman' by applying the observations of post-colonial theory, Christianity is seen, clearly, as a colonising force. Particular circumstances of Scottish history and culture allow such colonisation, it can be argued. These circumstances originate, generally, from 'the south', from Knoxian (Lowland Scottish) Calvinism, which from the Reformation down to the nineteenth century saw the Highlands as especially difficult, potentially backsliding missionary territory, and from southern-educated landlords. In the light of the evidence of this poem, then, to what extent can colonisation be said to be any kind of national (England mastering Scotland) project, or should colonisation be seen as something involving essentially different, more complex forces?
- Is the reading of 'The Two Drovers' mounted in this chapter credible, or is it unfair to impose upon it larger cultural and international contexts than are actually, explicitly, present in the text?
- What might the comparative context, looking at Scottish literature in relation to other national literatures, tell us about Scottish literature?

GLOSSARY OF 'SCOTTISH' STANZAS (PARTICULARLY REFERRED TO IN THE TEXT)

Cherrie and Slae stanza

Named after the poem by Alexander Montgomerie, consisting of fourteen lines rhymed most commonly, as below, aabccbdedefgfg, in iambic (short, long stress) tetrameter for two lines, followed by one of iambic trimeter, two of iambic tetrameter, one of iambic trimeter, one of iambic tetrameter, one of iambic trimeter, one of iambic tetrameter, one of iambic trimeter, one of iambic dimeter, one of iambic trimeter, one of iambic dimeter, one in iambic trimester. This example is stanza 3 from *The Cherrie and the Slae* (see Jack and Rozendaal (eds), *The Mercat Anthology of Early Scottish Literature*, p. 291):

I saw the hurcheon and the hare [hedgehog]
In coverts hirpling heere and there, [playing in coverts]
To mak their morning mange; [chorus]
The con, the conny and the cat, [squirrel; rabbit]
Whose dainty dounes with dew were wat [furs; wet]
With stiff mustaches strang;
The hart, the hynd, the dae, the rae, [doe; roe deer]
The fulmart and false foxe; [polecat]
The bearded buck clamb up the brae [climbed; hill]
With birsie baires and brocks; [bristly; badgers]
Some feeding, some dreading
The hunters subtile snares,
With skipping and tripping,
They plaid them all in paires. [gambolled]

'Christ's (or Christis) Kirk' stanza

Named after the poem of the same name, usually comprising an octave with alternating iambic (short, long stress) tetrameters and trimeters, followed by the so-called 'bob-wheel' (two lines comprising a monometer and trimeter), though in later usage the bob-wheel became a single dimeter closing the stanza.

The opening stanza from, 'Christis Kirk on the Grene' (see MacLaine (ed.), *The Christis Kirk Tradition*, pp. 10–11):

Was nevir in Scotland hard nor sene [heard]
Sic dansing nor deray [such; disorder]
Nowthir at Falkland on the grene
Nor Peblis to the play,
As wes of wowaris, as I wene, [wooers; think]

At Christ Kirk on ane day.
That come our kitties weschin clene [maidens; washed clean]
In thair new kirtillis of gray [gowns]
Full gay,
At Christis Kirk of the grene.

Robert Burns's opening stanza from 'The Holy Fair' (see Kinsley (ed.), *Burns: Poems and Songs*, p. 103):

Upon a simmer Sunday morn [summer]
When Nature's face is fair,
I walked forth to view the corn,
An' snuff the callor air: [fresh]
The rising sun, owre Galston muirs, [over]
Wi' glorious light was glintan;
The hares were hirplin down the furrs, [limping; furrows]
The lav'rocks they were chantan
Fu sweet that day.

'Habbie' (or 'Standard Habbie', or 'Habbie Simson', or 'Burns') stanza

Named after the 'The Life and Death of the Piper of Kilbarchan, or the epitaph of Habbie Simson'. A six-line vehicle, consisting usually of a couplet followed by a quatrain, rhyming, most often aaabab, three lines of iambic (short, long stress) tetrameter, followed by one of iambic dimeter, one of iambic tetrameter, one of iambic tetramter and a closing line of iambic dimeter.

Robert Fergusson's opening stanza from 'The Daft-Days' (see McDiarmid (ed.), *The Poems of Robert Fergusson*, p. 32):

Now mirk December's dowie face [dark; sad]
Glours our the rigs wi' sour grimace, [over]
While thro' his minimum of space,
The bleer-ey'd sun,
Wi' blinkin light and stealing pace,
His race doth run.

'Rhyme Royal' stanza

Of seven lines, most frequently in iambic pentameter (meter of five feet, each foot comprised of a short followed by a long syllable) rhymed ababbcc. Structure usually comprises the arrangement of a tercet (aba) and two couplets (bb cc), or a quatrain (abab) and a tercet (bcc). The example which follows is stanza 2 from *The Kingis Quair* (see Jack and Rozendaal (eds), *The Mercat Anthology of Early Scottish Literature*, p. 18):

> Quhen as I lay in bed alone waking,
> New partit out of slepe a lyte tofore, [a short time before]
> Fell me to mynd of mony diverse thing,
> Of this and that; can I nought say quharfore,
> Bot slepe for craft in erth might I no more [skill]
> For quhich, as tho, coude I no better wyle, [at that time; strategy]
> But toke a boke, to rede upon a quhile

REFERENCE MATERIALS

There is a wide, but arguably rather patchy (hugely variable in quality), set of published and institutional resources for the study of Scottish Literature. Those which follow are particularly recommended.

A number of journals publish extensive criticism in Scottish Literature, especially *Studies in Scottish Literature* (founded 1963) produced from the University of South Carolina in Columbia, under the continuous editorship of Professor G. Ross Roy, and *Scottish Studies Review* (founded 2000; previously the *Scottish Literary Journal*, founded 1974, but re-formed in an amalgamation with the periodical *Scotlands*, 1994–98), which is overseen by the Association for Scottish Literary Studies. The modern *Edinburgh Review* (the *New Edinburgh Review*, 1969–84; the *Edinburgh Review* from 1984), *Cencrastus* (founded 1979), *Chapman* (founded 1970), *The Drouth* (founded 2001), the *Journal of Irish and Scottish Studies* (founded 2007), *Lallans* (in Scots; founded 1973), the *Review of*

Scottish Culture (founded 1984), all feature a variety of accessible and specialist commentary on Scottish Literature. *Gairm*, a Gaelic quarterly (founded 1952), also carries material of interest with regard to 'Scottish Literature'.

The Association for Scottish Literary Studies (7 University Gardens, University of Glasgow G12 8QH), founded in 1970, offers a variety of membership packages and, as well as *Scottish Studies Review*, publishes *Scottish Language* (founded 1982), *New Writing Scotland* (founded 1983), *Scotlit* (founded in 1989 and particularly aimed at schools), an annual volume (or critical edition, since 1971), the *Scotnotes* series (study notes on a wide range of Scottish authors and texts including so far: The Ballads, Iain Banks, George Douglas Brown, George Mackay Brown, John Buchan, Robert Burns, William Dunbar, Lewis Grassic Gibbon, Robert Henryson, James Hogg, Robin Jenkins, Liz Lochhead, Norman MacCaig, Hugh MacDiarmid, William McIlvanney, Naomi Mitchison, Edwin Morgan, Iain Crichton Smith, Muriel Spark, and Robert Louis Stevenson) and also other occasional volumes, as well as the e-zines, *The International Journal of Scottish Literature* (founded 2006) and *The Bottle Imp* (founded 2006), both of which are accessible via the ASLS website. The ASLS runs an annual scholarly conference in the spring of each year and another conference in the autumn aimed especially at teaching Scottish Literature in schools. The ASLS website has a very useful set of links to other cognate sites. Conferences of a literary nature are also regularly organised by The Saltire Society (founded 1936), whose 'Book of the Year' award (established 1981) is a particularly noteworthy event, and The Scots Language Society (founded 1972).

Other literary societies and associations whose activities and websites yield much useful information are the Robert Henryson Society, the Walter Scott Club, the James Hogg Society the Robert Louis Stevenson Society, the Neil Munro Society, The Friends of the Lewis Grassic Gibbon Centre and The Muriel Spark Society. Annually held are the Edinburgh Book Festival (administered by the Scottish Book Centre) during the Edinburgh International Festival, the Aye Right festival (at the Mitchell Library, Glasgow), StAnza (Scotland's Poetry Festival held in St Andrews) and Word (the University of Aberdeen's Writers Festival). National Poetry

Day is held in October, with a range of events by the Scottish Poetry Library and other organisations.

Specialist editions of Scottish writers have come to the fore in recent years, especially the Edinburgh Edition of the Waverley Novels (Walter Scott) published by Edinburgh University Press (and directed from the Walter Scott Research Centre at the University of Aberdeen); the Stirling/South Carolina edition of the work of James Hogg (Edinburgh University Press); and the collected works of Hugh MacDiarmid (Carcanet). Of longstanding excellence are the volumes produced by the Scottish text Society which, since its inception in 1882, has published 150 volumes (with particular emphasis upon the medieval area). The 'Canongate [Scottish] Classics' series (published by Canongate Publishing of Edinburgh) offers a particularly wide range of Scottish literary texts and a new multi-series of editions of Scottish Literature has recently been established by the publisher Kennedy & Boyd in Glasgow.

Places to visit include, especially, Abbotsford (Walter Scott's home and library of around 12,000 books), near Melrose; Brownsbank Cottage (the home of Hugh MacDiarmid) in Biggar; the Burns Cottage museum in Alloway (see also the poet's house in Dumfries); Thomas Carlyle's house in Ecclefechan; the John Buchan Centre in Broughton; the Lewis Grassic Gibbon Centre in Arbuthnott; and The Writer's Museum (dedicated to Burns, Scott and Stevenson) in Edinburgh.

The website of SCRAN (Scottish Cultural Resources Access Network) digitises many aspects of Scottish culture, including literary material. STELLA (Software for Teaching English Language and Literature and its Assessment) at the University of Glasgow offers various materials for the teaching and learning of Scottish Literature and Language. All of The British Library (London), the National Library of Scotland (Edinburgh), Edinburgh Central Library and the Mitchell Library, Glasgow (which has a highly specialised collection in poetry accessed via its 'Scottish Poetry Catalogue'), as well as all the major university libraries in Scotland have extensive holdings in Scottish Literature. Of particular speciality are the independent Scottish Poetry Library, 5 Crichton Close, Canongate, Edinburgh, and the Scottish Theatre Archive held in the University of Glasgow Library. In the United States and Canada, many libraries have extensive holding of Scottish Literature, but the Thomas Cooper Library, University of South Carolina, has the most dedicated collection of Scottish poetry and criticism in North America. An extensive sound archive of literary material in Scots is commercially available from 'Scotsoun' (www.Lallans.co.uk). Hugely useful online is 'The Dictionary of the Scots Language', comprising *The Dictionary of the Older Scottish Tongue* (including additions to this originally printed publication) and the *Scottish National Dictionary* (including supplements to the originally printed version).

Guide to Further Reading

Clearly, the reading below is far from exhaustive given the wide-ranging field covered in this book. It includes particularly reliable or accessible editions of work which sometimes, then, will be dated differently below from dates given for the same texts in the main chapters, which usually provide date of first publication. Also, for instance, some particular criticism of Walter Scott is highlighted, though in the case of Robert Burns this is not the case, the logic being that the former needs a little more signposting than the criticism of the latter, around which it is fairly easy for the uninitiated to navigate.

Primary Sources

Anthologies

Bawcutt, Priscilla and Riddy, Felicity (eds), *Longer Scottish Poems. Volume One:* 1375–1650. Edinburgh: Scottish Academic Press, 1987.

Carruthers, Gerard (ed.), *Scottish Poems*. New York, London and Toronto: Alfred A. Knopf, 2009.

Clancy, Thomas Owen and Márkus, Gilbert (eds), *Iona: The Earliest Poetry of a Celtic Monastery*. Edinburgh: Edinburgh University Press, 1995.

Clancy, Thomas Owen (ed.), *The Triumph Tree: Scotland's Earliest Poetry AD* 550–1350. Edinburgh: Canongate, 1998.

Corbett, John and Bill Findlay (eds), *Serving Twa Maisters: Five Classics Plays in Scots Translation*. Glasgow: Association for Scottish Literary Studies, 2005.

Craig, Cairns and Randall Stevenson (eds), *Twentieth Century Scottish Drama*. Edinburgh: Canongate, 2001.

Crawford, Robert and Mick Imlah (eds), *The New Penguin Book of Scottish Verse*. Harmondsworth: Penguin, 2000.

Crawford, Thomas, David Hewitt and Alexander Law (eds), *Longer Scottish Poems Volume Two:* 1650–1830. Edinburgh: Scottish Academic Press, 1987.

Davidson, Toni (ed.), *And Thus Will I Freely Sing: An Anthology of Gay and Lesbian Writing from Scotland*. Edinburgh: Polygon, 1989.

Gifford, Douglas and Alan Riach (eds), *Scotlands: Poets and the Nation*. Manchester: Carcanet, 2004.

Jack, R. D. S. and P. A. T. Rozendaal (eds), *The Mercat Anthology of Early Scottish Literature* 1375–1707. Edinburgh: Mercat Press, 1997.

Jack, Ronald D. S., *Scottish Prose* 1550–1700. London: Calder & Boyers, 1971.

Leonard, Tom (ed.), *Radical Renfrew: Poetry from the French Revolution to the First World War*. Edinburgh: Polygon, 1990.

MacAulay, Donald (ed.), *Nua-Bhardachd Ghaidhlig: Modern Scottish Gaelic Poems*. Edinburgh: Canongate, 1995.

McCulloch, Margery Palmer (ed.), *Modernism and Nationalism: Literature and Society* 1918–1939. Glasgow: Association for Scottish Literary Studies, 2004.

McGonigal, James and Donny O'Rourker and Hamish Whyte (eds), *Across the Water: Irishness in Modern Scottish Writing*. Argyll: Glendaruel, 2000.

MacLaine, Allan H. (ed.), *The Christis Kirk Tradition: Scots Poems of Folk Festivity*. Glasgow: Association for Scottish Literary Studies, 1996.

MacQueen, John and Tom Scott (eds), *The Oxford Book of Scottish Verse*. Oxford and New York: Oxford University Press, 1989.

Morrison, Robert and Chris Baldick (eds), *Tales of Terror from Blackwood's Magazine*. Oxford: Oxford University Press, 1995.
Thomson, Derick S. (ed.), *Gaelic Poetry in the Eighteenth Century*. Aberdeen: Association for Scottish Literary Studies, 1993.

Individual Writers

Aird, Thomas, *The Old Bachelor in the Old Scottish Village*. Edinburgh: Blackwood and Sons, 1857.
Alexander, William, *Johnny Gibb of Gushetneuk*, introduced by William Donaldson. East Linton: Tuckwell, 1995.
Barbour, John, *The Bruce*, ed. A. A. M. Duncan. Edinburgh: Canongate, 1999.
Barrie, J. M., *Farewell Miss Julie Logan*. Edinburgh: Scottish Academic Press, 1989.
Boswell, James, *The Journal of A Tour to the Hebrides*, ed. Peter Levi. Harmondsworth: Penguin, 1984.
Brown, George Douglas, *The House with the Green Shutters*, ed. Cairns Craig. Edinburgh: Canongate, 1996.
Brown, George Mackay, *Andrina and Other Stories*. London: Chatto & Windus, 1983.
— *Collected Poems*, ed. Archie Bevan and Brian Murray. London: John Murray, 2005.
Buchan, John, *The Thirty-Nine Steps*, ed. Christopher Harvie. Oxford: Oxford University Press, 1999.
— *Witch Wood*, ed. James Grieg. Oxford: Oxford University Press, 1993.
Buchanan, Robert Williams, *The New Rome: Poems and Ballads of our Empire*. London: Walter Scott, 1899.
Burns, Robert, *Burns: Poems and Songs*, ed. James Kinsley. Oxford: Oxford University Press, 1969.
Carlyle, Thomas, *The French Revolution*, ed. K. J. Fielding and David Sorensen. Oxford: Oxford University Press, 1989.
— *Selected Writings*, ed. Alan Shelston. Harmondsworth: Penguin, 1971.
Carswell, Catherine, *Open the Door!* Edinburgh: Canongate, 1996.
Craig, Alexander, *Poems of Alexander Craig*. Glasgow: Hunterian Club, 1873.

Davidson, John, *Baptist Lake*. London: Bodley Head, 1894.
— *Collected Poems*, ed. Andrew Turnbull. Edinburgh: Scottish Academic Press, 1973.
Doyle, Arthur Conan, *The Hound of the Baskervilles*, ed. Christopher Frayling. London: Penguin, 2001.
Fergusson, Robert, *The Poems of Robert Fergusson*, ed. M. P. McDiarmid. Edinburgh: Blackwoods for the Scottish Text Society, 1955–56.
Ferrier, Susan, *Marriage*. Bampton: Three Rivers Books, 1984.
Friel, George, *Mr Alfred MA*. Edinburgh: Canongate, 1999.
Galloway, Janice, *The Trick is to Keep Breathing*. London: Vintage, 1999.
Galt, John, *Annals of the Parish*, ed. James Kinsley. London: Oxford University Press, 1972.
— *The Entail*, ed. Ian Gordon. Oxford: Oxford University Press, 1984.
— *Ringan Gilhaize*, introduced by Patricia J. Wilson. Edinburgh: Canongate, 1995.
Geddes, James Young, *In the Valhalla and other poems*. Dundee: J. Leng & Co., 1891.
Grassic Gibbon, Lewis, *Smeddum: A Lewis Grassic Gibbon Anthology*, ed. Valentina Bold. Edinburgh: Canongate, 2001.
— *Sunset Song*, introduced by Tom Crawford. Edinburgh: Canongate, 1988.
Gray, Alasdair, *Lanark: A Life in Four Books*. Edinburgh: Canongate, 1981.
— *Unlikely Stories Mostly*. London: Penguin, 1984.
Gunn, Neil, *Butcher's Broom*. Edinburgh: Porpoise Press, 1934.
— *Highland River*. Edinburgh: Canongate, 1991.
— *The Silver Darlings*. London: Faber and Faber, 1969.
Hogg, James. See the *Stirling-South Carolina Edition of James Hogg*, gen. ed. Douglas Mack. Edinburgh: Edinburgh University Press, 1995 to the present.
— *Private Memoirs and Confessions of a Justified Sinner*, ed. André Gide. London: Cresset Press, 1947.
Home, John, *Douglas*. Edinburgh: Oliver & Boyd, 1972.
Hume, David, *The Letters of David Hume*, ed. J. Y. T. Greig. Oxford: Clarendon Press, 1969.

Jenkins, Robin, *The Cone-Gatherers*. London: Macdonald, 1955.
— *The Changeling*. London: Macdonald, 1958.
— *Dust on the Paw*. London: Macdonald, 1961.
— *The Sardana Dancers*. London: Jonathan Cape, 1964.
Kennedy, A. L., *So I Am Glad*. Jonathan Cape: London, 1996.
Leonard, Tom, *Intimate Voices* 1965–1983. Newcastle upon Tyne: Galloping Dog Press, 1984.
Lindsay, David, *Ane Satyre of the Thrie Estaitis*, ed. R. J. Lyall. Edinburgh: Canongate, 1989.
Linklater, Eric, *Magnus Merriman*. Edinburgh: Canongate, 1990.
— *Private Angelo*. Edinburgh: Canongate, 1992.
Lockhart, John Gibson, *Peter's Letter to his Kinsfolk*. London: Thomas Nelson, 1952.
Lochhead, Liz, *Dreaming Frankenstein* and *Collected Poems*. Edinburgh: Polygon, 2003.
MacCaig, Norman, *Collected Poems*. London: Chatto & Windus, 1988.
MacColla, Fionn, *The Albannach*. London: Souvenir Press, 1984.
— *And the Cock Crew*. Edinburgh: Canongate, 1995.
MacDiarmid, Hugh *A Drunk Man Looks at the Thistle*, ed. Kenneth Buthlay. Edinburgh: Scottish Academic Press, 1987.
— *Hugh MacDiarmid: Selected Prose*, ed. Alan Riach. Manchester: Carcanet, 1992.
— *Selected Poetry*, ed. Alan Riach and Michael Grieve. Manchester: Carcanet, 1992.
MacDonald, George, *Lilith*. Holicong, PA: Wildside Press, 1999.
— *Phantastes: A Faerie Romance for Men and Women*, ed. Greville MacDonald. Whitehorn, CA: Johannesen, 1994.
McGonagall, William, *Poetic Gems*. Edinburgh: Birlinn, 1992.
McIlvanney, William, *The Kiln*. London: Sceptre, 1996.
Mac Laverty, Bernard, *Grace Notes*. London: Vintage, 1998.
MacLeod, Alistair, *No Great Mischief*. London: Jonathan Cape, 2000.
Mackenzie, Henry, *The Man of Feeling*, ed. Brian Vickers. Oxford and New York: Oxford University Press, 1987.
MacLean, Sorley, *From Wood to Ridge: Collected Poems*. Manchester: Carcanet/Birlinn, 1999.

Macpherson, James, *The Poems of Ossian*, ed. Howard Gaskill. Edinburgh: Edinburgh University Press, 1996.
Massie, Allan, *A Question of Loyalties*. London: Sceptre, 1990.
Mitchison, Naomi, *The Bull Calves*. Glasgow: Richard Drew, 1985.
Morgan, Edwin, *Collected Poems*. Manchester: Carcanet, 1990.
Morrison, Nancy Brysson, *The Gowk Storm*. Edinburgh: Canongate, 1989.
Muir, Edwin, *Complete Poems*, ed. Peter Butter. Aberdeen: Association for Scottish Literary Studies, 1991.
— *Scottish Journey*. Edinburgh: Mainstream, 1979.
Muir, Willa, *Imagined Corners*. Edinburgh: Canongate, 1987.
Munro, Neil, *The New Road*. Edinburgh: B. & W. Publishing, 1994.
Oliphant, Margaret, *A Beleaguered City and other tales of the Seen and Unseen*, ed. Jenni Calder. Edinburgh: Canongate, 2000.
— *Kirsteen*, introduced by Merryn Williams. London: Dent, 1984.
— *Miss Marjoribanks*, ed. Elisabeth Jay. London: Penguin, 1998.
Ramsay, Allan, 'Allan Ramsay's first published poem: the poem to the memory of Dr Archibald Pitcairne', ed. F. W. Freeman and Alexander Law. *The Bibliotheck* 9, 7 (1979), pp. 153–60.
— *The Works of Allan Ramsay*, 6 volumes, ed. Burns Martin, John W. Oliver, Alexander M. Kinghorn and Alexander Law. Edinburgh and London: Blackwoods for the Scottish Text Society: Edinburgh and London, 1951–74.
— *Poems by Allan Ramsay & Robert Fergusson*, ed. Alexander Kinghorn and Alexander Law. Edinburgh: Scottish Academic Press, 1985.
Scott, Walter. See the *Edinburgh Edition of the Waverley Novels*, 30 volumes, editor-in-chief David Hewitt. Edinburgh: Edinburgh University Press, 1993 to the present.
Shepherd, Nan, *The Quarry Wood*. Edinburgh: Canongate, 1987.
Smith, Ian Crichton, *Selected Poems*. Manchester: Carcanet, 1985.
Smollett, Tobias, *The Expedition of Humphry Clinker*, ed. Lewis Knapp and Paul Gabriel Boucé. Oxford: Oxford University Press, 1984.
Spark, Muriel, *The Ballad of Peckham Rye*. London: Penguin, 1963.

— *The Prime of Miss Jean Brodie*. London: Penguin, 1965.
Stevenson, Robert Louis, *Kidnapped*, ed. Donald McFarlan. Penguin: London, 1994.
— *The Master of Ballantrae* & *Weir of Hermiston*, introduced by Claire Harman. London: Dent, 1992.
— *South Sea Tales*, ed. Roslyn Jolly. Oxford: Oxford University Press, 1996.
— *The Strange Case of Dr Jekyll and Mr Hyde*, ed. Robert Mighall. London: Penguin, 2002.
Thomson, James, *The Seasons* and *The Castle of Indolence*, ed. James Sambrook. Oxford: Oxford University Press, 1987.
Thomson ('B. V.'), James, *The City of Dreadful Night*, introduced by Edwin Morgan. Edinburgh: Canongate, 1993.
Welsh, Irvine, *Trainspotting*. London: Minerva, 1996.
Wordsworth, William, *The Oxford Authors: William Wordsworth*, ed. Stephen Gill. Oxford: Oxford University Press, 1984.

Secondary Sources

Reference

Aitken, W. R., *Scottish Literature in English and Scots: A Guide to Information Sources*. Detroit: Gale Research Company, 1982.
Donaldson, Gordon (ed.), *Scottish Historical Documents*. Glasgow: Neil Wilson Publishing, 1974.
Donaldson, Gordon and Robert S. Morpeth, *A Dictionary of Scottish History*. Edinburgh: John Donald, 1977.
Robinson, Mairi (editor-in-chief), *The Concise Scots Dictionary*. Aberdeen: Aberdeen University Press, 1987. See also the useful online resource for the Scots language mentioned in the Resources section.
Royle, Trevor, *The Mainstream Companion to Scottish Literature*. Edinburgh and London: Mainstream, 1993.

Criticism

Alexander, J. H. and David Hewitt (eds), *Scott and His Influence*. Aberdeen: Association for Scottish Literary Studies, 1983.

Anderson, Carol and Aileen Christianson (eds), *Scottish Women's Fiction* 1920*s to* 1960*s*. East Linton: Tuckwell Press, 2000.

Arnold, Matthew, 'John Keats', in R. H. Super (ed.), *The Complete Works of Matthew Arnold*, Vol. IX. Ann Arbor, MI: University of Michigan Press, 1973.

— *Lectures and Essays in Criticism*, ed. R. H. Super. Ann Arbor, MI: University of Michigan Press, 1962.

Baldick, Chris, *Criticism and Literary Theory,* 1890 *to the Present.* Harlow: Longman, 1996.

— *The Social Mission of English Criticism* 1848–1932. Oxford: Clarendon Press, 1983.

Barthes, Roland, 'From Work to Text' (1971), reprinted in Niall Lucy (ed.), *Postmodern Literary Theory*. Oxford: Blackwell, 2000, pp. 285–92.

Bell, Eleanor and Gavin Miller (eds), *Scotland in Theory*. Amsterdam and New York: Rodopi, 2004.

Brown, Ian, Thomas Owen Clancy, Susan Manning and Murray Pittock (eds), *The Edinburgh History of Scottish Literature Volume* 1*: From Columba to the Union (until* 1707*)*. Edinburgh: Edinburgh University Press, 2007.

— *The Edinburgh History of Scottish Literature Volume* 2*: Enlightenment, Britain and Empire (*1707–1918*)*. Edinburgh: Edinburgh University Press, 2007.

— *The Edinburgh History of Scottish Literature: Volume* 3*: Modern Transformations, New Identities (from* 1918*)*. Edinburgh: Edinburgh University Press, 2007.

Carpenter, Sarah, 'Early Scottish Drama', in R. D. S. Jack (ed.), *The History of Scottish Literature*, Vol. I, pp. 199–212.

Carruthers, Gerard, 'Fictions of Belonging: National Identity and the Novel in Ireland and Scotland', in Brian W. Shaffer (ed.), *A Companion to the British and Irish Novel,* 1945–2000. Oxford: Blackwell, 2005, pp. 112–27.

— 'James Thomson and Eighteenth-Century Scottish Literary Identity', in Richard Terry (ed.), *James Thomson: Essays for the Tercentenary*. Liverpool: Liverpool University Press, 2000, pp. 165–90.

— 'Remaking Romantic Scotland: Lockhart's Biographies of Burns

and Scott', in Arthur Bradley and Alan Rawes (eds), *Romantic Biography*. Aldershot: Ashgate, 2003, pp. 93–108.
— 'Revisionism in Irish and Scottish Literature: How Far Can We Go?' in *English Subject Centre Newsletter* 10 (June 2006), pp. 8–10.
— 'Scottish Literature: Second Renaissance', in Laura Marcus and Peter Nicholls (eds), *The Cambridge History of Twentieth Century English Literature*. Cambridge: Cambridge University Press, 2004, pp. 668–84.
Carruthers, Gerard and Sarah Dunnigan, '"A reconfused chaos now": Scottish Poetry and Nation from the Medieval Period to the Eighteenth Century', *Edinburgh Review* 100 (1999), pp. 81–94.
Carruthers, Gerard, David Goldie and Alastair Renfrew (eds), *Beyond Scotland: New Contexts for Twentieth-Century Scottish Literature*. Amsterdam and New York: Rodopi, 2004.
Christianson, Aileen and Alison Lumsden (eds), *Contemporary Scottish Women Writers*. Edinburgh: Edinburgh University Press, 2000.
Clancy, Thomas Owen and Murray Pittock (eds), *The Edinburgh History of Scottish Literature. Volume 1: From Columba to the Union (until 1707)*. Edinburgh: Edinburgh University Press, 2007.
Clive, John and Bernard Bailyn, 'England's Cultural Provinces: Scotland and America', *William and Mary Quarterly* 3rd series No. 11 (1954), pp. 200–13.
Corbett, John, *Language and Scottish Literature*. Edinburgh: Edinburgh University Press, 1997.
Cowan, Edward J. *Scottish History and Scottish Folk* (Inaugural Lecture, 15 March 1995, printed at the University of Glasgow).
Craig, Cairns, *The History of Scottish Literature Volume 4: Twentieth Century*. Aberdeen: Aberdeen University Press, 1987.
— *The Modern Scottish Novel: Narrative and the National Imagination*. Edinburgh: Edinburgh University Press, 1999.
— *Out of History: Narrative Paradigms in Scottish and English Culture*. Edinburgh: Polygon, 1996.
— 'Scotland and Hybridity', in Carruthers et al. (eds), *Beyond Scotland: New International Contexts for Twentieth-Century Scottish Literature*, pp. 229–53.

Craig, David, *Scottish Literature and the Scottish People 1680–1830*. London: Chatto & Windus, 1961.
Crawford, Robert, *Devolving English Literature*. Oxford: Clarendon Press, 1992.
— *Scotland's Books*. London: Penguin, 2007.
— 'Scottish Literature and English Studies', in Robert Crawford (ed.), *The Scottish Invention of English Literature*. Cambridge: Cambridge University Press, 1998.
Crawford, Tom, *Walter Scott*. Edinburgh: Scottish Academic Press, 1982.
Daiches, David, *Literature and Gentility in Scotland*. Edinburgh: Edinburgh University Press, 1982.
— *The Paradox of Scottish Culture: The Eighteenth Century Experience*. London: Oxford University Press, 1964.
Donaldson, William, *Popular Literature in Victorian Scotland*. Aberdeen: Aberdeen University Press, 1986.
Douglas, George, *Scottish Poetry: Drummond of Hawthornden to Fergusson*. Glasgow: J. Maclehose, 1911.
Duncan, Ian, 'Adam Smith, Samuel Johnson and the Institutions of English', in Crawford (ed.), *The Scottish Invention of English Literature*, pp. 37–54.
Dunnigan, Sarah, *Eros and Poetry at the Courts of Mary Queen of Scots and James VI*. Basingstoke: Palgrave Macmillan, 2002.
Dunnigan, Sarah M., C. Marie Harker and Evelyn S. Newlyn (eds), *Woman and the Feminine in Medieval and Early Modern Scottish Writing*. Basingstoke: Palgrave Macmillan, 2004.
Dunnigan, Sarah, 'A New Critical Cartography: Pre- and Post-Union Scottish Renaissance', in Marco Fazzini (ed.), *Alba Literaria: A History of Scottish Literature*. Amos Edizioni: Venezia, 2005, pp. 99–119.
Eliot, T. S., 'The Metaphysical Poets', in *Selected Prose*, ed. John Hayward. Harmondsworth: Penguin, 1953, pp. 281–91.
— 'Was there a Scottish Literature?' *The Athenæum* (1 August 1919), reprinted in Margery Palmer McCulloch (ed.), *Modernism and Nationalism: Literature and Society in Scotland 1918–1939*. Glasgow: Association for Scottish Literary Studies, 2004, pp. 7–10.
Fleming, Morna, 'Kin[g]es be the glas, the verie scole, the booke,

/ Where priuate men do learne, and read, and looke': The Translation of James VI to the Throne of England', in van Heijnsbergen & Royan (eds), *Literature, Letters and the Canonical in Early Modern Scotland*, pp. 90–110.

Freeman, F. W., *Robert Fergusson and the Scots Humanist Compromise*. Edinburgh: Edinburgh University Press, 1984.

Gaskill, Howard (ed.), *Ossian Revisited*. Edinburgh: Edinburgh University Press, 1991.

Geddes, Patrick, 'The Scots Renascence', *Evergreen: A Northern Seasonal* 1, Spring. London, 1895, pp. 191–3.

Gifford, Douglas (ed.), *The History of Scottish Literature: Volume 3, Nineteenth Century*. Aberdeen: Aberdeen University Press, 1988.

Gifford, Douglas, 'Remapping Renaissance in Modern Scottish Literature', in Carruthers, Goldie and Renfrew (eds), *Beyond Scotland: New Contexts for Twentieth Century Scottish Literature*, pp. 17–38.

Gifford, Douglas, Sarah Dunnigan and Alan MacGillivray (eds), *Scottish Literature: in English and Scots*. Edinburgh: Edinburgh University Press, 2002.

Gifford, Douglas and Dorothy McMillan (eds), *A History of Scottish Women's Writing*. Edinburgh: Edinburgh University Press, 1997.

Gonda, Caroline (ed.), *Tea and Leg-Irons: New Feminist Readings from Scotland*. London: Open Letters, 1992.

Harker, C. Marie, 'John Knox, *The First Blast*, and the Monstrous Regiment of Gender', in Theo van Hiejnsbergen and Nicola Royan (eds), *Literature, Letters and the Canonical in Early Modern Scotland*. East Linton: Tuckwell Press, 2002, pp. 35–51.

Hart, F. R., *The Scottish Novel from Smollett to Spark*. London: J. Murray, 1978.

Hewitt, David, 'Walter Scott', in the *New Dictionary of National Biography*. Oxford: Oxford University Press, 2004.

Hook, Andrew, 'David Daiches on Scottish Literature', in William Baker and Michael Lister (eds), *David Daiches, A Celebration of His Life and Work*. Eastbourne: Sussex Academic Press, 2007, pp. 71–7.

— *History of Scottish Literature Volume 2: Eighteenth Century*. Aberdeen: Aberdeen University Press, 1987.

— *From Goosecreek to Gandercleugh: Studies in Scottish-American Literary and Cultural History*. East Linton: Tuckwell Press, 1999.

Irving, David, *The Lives of the Scottish Poets*. Edinburgh: Alexander Lawrie, 1804.

Jack, R. D. S. (ed.), *The History of Scottish Literature Volume 1: Origins to 1660*. Aberdeen: Aberdeen University Press, 1988.

Jessop, Ralph, *Carlyle and Scottish Thought*. Basingstoke: Macmillan, 1997.

Kidd, Colin, *Subverting Scotland's Past*. Cambridge: Cambridge University Press, 1993.

Kovesi, Simon, *James Kelman*. Manchester and New York: Manchester University Press, 2007.

Lang, Andrew, 'The Celtic Renascence', *Blackwood's Magazine* Vol. 926 (February 1897), pp. 191–5.

Leonard, Tom, *Places of the Mind: The Life and Work of James Thomson ('B. V.')*. London: Jonathan Cape, 1993.

McGonigal, James and Kirsten Stirling (eds), *Ethically Speaking: Voice and Values in Modern Scottish Writing*. Amsterdam and New York: Rodopi, 2006.

McGuire, Matt, *The Essential Guide to Contemporary Scottish Literature*. Basingstoke: Palgrave MacMillan, 2008.

MacQueen, John, *Progress and Poetry*. Edinburgh: Scottish Academic Press, 1982.

— *The Rise of the Historical Novel*. Edinburgh: Scottish Academic Press, 1989.

Mack, Douglas, *Scottish Fiction and the British Empire*. Edinburgh: Edinburgh University Press, 2006.

Manning, Susan, *Fragments of Union: Making Connections in Scottish and American Writing*. Basingstoke: Palgrave Macmillan, 2002.

— *The Puritan-Provincial Vision: Scottish and American Literature in the Nineteenth Century*. Cambridge: Cambridge University Press, 1990.

Mapstone, Sally (ed.), *William Dunbar, 'The Nobill Poet'*. East Linton: Tuckwell Press, 2001.

Millgate, Jane, *Walter Scott: the Making of the Novelist*. Edinburgh: Edinburgh University Press, 1984.

Millar, J. H., *A Literary History of Scotland*. London: T. Fisher Unwin, 1903.

Moore, Dafydd, *Enlightenment and Romance in James MacPherson's Poems of Ossian*. Aldershot: Ashgate, 2003.

Muir, Edwin, 'The Meaning of Romanticism', *Chapman* 49 (Summer 1987), pp. 1–10.

— *Scott and Scotland: The Predicament of the Scottish Writer*. Edinburgh: Polygon, 1982.

Murray, Isobel and Bob Tait, *Ten Modern Scottish Novels*. Aberdeen: Aberdeen University Press, 1984.

Noble, Andrew, 'John Wilson (Christopher North) and the Tory Hegemony', in Douglas Gifford (ed.), *The History of Scottish Literature: Vol. 3, Nineteenth Century*. Aberdeen: Aberdeen University Press, 1988, pp. 125–52.

— 'Urbane Silence: Scottish Writing and the Nineteenth-Century City', in George Gordon (ed.), *Perspectives of the Scottish City*. Aberdeen: Aberdeen University Press, 1985, pp. 64–90.

Oliphant, Margaret, *Annals of a Publishing House*. Edinburgh: Blackwood & Son, 1897–8.

Petrie, Duncan, *Contemporary Scottish Fictions*. Edinburgh: Edinburgh University Press, 2004.

Pittock, Murray, *The Invention of Scotland: The Stuart Myth and Scottish Identity, 1638 to the Present*. London: Routledge, 1991.

— *Poetry and Jacobite Politics in Eighteenth Century Britain and Ireland*. Cambridge: Cambridge University Press, 1994.

— *Scottish and Irish Romanticism*. Oxford: Oxford University Press, 2008.

Riach, Alan, *Representing Scotland in Literature, Popular Culture and Iconography*. Basingstoke: Palgrave Macmillan, 2005.

Riddy, Felicity, 'The Alliterative Revival', in R. D. S. Jack (ed.), *The History of Scottish Literature: Volume 1, Origins to 1660*, pp. 39–54.

Robb, David, *Auld Campaigner: A Life of Alexander Scott*. Edinburgh: Dunedin Academic Press, 2007.

— *George MacDonald*. Edinburgh: Scottish Academic Press, 1987.

Ross, John, *Scottish History and Literature to the Period of the Reformation*. Glasgow: J. Maclehose and Sons, 1884.

Ryan, Ray, *Ireland and Scotland: Literature and Culture, State and Nation, 1966–2000*. Oxford: Oxford University Press, 2002.

Sassi, Carla, *Why Scottish Literature Matter*. Edinburgh: Saltire, 2005.

Schoene, Berthold (ed.), *The Edinburgh Companion to Contemporary Scottish Literature*. Edinburgh: Edinburgh University Press, 2007.

Scott, Andrew Murray, *Alexander Trocchi: The Making of the Monster*. Edinburgh: Polygon, 1991.

Scott, Mary Jane, *James Thomson, Anglo-Scot*. Athens, GA and London: University of Georgia Press, 1988.

Simpson, Kenneth, *The Protean Scot: the Crisis of Identity in Eighteenth Century Scottish Literature*. Aberdeen: Aberdeen University Press, 1988.

Smith, G. Gregory, *Scottish Literature: Character and Influence*. London: Macmillan, 1919.

Smith, J.C. *Some Characteristics of Scots Literature*. London: Published for the English Association, 1912.

Speirs, John, *The Scots Literary Tradition*. London: Faber and Faber, 1961.

Spiller, Michael, 'The Scottish Court and the Scottish Sonnet at the Union of Crowns', in Sally Mapstone (ed.), *The Rose and the Thistle: Essays on the Culture of Late Medieval and Renaissance Scotland*. East Linton: Tuckwell, 1998, pp. 101–15.

Stafford, Fiona, *Starting Lines in Scottish, Irish and English Poetry from Burns to Heaney*. Oxford: Oxford University Press, 2000.

— *The Sublime Savage*. Edinburgh: Edinburgh University Press, 1988.

Sutherland, John, *The Life of Walter Scott: A Critical Biography*. Oxford: Blackwell, 1995.

Thomson, Alex, '"You can't there from here': Devolution and Scottish Literary History', *International Journal of Scottish Literature*. Issue 3 (Autumn/Winter 2007) [online].

Trumpener, Katie, *Bardic Nationalism: The Romantic Novel and the British Empire*. Princeton, NJ: Princeton University Press, 1997.

Veitch, John, *The Feeling for Nature in Scottish Poetry*. Edinburgh: Blackwood, 1887.

Walker, Marshall, *Scottish Literature since 1707*. London and New York: Longman, 1996.

Watson, Roderick, *The Literature of Scotland*. New York: Palgrave, 2007.

Whyte, Christopher, 'Bakhtin at Christ's Kirk: Carnival and the Scottish Renaissance', *Studies in Scottish Literature* XXVIII (1993), pp. 178–203.

— 'Bakhtin at Christ's Kirk (Part II) Carnival and the Vernacular Revival', *Studies in Scottish Literature* XXIX (1996), pp. 133–57.

— Whyte, Christopher (ed.), *Gendering the Nation: Studies in Modern Scottish Literature*. Edinburgh: Edinburgh University Press, 1995.

— *Modern Scottish Poetry*. Edinburgh: Edinburgh University Press, 2004.

Wickman, Matthew, *The Ruins of Experience: Scotland's 'Romantick' Highlands and the Birth of Modern Witness*. Philadelphia: University of Pennsylvania Press, 2007.

— 'Scotland – The Event; or Theory after Muir', *International Journal of Scottish Literature*. Issue 3 (Autumn–Winter 2007), online.

Williams, Raymond, *The Country and the City*. London: Hogarth Press, 1985.

Wilson, A. N., *A Life of Walter Scott*. Oxford: Oxford University Press, 1980.

Wittig, Kurt, *The Scottish Tradition in Literature*. Edinburgh: Oliver & Boyd, 1958.

Index